S0-CFM-001

Emotion, Cognition, Health, and Development in Children and Adolescents

Emotion, Cognition, Health, and Development in Children and Adolescents

Edited by
Elizabeth J. Susman
Lynne V. Feagans
William J. Ray
The Pennsylvania State University

LEA LAWRENCE ERLBAUM ASSOCIATES, PUBLISHERS
1992 Hillsdale, New Jersey Hove and London

Lawrence Erlbaum Associates, Inc., Publishers
365 Broadway
Hillsdale, New Jersey 07642

Library of Congress Cataloging-in-Publication Data

Emotion, cognition, health, and development in children and adolescents / edited by Elizabeth J. Susman, Lynne V. Feagans, William J. Ray.
p. cm.
Includes bibliographical references and index.
ISBN 0-8058-0548-6
1. Health behavior in children—Congresses. 2. Health behavior in adolescents—Congresses. I. Susman, Elizabeth J. II. Feagans, Lynne V. III. Ray, William J., 1945-
RJ47.53.E46 1992
618.92—dc20 91-32896
CIP

Printed in the United States of America
10 9 8 7 6 5 4 3 2 1

Contents

Historical and Theoretical Perspectives on Behavioral Health in Children and Adolescents: An Introduction **1**
Elizabeth J. Susman, Lorah D. Dorn, Lynne V. Feagans, and William J. Ray

1 Here's Looking at You, Kid! New Ways of Viewing the Development of Health Cognition **9**
David S. Gochman

PART I DEVELOPMENTAL TRAJECTORIES IN BEHAVIORAL HEALTH **25**

2 Development of Attachment, Health Risks, and Health Control **27**
Colleen Frobose and Elizabeth J. Susman

3 The Role of Individual Differences in Infant Personality in the Formation of Attachment Relationships **31**
Nathan A. Fox

4 The Development of Autonomy in Children's Health Behaviors **53**
Ronald J. Iannotti and Patricia J. Bush

5 Risk-Taking Behaviors and Biopsychosocial Development During Adolescence **75**
Charles E. Irwin, Jr. and Susan G. Millstein

PART II DEVELOPMENTAL PROCESSES AND DISEASE 103

6 Disease Processes and Behavior 105
William J. Ray

7 Iron Deficiency Anemia and Infant Behavior 111
Betsy Lozoff

8 Cognitive Maturity, Stressful Events, and Metabolic Control Among Diabetic Adolescents 121
Gary M. Ingersoll, Donald P. Orr, Michael D. Vance, and Michael P. Golden

9 Ego Development Paths and Adjustment to Diabetes: Longitudinal Studies of Preadolescents and Adolescents With Insulin-Dependent Diabetes Mellitus 133
Stuart T. Hauser, Alan Jacobson, Janet Milley, Donald Wertlieb, Joseph Wolfsdorf, Raymonde D. Herskowitz, Phillip Lavori, and Robin L. Bliss

PART III NEW PERSPECTIVES ON HEALTH AND DEVELOPMENT 153

10 Wellness, Illness, Health, and Disease Concepts 155
Arthur H. Parmelee, Jr.

11 Intervention Strategies to Promote Healthy Children: Ecological Perspectives and Individual Differences in Development 165
Lynne V. Feagans

Author Index 171

Subject Index 179

Historical and Theoretical Perspectives on Behavioral Health in Children and Adolescents: An Introduction

Elizabeth J. Susman
The Pennsylvania State University

Lorah D. Dorn
National Institute of Mental Health, Bethesda, MD

Lynne V. Feagans
The Pennsylvania State University

William J. Ray
The Pennsylvania State University

The scientific study of health and behavior has been integrated over the past two decades to form entirely new interdisciplinary areas of inquiry. These new disciplines focus on health, illness, and behavior as processes reciprocally influencing each other. The existing literature emphasizes these processes primarily in adults rather than in children and adolescents, and the research tends not to address the issue of change across the life span. Consequently, developmental considerations have been underemphasized in theoretical and research perspectives. This volume attempts to fill that gap by including chapters that focus on emotion, cognition, and health as important developmental processes in a new scientific frontier, behavioral health in children and adolescents.

A developmental perspective in behavioral health is important because biological and behavioral processes unique to each developmental period have far-reaching implications for health promotion, disease prevention, and disease recovery in childhood and adolescence. Promotion of health during childhood and adolescence is important because it is during these early critical periods that major organ systems develop and learning of health-related behaviors, attitudes, values, and perceptions takes place. The development of a healthy lifestyle during childhood and adolescence will cast the mold for a similar lifestyle throughout the life span. Prevention of disease and rapid recovery from illness at all phases of the life span are byproducts of a healthy lifestyle in the early years.

This book is an outgrowth of a conference on emotion and cognition as antecedents and consequences of health and disease processes in children and adolescents. The theoretical rationale for the conference was based on the assumption that the development of emotion, cognition, health, and illness are processes that influence each other through the life span and that these reciprocal interactions begin in infancy. In the chapters to follow, developmental theories, research, and implications for interventions are discussed as they relate to promoting health, preventing disease, and treating illness in children and adolescents.

HISTORICAL PERSPECTIVE ON BEHAVIORAL HEALTH

The modern integration of mind and body in the scientific literature has provided the foundation for the evolution of multiple new frontiers devoted to explaining the development of health and illness. These new fields include behavioral medicine, health behavior, health psychology, and the more inclusive term for considering all of these fields, *behavioral health* (Matarazzo, 1984). Behavioral medicine was the first new discipline to emerge. It is defined as an interdisciplinary field concerned with the development and integration of behavior and the biomedical sciences (Schwartz & Weiss, 1978). The focus of behavioral medicine is on how behavior influences disease processes and on treatment rather than on prevention. A later discipline, health behavior, focuses on personal attributes (e.g., beliefs and expectations), personality characteristics, emotions and cognitions that relate to health maintenance, and health restoration and improvement (Gochman, 1982). A discipline evolving parallel to health behavior is health psychology. In 1980 at the annual meeting, the Division of Health Psychology adopted an official working definition of the field of health psychology:

> Health psychology is the aggregate of the specific educational, scientific, and professional contributions of the disciplines of psychology to the promotion and maintenance of health, the prevention and treatment of illness, the identification of etiologic and diagnostic correlates of health, illness, and related dysfunction, and the analysis and improvement of the health care system and health policy formation. (Stone, 1987, p. 27)

In this introduction, behavioral health is used as an inclusive term to represent the new disciplines discussed as well as other interdisciplinary efforts that focus on the integration of health, illness, and behavior.

Although behavioral health in children and adolescents has only recently begun to receive systematic attention, behavioral pediatrics has been in existence for about a decade. Behavioral pediatrics is developmentally oriented because of the nature of the discipline of pediatrics itself. Within the behavioral pediatrics perspective, Krasnegor, Arasteh, and Cataldo (1986) published one of the first books examining child health and behavior in terms of perspectives, determinations, prevention, and treatment. Recently, child health and behavior was the focus of a national working conference on health and behavior (Drotar et al.,

1989). The new focus on child health and behavior offers the potential for promoting optimal health in the current generation of children as well as in future generations.

Behavioral health in childhood and adolescence may not have gained in prominence because, historically, these periods have been considered healthy stages of the life span. In childhood, chronic and debilitative diseases are not prominent. With the advent of antibiotic therapy to treat infectious diseases, mortality now is confined primarily to accidents, genetic diseases, and neoplasms. Morbidity in childhood currently tends to be the result of preventable nutritional deficits (e.g., iron deficiency) and infectious processes. Both conditions were assumed, heretofore, to be benign conditions (e.g., otitis media). Nonetheless, these conditions may adversely affect the emotional and cognitive development of children resulting in less than optimal adult health and functioning.

In adolescence, morbidity and mortality often are the result of preventable social, environmental, and behavioral factors (Irwin & Millstein, 1986). Preventable morbidity and mortality include accidents, homicide, suicide, and injury. Thus, there remains reason for concern for the health of children and adolescents in spite of overall prevention and treatment of major life-threatening childhood illnesses.

BEHAVIORAL HEALTH IN CHILDREN AND ADOLESCENTS

In the past, when children were considered in behavioral health, research, or clinical practice, it was in terms of how child health behavior affects adult health (Maddux, Roberts, Sledden, & Wright, 1986). This focus led to a lack of theory on the integration of health and behavior in children and adolescents. The developmental perspective on behavioral health, in this volume, is different from this earlier approach in terms of its conceptualization and the importance it places on health and behavior during childhood and adolescence. Theoretical perspectives on child and adolescent health and health behaviors should be different from those for adults, primarily because of physical, emotional, cognitive, and social developmental differences between children, adolescents, and adults. When considering strategies for optimizing health and development, the uniqueness of emotional and cognitive processes in early developmental periods should be considered. The immature emotional and cognitive status of children and adolescents may impede efforts to change their behavior to promote health or adaptation to disease states. Nonetheless, in spite of immaturity in emotional and cognitive processes, plasticity in psychological and organ systems is a major advantage in the child and adolescent years in developing a lifestyle conducive to optimizing health and development throughout the life span.

COGNITION AND EMOTIONS IN BEHAVIORAL HEALTH

Cognition

Cognitive developmental stage is an important concept in behavioral health in children and adolescents. Stage of cognitive development reflects how children think about and process information about their external physical world as well as their internal emotional world. A child's ability to process information about internal and external events has important implications for health. Before children can regulate their behavior to promote health or prevent disease, they must possess some concept of the relationship between behavior and health that entails the ability to think about the abstract concept of health. The ability to think abstractly, the stage of formal operational thought, emerges at approximately age 13 to 14. There is, however, interindividual variability in the age at which, or whether, abstract thinking emerges. The ability to think abstractly about health develops parallel to the ability to think abstractly about other concepts and ideas (Bibace & Walsh, 1980). Concepts of illness and treatment show a similar developmental trajectory in children and adolescents who were themselves victims of serious diseases (Susman, Dorn, & Fletcher, 1987).

Differences in cognitive abilities between children and adults have implications for compliance with health promotion, preventive interventions, and health teaching, particularly in adolescence (see chapters in this volume by Hauser et al. and Ingersoll, Orr, Vance, & Golden). Possessing the ability to think abstractly, in this case, to comprehend the connection between one's behavior and the promotion or restoration of health, adolescents are assigned by parents, health professionals, and society added responsibility for maintaining their health. With additional responsibility, the issue of noncompliance becomes a central concern for parents and health care providers. Conflicts may arise as a result of adolescents' need for independence and control and parents' need to monitor and control the health-enhancing behavior of adolescents.

Emotions

Emotions as causes and sequela of health and disease play a central role in psychoanalytic theories. Stress-related emotions now are central concepts in theoretical perspectives in behavioral health. Stress-related emotional arousal is assumed to adversely affect health and is considered an etiological factor in disease processes. Sweeping advances have been made linking stress-related emotional arousal and the potentially harmful physiological cascade of events that follows its instigation. These physiological changes include an increase in the production of corticotropin releasing hormone, adrenocorticotropin hormone, and cortisol.

Although the exact mechanism whereby these hormones affect the development of disease is unknown (e.g., cardiovascular disease), there are a myriad of theories regarding the links between negative emotionality, the physiology of stress, and disease. In addition to neuroendocrine changes, immunological changes accompanying periods of grief, depression, and emotional distress reflect an association between emotions and disease processes (Geiser, 1989). Likewise, psychophysiological measures reflecting sympathetic/parasympathetic activity are also associated with negative emotions and arousal with pathophysiology (Dienstbier, 1989). On the positive side, social support and its related positive emotionality are associated with reduced physiological reactivity and less morbidity/mortality in a variety of studies. The social support protective factor makes the work of Fox (chapter 3, this volume) concerning emotional attachment particularly intriguing.

THEORETICAL PERSPECTIVE ON BEHAVIORAL HEALTH

The theoretical framework that guided this volume was based on a life-span developmental perspective. This perspective is particularly well suited to considering issues related to emotion, cognition, health, and development. Within this perspective are two propositions: (1) Health and behavior should be oriented toward dynamic developmental processes that characterize children and adolescents, and (2) health and behavior should be considered in the specific contexts (e.g., home, peer group, family, school, and community) in which children and adolescents develop. These two propositions are based on Lerner's (1979, 1987) life-span perspective for conceptualizing biological and psychological development throughout the life span.

Within the Lerner model, three concepts are central to explaining development: (1) *organismic* (individual) *variables,* (2) *contextual variables,* and (3) the *goodness of fit* between organismic and contextual variables. Organismic variables within the individual child or adolescent have the potential for affecting health and include the dynamic processes of biological changes (e.g., growth) and emotional and cognitive psychological processes. Contextual variables include peer, family, school, and community influences. Development and change at either the organismic or contextual level influence development and change on the other level. Goodness of fit refers to the extent to which individual characteristics fit with a given context. With regard to health, children may possess the individual characteristics to act in ways that promote optimal health and compliance with treatment regimens, however, the context may not allow for accessibility of the needed resources (e.g., nutritional food), or the availability of resources may be limited. Thus, the goodness of fit between the organismic health needs of the child and the context is not optimal.

Throughout this book, chapters focus on issues of emotion, cognition, health, and development with an orientation to organismic variables, contextual variables, or the goodness of fit between the two. Although not always explicitly stated within the life-span theoretical model, each chapter offers an in-depth orientation of the importance of specific developmental processes and the contribution of these processes to understanding the reciprocity between health and behavior.

ORGANIZATION OF CONTENT

The chapters are organized around four thematic issues related to emotion, cognition, health, and development: (I) Historical and theoretical perspectives on health and behavior in children and adolescents; (II) Development of attachment, autonomy, and risk taking; (III) Disease processes and behavior; and (IV) New perspectives on health and implications for intervention. The second and third themes are preceded by chapters designed to orient the reader to the importance of each theme in the health and development of children and adolescents.

The historical background of the entire field, with recommendations for the future, is succinctly covered by Gochman (chapter 1). The developmental trajectories of cognitions and their implications for a child's understanding of health and illness are discussed. He leaves the reader with a wealth of information on the complexities of psychological and behavioral processes in modulating health and illness during the child and adolescent years.

Frobose and Susman (chapter 2) present an overview of the developmental trajectory of attachment, autonomy, and risk taking. Attachment and temperament, two critical concepts for understanding emotional development, are discussed by Fox (chapter 3). Secure and insecure attachment have implications for a child's reactions to health-care personnel, compliance with treatment regimens, and autonomy in health behaviors. Temperament may either predispose individuals to certain diseases or act as a protective factor against diseases (e.g., cardiovascular disease). Although the concepts of attachment and temperament are discussed in relation to infancy, their implications for behavioral health throughout the life span are apparent.

Iannotti and Bush (chapter 4) describe a unique cross-sectional and longitudinal study that incorporates both organismic and contextual factors and the goodness of fit between the two sets of developmental processes. They include findings on the development of autonomy in the domains of nutrition and self-medication. Children and mothers are interviewed with regard to aspects of their own behavior regarding food and medications. The contexts in which these behaviors are engaged are discussed.

The development of risk taking in adolescence and its developmental and contextual aspects are discussed by Irwin and Millstein (chapter 5). The richly detailed chapter presents a definition of risk taking, a review of national data on mortality and morbidity, morbidity data on three risk behaviors, and a biopsychosocial model of risk taking. The chapter concludes with data on risk taking in adolescents.

After the introduction by Ray (chapter 6), the next three chapters address developmental issues related to specific disease states. Lozoff (chapter 7) describes a cross-cultural research program directed toward iron deficiency. In her highly original research in Central America, Dr. Lozoff discovered that developmental test score findings in children were also sensitive in one particular group to behavioral distress. For our purposes, her work points to emotional/behavioral patterns in mother-infant pairs. The findings do not support the position that anemic infants are unresponsive to mother-infant interactions. The works of Ingersoll, Orr, Vance, and Golden (chapter 8) and of Hauser and colleagues (chapter 9) focus on diabetes. Both chapters emphasize cognitive and ego development as important considerations for understanding how adolescents respond to their illness. Overall, these works emphasize the well-known traditional statement that who has the disease is as important as the disease this person has.

The chapter by Parmelee (chapter 10) on illness, health, and disease concepts and the final chapter by Feagans on implications for intervention suggest new directions for behavioral health of children and adolescents. These concluding chapters, in combination with all the preceding chapters, have the potential for advancing the relatively nascent field because each is firmly grounded in developmental theory and empirical research. Each chapter also synthesizes the literature to offer conclusions with relevance to the multiple disciplines interested in the health and behavior of children and adolescents. The multiple suggestions for needed research most assuredly will lead to exciting future research and scholarship.

REFERENCES

Bibace, R., & Walsh, M. E. (1980). Development of children's concepts of illness. *Pediatrics, 66,* 912-917.

Dienstbier, R. (1989). Arousal and physiological toughness: Implications for mental and physical health. *Psychological Bulletin, 96,* 84-100.

Drotar, D., Johnson, S. B., Iannotti, R., Krasnegor, N., Matthews, K. A., Melamed, B. G., Millstein, S., Peterson, R. A., Popiel, D., & Routh, D. D. (1989). Child health psychology. [Special issue], *Health Psychology, 8,* 781-784.

Geiser, D. (1989). Psychosocial influences on human immunity. *Clinical Psychology Review, 9,* 689-715.

Gochman, D. S. (1982). Labels, systems, and motives: Some perspectives for future research. *Health Education Quarterly, 9,* 167-174.

Irwin, C. E., & Millstein, S. G. (1986). Biopsychosocial correlates of risk-taking behaviors during adolescence. *Journal of Adolescent Health Care, 7,* 82-93.

Krasnegor, N. A., Arasteh, J. D., & Cataldo, M. F. (Eds.). (1986). *Child health behavior: A behavioral pediatrics perspective.* New York: Wiley.

Lerner, R. M. (1979). A life-span review of human development: The sample case of aging. *Contemporary Psychology, 24,* 1,008-1,009.

Lerner, R. M. (1987). A life-span perspective for early adolescence. In R. M. Lerner & T. T. Foch (Eds.), *Biological-psychosocial interactions in early adolescence: A life-span perspective* (pp. 1-6). Hillsdale, NJ: Lawrence Erlbaum Associates.

Maddux, J. E., Roberts, M. C., Sledden, E. A., & Wright, L. (1986). Developmental issues in child health psychology. *American Psychologist, 41,* 25-34.

Matarazzo, J. D. (1984). Behavioral health: A 1990 challenge for the health sciences professions. In J. D. Matarazzo, S. M. Weiss, J. A. Herd, N. E. Miller, & S. M. Weiss (Eds.), *Behavioral health: A handbook of health enhancement and disease prevention* (pp. 3-40). New York: Wiley.

Schwartz, G. E., & Weiss, S. M. (1978). Yale Conference on Behavioral Medicine: A proposed definition and statement of goals. *Journal of Behavioral Medicine, 1,* 3-12.

Stone, G. (1987). The scope of health psychology. In G. Stone, S. Weiss, J. Matarazzo, N. Miller, J. Rodin, C. Belar, M. Follick, & J. Singer (Eds.), *Health psychology* (pp. 27-40). Chicago: University of Chicago Press.

Susman, E. J., Dorn, L. D., & Fletcher, J. C. (1987). Reasoning about illness in ill and healthy children and adolescents: Cognitive and emotional developmental aspects. *Journal of Developmental and Behavioral Pediatrics, 8,* 266-273.

1

Here's Looking at You, Kid! New Ways of Viewing the Development of Health Cognition[1]

David S. Gochman
University of Louisville

This chapter provides a picture of what we currently know about health cognitions in young populations. In this chapter, the term *cognition* denotes "those personal thought processes that serve as frames of reference for organizing and evaluating experiences. Beliefs, expectations, perceptions, values, motives, and attitudes all provide the person with ways of filtering, interpreting, understanding, and predicting events" (Gochman, 1988b, p. 21). *Health cognitions,* then, refer broadly to those beliefs, expectations, perceptions, values, motives, and attitudes that serve as personal frames of reference for organizing and evaluating health, regardless of whether those cognitions have demonstrable empirical linkages with health status and regardless of whether they are "objectively valid."

The chapter then identifies some critical areas for future research and concludes with a discussion of how we ought to think about and how we ought to conduct this research. The chapter is thus a background and introduction to the overall themes of the book namely, emotion, cognition, health, and development in children and adolescents.

---

[1]With apologies to Humphrey Bogart; Hal B. Wallis (producer); Michael Curtiz (director); Julius J. Epstein, Philip G. Epstein, and Howard Koch (screenplay); and Warner Brothers films for appropriation of these classic lines from "Casablanca" (1942), based on "Everybody Comes to Rick's," an unproduced play by Murray Burnett and Joan Alison.

WHAT DO WE KNOW ABOUT HEALTH COGNITIONS IN YOUNG POPULATIONS?

We know a little—but very little—about some areas of youngsters' health cognitions. For example, in addition to some knowledge about locus of control and the development of autonomy related to health (see Iannotti and Bush, chapter 4), we have some data-based knowledge about youngsters' beliefs about the causes of illness, about body parts, about their definitions and conceptions of health and illness, about their perceptions of vulnerability, and about their health-related motivation.

Causes of Illness

From Nagy's (1951, 1953) explorations of beliefs about germs and contagion, we have learned ways in which beliefs about causes of illness changed with age: Children younger than 5 seem incapable of grasping the real origins of illness, whereas those 6 and older appear to be able to apply the concepts of infection, and their precision in doing so increases developmentally.

Body Parts

From the observations gleaned by Gellert (1962, 1978) through her standardized questionnaire, we have learned that egocentrism and concreteness tend to be more characteristic of the way in which younger children—in contrast to older ones—view their bodies and that older children tend to demonstrate greater degrees of articulation of parts of the various body systems and increased conceptions of their permanence.

Definitions and Conceptions of Health and Illness

From Rashkis's (1965) observations based on play-period interviews with elementary school children, we have learned that older youngsters more than younger ones equate being well with positive, pleasant states. Younger respondents are apparently unable to integrate their health-related feelings and experiences into a clear, conscious conception of health as a positive state.

From Natapoff's data (1982) we have learned that youngsters equate being healthy with (in order of preference) feeling good, with the ability to do the things they want to do, and with not being sick. They are least likely to equate being healthy with being happy or with having a strong body. They equate not being healthy with being sick and with not being able to do things. We have also learned, as might be expected, that older children demonstrate greater analytic processes, greater levels of abstraction in their thinking, and greater ability to see part–whole relationships than do younger ones. Thus, older children and adolescents are able to think beyond their current sensory inputs to consider hypotheses about health and illness and to project linkages between health and the future; younger children remain bound by the specifics of health cues that are immediate to the senses and think primarily about health in the present. Simeonsson, Buckley, and Monson (1979) reported similar findings in their study of conceptions of health and illness in hospitalized youngsters. From Campbell's work (1975a, 1975b), we have learned that youngsters and their mothers show strong consensus about the relative importance of specific signs and symptoms as indicators of illness (e.g., fever, vomiting).

Perceived Vulnerability to Health Problems

From data derived from the health-belief model (e.g., Gochman, 1986), we learn that perceptions of being vulnerable to health problems are relatively stable between ages 8 and 14 or 15; that perceived vulnerability can be thought of as a consistent personality characteristic; that youngsters on the average see themselves as neither especially vulnerable or invulnerable to health problems; and that perceived vulnerability is negatively related to self-concept or self-esteem (Gochman & Saucier, 1982), is related more to self-concept than to prior traumatic experiences (Gochman, 1977), and is directly related to anxiety (Gochman & Saucier, 1982). This last finding suggests that perceived vulnerability is not a "pure" cognition but one that has an affective or emotional component, making it especially relevant to both the emotional and cognition focal points of this volume.

Health Motivation

We have learned that health is not an especially salient motive, preference, value, or priority for youngsters (Gochman, 1986) and that it declines appreciably in relation to appearance or cosmetic concerns between ages 8 and 15 (Gochman, 1986). Of course, this conclusion may be overly simplistic; the observed lack of potency in relation to appearance may disappear when comparisons are made with other motives.

Michela and Contento's innovative study (1986) of health orientations, taste orientations, and multiple-motive orientations, which integrated Piagetian developmental concepts with value–expectancy theory, is one of the few rigorous investigations in this area. Their findings reveal complex linkages between patterns of motivation within individual youngsters, levels of cognitive development, and youngsters' food decisions and eating behaviors.

AN AGENDA FOR FUTURE RESEARCH

From these beginnings, available evidence is congruent with both Piagetian and Lewinian models of conceptual growth and development. No single theoretical model has an advantage in accounting for or making predictions about aspects of the development of health related cognitions. Despite these important starts, consensus exists that much more needs to be learned (Bruhn & Parcel, 1982). What we currently know reflects a lack of systematic efforts at developing this knowledge. In terms of a *sociology of knowledge* (e.g., Hayes-Bautista, 1978), what we currently know as professionals is lacking in depth, coherence, and organization. Literature reviews (e.g., Burbach & Peterson, 1986; Gochman, 1985, 1988a, 1988c, 1988d; Kalnins & Love, 1982) affirm that there have been few systematic replications, little effort directed at broadening samples, and little done to move beyond specific cultural frameworks.

It is implicit from this overview of what is currently known that even in the areas where some knowledge exists, there is an urgent need to expand this knowledge systematically. A future research agenda for young persons' health cognitions should assign high priority to the following five areas: the origins and development of health cognitions, the role of the family as a determinant of these cognitions, health-germane motivation, cognitions related to coping, and searches for meaning.

Origins and Development of Health Cognitions

A gap exists in our knowledge about the roots or sources of health cognitions, as it does in our knowledge of health behavior in general. Much research has been undertaken to shape and modify selected health cognitions and other health behaviors, but few investigations have attempted systematically to explore their origins.

Coupled with the need for greater knowledge and understanding about the origins of health cognitions is the need for greater knowledge and understanding about how such cognitions develop. Although perceived vulnerability appears to be one of the most systematically examined health cognitions in younger populations, its origins in family, peer, media, and experiential factors remain unstudied. The dearth of well-conducted, rigorous research in this area has been noted repeatedly (e.g., Bruhn & Parcel, 1982; Gochman, 1985, 1988a, 1988c, 1988d; Kalnins & Love, 1982).

Questions arise about the importance of a range of factors such as the family, friends, peer groups, social relationships, and societal and cultural values and institutions in the origins and development of such cognitions.

Basic research into the origins of health cognitions and how they develop is thus a major challenge for the future and leads directly to the second area identified for future research—the family.

The Family and Health Cognitions

Although the family is presumed to be a major determinant of health cognitions, and although Campbell (1978), for example, has shown how some maternal values serve as determinants of youngsters' conceptions of sick role, reviews of the literature (e.g., Baranowski & Nader, 1985; Gochman, 1985, 1988c) attest to the virtual nonexistence of knowledge about relationships between family characteristics and children's health cognitions. Baranowski and Nader described this relationship as "almost ignored" (1985, p. 53), Sallis and Nader (1988) noted the paucity of documentation of mechanisms of family influence, and Drotar et al. (1989) continued to point to the need to expand knowledge in this area. Moreover, Dielman, Leech, Becker, Rosenstock, and Horvath (1982), noting that studies relating parental and youngsters' health beliefs have been "relatively rare," were unable in their own investigation to demonstrate any relationships. They asserted, "Child health beliefs are scarcely influenced by parental characteristics" (p. 63).

Possibly, the failure to discover the roots of children's health behavior in family characteristics reflects an unfortunate combination of inadequate conceptualizations of the family together with a small number of studies conducted in this area. Research has seldom looked at the family as an entity or unit, that is, as a social group or social system. More often than not, research has considered family solely in terms of some personal or demographic characteristic of one or both parents or in terms of its size.

Future research into youngsters' health cognitions should examine the family in terms of its characteristics as an integral social unit, that is, its role structure, norms, values, and patterns of communication. Pratt (1976) has developed one of the few extant conceptual models available that considers the family in this way, and studies based on her model, or similarly coherent ones, are sorely needed.

Health-Germane Motivation

Few studies have been conducted on health, the desire for health, or the wish to possess good health as motives. This is a research arena in which cognitions have affective or emotional components and thus is especially important to the theme of this volume. Moreover, it is increasingly important to differentiate between health as a motive and health-germane motives, those motives that can effectively be drawn on to generate health actions. Thus, a more basic question for future research is: What are the motives that generate health actions in young populations? The desires of young people to be physically or socially active, to be academically successful, to be athletically proficient, or to engage responsibly in family and peer roles may be more critical to health actions than the value of health itself.

Moreover, future research in youngsters' health cognitions needs to address issues such as those raised by Burt (1984) of whether youngsters perceive health as juxtaposed with pleasure, indicating that actions considered to be healthy are often thought to be unappealing, distasteful, and otherwise noxious; and those raised by Bruhn (1988) about the conflict between personal risk and other motives and values and about the trade-offs involved in changing behaviors. For adolescents, for example, what are the trade-offs for eating a nonjunkfood diet? Or, for not engaging in sexual behavior, or, more realistically, for engaging in safe or protected sexual behavior?

Cognitive Aspects of Coping

Among the coping mechanisms related to health status are cognitive skills that control or modify the meaning of stress-inducing situations (e.g., Ben-Sira & Padeh, 1978; Pearlin & Schooler, 1978).

Antonovsky (1984) identified one such cognitive skill as an ability to set boundaries around events that are stress producing. Such a skill creates the belief that these problems do not have much priority, do not matter sufficiently, and thus need not be made manageable. Such coping skills and their origins and developmental patterns provide another important arena for future research in youngsters' health cognitions. Zastowny, Kirschenbaum, and Meng (1986) have shown that providing instruction in coping techniques for parents whose children were about to undergo elective surgery resulted in the children showing greater levels of adaptive behaviors during their hospital stay. Additional studies are needed to determine how coping skills are related more broadly to a range of health behaviors.

Meanings of Health, Illness, and Treatment

Health as a motive, motives relevant to health, and cognitive responses that have the capacity to change the meaning of situations, lead to questions about the salience or deeper meaning of health, illness, and treatment. It is here that we approach more closely a genuine intertwining of cognition and emotion.

The profession of social work has a tradition of borrowing from a variety of disciplines rather than developing its own concepts and techniques (e.g., Bartlett, 1961). Yet in one critical area it can claim proper ownership. It is the particular responsibility of the professional social worker on the interdisciplinary care team to explore, understand, and work with the "meaning" of an illness or a condition for the patient and the patient's family (Bartlett, 1961, pp. 134–135). In such a context, meaning differs from what illness means in general, dictionary terms. In such a context, the meaning of illness represents its salience and implications—often highly emotional—for the patient, for the family, and for significant others. Ben-Sira (1977) addressed this deeper meaning of illness in his study of the person's "image" of an illness, or "involvement" with a disease. Moreover, he (1988) further amplified the role of the meaning of illness through discussion of "lay-intelligible explanations" and the importance of relief from the illness-generated anxiety as an objective in the patient's interactions with a health-care practitioner. Similarly, Stimson and Webb (1975) pointed out how patients attempt to make sense out of what has happened to them. These deeper meanings of the illness experience have important implications for health actions such as preventive activities, acceptance of a regimen, giving up sick role, and rehabilitation.

As we look at young persons then, we want to know more about what their illnesses mean to them, about the anxieties their illnesses generate, and about the impact of their illnesses on their total personal and social functioning.

Moving away from scientifically and medically correct descriptions of the disease process toward increasing understanding of personal or phenomenological definitions or conceptions of the disease process, researchers are beginning to explore "common sense" views or "schemas" of disease (Bishop & Converse, 1987; Lau & Hartman, 1983; Leventhal, Prohaska, & Hirschman, 1983). Lau and Hartman reasoned that it is at the point when individual common sense or personal "lay schemes" for evaluating or interpreting signs and symptoms no longer provide an adequate "fit," that is, when they no longer account for what persons are experiencing, that persons are inclined to believe they have something seriously wrong with themselves and take some appropriate action. Such "personal constructions" of disease in young populations should be systematically explored.

As Ben-Sira (1988) and Roter (1988) made clear, the affective components of treatment—what treatment means in terms of the feelings and emotional needs of the patient—in contrast to the instrumental or technical components are increasingly important areas for systematic future research. Moreover, compliance studies are increasingly identifying what medication means to the patient. Conrad (1985), for example, has shown that for certain conditions (e.g., epilepsy), compliance can be a reminder that the patient has a stigmatized condition, a reminder that often has a strong negative emotional component.

Thus, the meaning of treatment, again in relation to personal needs and values and individual conceptions of what constitutes quality of life, appears to be an important factor in reconsidering definitions of *compliance, adherence,* or *acceptance* of treatment in youngsters and is thus a promising area for future research into their health cognitions.

HEALTH BEHAVIOR: A FRAME OF REFERENCE

To increase the likelihood that such a research agenda will be productive, I advocate a *health behavior* perspective. What this means and what its implications are comprise this chapter's final section, and generate the presentation's title. I am concerned about ways of looking at health cognitions and other health behaviors in young people and hope to change the way we do so.

Health Behavior as Basic Research

Health behavior is not a traditional discipline but a newly emerging interdisciplinary field still in the process of establishing its identity. Although health behavior's boundaries have not yet been rigidly or categorically set, and its definition has not yet been hardened in concrete, a working definition, emerging from an earlier task (Gochman, 1981), establishes health behavior as:

> Those personal attributes such as beliefs, expectations, motives, values, perceptions, and other cognitive elements; personality characteristics, including affective and emotional states and traits; and overt behavior patterns, actions and habits that relate to health maintenance, to health restoration and to health improvement. (Gochman, 1982, p. 169)

Health behavior research, then, is the systematic, scientific, interdisciplinary examination of these behaviors and their determinants. Health behaviors, including relevant affective and emotional states and traits, health beliefs, attitudes, and other cognitions, can be analyzed in at least three ways: (a) as antecedents or causes of diseases, illnesses, and health status (e.g., Belloc & Breslow, 1972); (b) as targets for systematic interventions directed at producing behavioral changes and ultimately at generating changes in health status (e.g., Breslow, 1978/1980). Such an approach is taken by health educators, by health promotion campaigns, and by public health programs; and (c) as interesting in their own right and as inherently worthy of serious scientific investigation. As such, health behaviors are looked upon as consequences, or outcomes, of a variety of diverse personal and social processes. This way of looking at health behaviors is the primary focus of this chapter.

A perspective that considers youngsters' health cognitions as phenomena worthy of being understood on their own terms and not studied simply because they affect health or because they can be modified to improve health may be more likely to generate basic, conceptually derived, rigorous, systematic scientific investigations and thus be more likely to lead to greater understanding of these cognitions, as well as of a broader range of health behaviors, than perspectives that place health behaviors in an ancillary position. The behavior itself must be the primary focus, not the treatment, the health promotion package or marketing attempt, the health education program, or the technology; the basics rather than the applications must be the focus.

Program Effectiveness. Attempts to change individual health cognitions or behaviors, either through individual therapeutic interventions or through larger scale health promotion or health education programs, have been less than impressive. Many attempts are *ad hoc,* hastily conceived and lacking in theoretical rationale or empirical foundation. A major reason for this is the lack of basic knowledge about the target behaviors, the contexts in which they occur, and the factors that determine and stabilize them. Basic research in health behavior, aside from being worthy of study in its own right, may very well increase the effectiveness of interventions and programs designed to bring about behavioral change. What is envisioned here is a continuous flow from basic to applied research and then back to basic research again.

What Health Behavior Research is Not

Health behavior is thus conceptually distinct from responses to treatment, from health care, from the organization or structure of the health delivery system, and from the technology of health interventions (Gochman, 1988c, 1988d). Yet it touches profoundly upon all of these. Health behavior research is concerned with the way such interventions and institutional structures affect the health behavior of individual youngsters. Health behavior research is not primarily concerned with health status. Yet a young person's perception of health status is assuredly an important health behavior.

Behavioral Medicine. Health behavior research is not identical to behavioral medicine, which has been defined as the "field concerned with the *development of behavioral science* knowledge and techniques relevant to the understanding of *physical health* and *illness* and the application of this knowledge and these techniques to prevention, treatment and rehabilitation" (Schwartz & Weiss, 1978, p. 4). Although some areas within behavioral medicine are also contained by health behavior, health behavior research is not ancillary to treatment or to the technology of treatment. Moreover, health behavior research does not automatically begin with a medical framework and its assumptions.

Behavioral Health. Health behavior research is not *behavioral health,* which has been defined as "an interdisciplinary field dedicated to promoting a philosophy of health that stresses *individual responsibility* in the application of behavioral and biomedical science knowledge and techniques to the maintenance of health and the prevention of illness and dysfunction" (Matarazzo, 1980, p. 813). Behavioral health thus appears to represent a primary commitment to the application of knowledge rather than to seeking and establishing basic knowledge. Furthermore, behavioral health (Matarazzo, 1984) emphasizes an ideology aimed at improving health status by the combination of applied knowledge and individual responsibility. Although health behavior research accepts the importance of applying knowledge, as an area of basic inquiry it must remain value free about how persons ought to behave and thus, must pursue neutrality about individual responsibility.

Furthermore, and directly related to this last point, the knowledge generated by health behavior research may well call attention to larger systems such as social, societal, community, or institutional factors that mediate health behaviors, present barriers to individual action, or present greater health-risk factors than personal habits. In this sense, health behavior research has implications not only for understanding personal and treatment dimensions but also for the development and implementation of social policies and health-service institutions (Kolbe, 1988).

Health Psychology. Finally, health behavior research is not *health psychology,* although much health behavior research has been, is, and will continue to be conducted by persons trained in psychology who are interested in health behaviors and health issues. Health psychology, however, is strongly identified with behavioral medicine (e.g., Taylor, 1990), and this is reflected in the content of nearly all of the articles appearing within the pages of its journal, *Health Psychology.* These reports of well-designed and rigorously conducted studies generally reflect a commitment to the medical model and concomitant clinical interventions related to risk factors and disease. Nearly all of a special issue on child health psychology (Melamed, Matthews, Routh, & Stabler, 1986) is devoted to programs and interventions relating to specific illnesses or medical processes. Although health is assuredly an ultimate interest, the issue deals more with child illness psychology than with the topic of its title. (Illness has always been more dramatic and compelling a topic than health, both in personal discourse and research.)

The special issue of *Health Psychology* reporting the proceedings of the National Working Conference on Research in Health and Behavior (Baum, 1989) is, in similar fashion, almost entirely devoted to pathology, vulnerability to infectious diseases, biobehavioral research on cardiovascular disorders, psychoimmunology, cancer, AIDS, and smoking. Here again, illness rather than health is the major focus.

Issues of Health Behavior's Identity

Because health behavior has not yet solidly achieved its own identity, there are few institutional arrangements, that is, departments or programs, that serve to attract numbers of health behaviorists. Most health behaviorists work in relative isolation from one another and lack the opportunity for the face-to-face interaction that generates conceptual breadth and enhances methodological strengths. Conferences such as the one that generated this book are often the only or the primary mechanism for this interaction. Health behavior seems to "fall between the cracks," institutionally and organizationally. Issues related to health behavior's identity must thus be satisfactorily resolved for it to move productively into the future. Among these issues are its relationship with medicine and medical schools, its interdisciplinary nature, and its location (Gochman, 1988d).

Health Behavior and Medicine. Health behavior research and behavioral medicine differ not only in their substantive definitions, but in their directional definitions as well. Directional definitions have labeling qualities that guide or impel movement along selected paths (Gochman, 1982). Behavioral medicine is an attractive and potent label with the capacity to direct research activities selectively. Researchers identifying with behavioral medicine are thus increasingly likely to accept and build upon the medical model, to conduct research addressing medical problems, and to subordinate basic research interests to those with immediately discernable medical applications.

Unquestionably, the practical and human value of such activities is worthwhile. But they do not routinely advance basic health behavior research—knowledge about the behavior itself. Basic research in health behavior will be productively developed and conducted to the degree that it can resist being labelled as behavioral medicine. Questions thus arise about the sustained effects of locating health behavior research within medical schools.

Health Behavior Research is Interdisciplinary

Health behavior research is not the exclusive turf or domain of any one discipline or profession. It must be conducted collaboratively by scientists in anthropology, dentistry, health and physical education, medicine, nursing, nutrition, psychiatry, psychology, public health, social work, and sociology. Each of these fields offers unique perspectives, skills, and interests. Productive, rigorous, basic health behavior research requires collegial borrowing among and sharing of the broad spectrum of available theories, concepts, and methods. Such interdisciplinary collaboration enhances the likelihood of increasing basic knowledge about child and adolescent health-related beliefs, attitudes, emotions, and behaviors. It is worth noting that where multidisciplinary partnerships are identified by health psychology, they include "epidemiologists, physiologists, pharmacologists, physicians, and the like" (Baum, 1989, p. 2). This can be interpreted as reflecting a medicocentric perspective, but it does not include nurses, dentists, or disciplines or professions focusing on health in larger social and community systems, such as anthropology, public health, social work, or sociology.

Locating Health Behavior Research

Basic health behavior research thus requires organizational and institutional structures that encourage such interdisciplinary efforts, that facilitate the interaction of researchers representing relevant disciplines and professions, and that establish and reinforce health behavior's identity. Ideally, such institutional structures would be departments or programs of health behavior made up of persons from several of these disciplines and professions who are engaged in and are committed to basic health behavior research. Ideally, their interdisciplinary research activities would be recognized as essentially scholarly in nature rather than as adjuncts to community service or to solving personal or community health and medical problems. Ideally, such structures would be located within the basic arts and sciences units of universities, with strong linkages to scholarly, substantive doctoral programs in relevant areas as well as to professional training programs in dentistry, medicine, nursing, and social work.

SUMMARY

These remarks identify the beginnings we have made in understanding youngsters' health cognitions and emotions and the gaps in our knowledge. Some important future research agendas are noted, particularly the origins and development of health cognitions, the role of the family, health-germane motivation, cognitive skills involved in coping, and searches for deeper meaning.

A health behavior perspective, emphasizing both basic research and interdisciplinary efforts and departing from and remaining independent of a medical model perspective, offers maximum promise of increasing our knowledge of youngsters' health cognitions and of remedying these gaps.

A basic health behavior perspective and youngsters' health-related cognitions . . . "This could be the beginning of a beautiful friendship" (see footnote 1).

ACKNOWLEDGMENTS

Selected copyrighted passages in this article are taken from *Health Behavior: Emerging Research Perspectives,* a book of original readings edited by the author and published by Plenum Publishing Corporation in 1988. The passages are parts of the author's chapters, "Health Behavior: Plural Perspectives" (chapter 1) and "Health Behavior Research: Present and Future" (chapter 23), and appear in this article with the kind permission of Plenum Publishing Corporation, which owns the copyright.

REFERENCES

Antonovsky, A. (1984). The sense of coherence as a determinant of health. In J. D. Matarazzo, S. M. Weiss, J. A. Herd, N. E. Miller, & S. M. Weiss (Eds.), *Behavioral health: A handbook of health enhancement and disease prevention* (pp. 114-129). New York: Wiley.

Baranowski, T., & Nader, P. R. (1985). Family health behavior. In D. C. Turk & R. D. Kerns (Eds.), *Health, illness, and families: A life-span perspective* (pp. 51-80). New York: Wiley.

Bartlett, H. M. (1961). *Social work practice in the health field.* New York: National Association of Social Workers.

Baum, A. (1989a). Preface. In A. Baum (Ed.), Proceedings of the National Working Conference on Research in Health and Behavior [Special issue], *Health Psychology, 8,* 629-630.

Baum, A. (Ed.). (1989b). Proceedings of the National Working Conference on Research in Health and Behavior [Special issue], *Health Psychology, 8.*

Belloc, N. B., & Breslow, L. (1972). Relationship of physical health status and health practices. *Preventive Medicine, 1,* 409-421.

Ben-Sira, Z. (1977). Involvement with a disease and health-promoting behavior. *Social Science and Medicine, 11,* 165-173.

Ben-Sira, Z. (1988). Affective behavior and perceptions of health professionals. In D. S. Gochman (Ed.), *Health behavior: Emerging research perspectives* (pp. 305-317). New York: Plenum.

Ben-Sira, Z., & Padeh, B. (1978). "Instrumental coping" and "affective defense": An additional perspective in health promoting behavior. *Social Science and Medicine, 12,* 163-168.

Bishop, G. D., & Converse, S. A. (1987). Illness representations: A prototype approach. *Health Psychology, 5,* 95-114.

Breslow, L. (1980). Risk factor intervention for health maintenance. In D. Mechanic (Ed.), *Readings in medical sociology* (pp. 68-79). New York: The Free Press. (Reprinted from *Science,* 1978, *200,* 908-912).

Bruhn, J. G. (1988). Life style and health behavior. In D. S. Gochman (Ed.), *Health behavior: Emerging research perspectives* (pp. 71-86). New York: Plenum.

Bruhn, J. G., & Parcel, G. S. (1982). Current knowledge about the health behavior of young children: A conference summary [Special issue]. *Health Education Quarterly, 9,* 142-166.

Burbach, D. J., & Peterson, L. (1986). Children's concepts of physical illness: A review and critique of the cognitive-developmental literature. *Health Psychology, 5,* 307-325.

Burt, J. J. (1984). Metahealth: A challenge for the future. In J. D. Matarazzo, S. M. Weiss, J. A. Herd, N. E. Miller, & S. M. Weiss (Eds.), *Behavioral health: A handbook of health enhancement and disease prevention* (pp. 1239-1245). New York: Wiley.

Campbell, J. D. (1975a). Attribution of illness: Another double standard. *Journal of Health and Social Behavior, 16,* 114-126.

Campbell, J. D. (1975b). Illness is a point of view: The development of children's concepts of illness. *Child Development, 46,* 92-100.

Campbell, J. D. (1978). The child in the sick-role: Contributions of age, sex, parental status, and parental values. *Journal of Health and Social Behavior, 19,* 35-51.

Conrad, P. (1985). The meaning of medications: Another look at compliance. *Social Science and Medicine, 20,* 29-37.

Dielman, T. E., Leech, S. L., Becker, M. H., Rosenstock, I. M., & Horvath, W. J. (1982). Parental and child health beliefs and behavior [Special issue]. *Health Education Quarterly, 9,* 60-77.

Drotar, D., Johnson, S. B., Iannotti, R., Krasnegor, N., Matthews, K. A., Melamed, B. G., Millstein, S., Peterson, R. A., Popiel, D., & Routh, D. K. (1989). Child health psychology [Special issue]. *Health Psychology, 8,* 781–784.

Gellert, E. (1962). Children's conceptions of the content and functions of the human body. *Genetic Psychology Monographs, 61,* 293-405.

Gellert, E. (1978). What do I have inside me? How children view their bodies. In E. Gellert (Ed.), *Psychosocial aspects of pediatric care.* New York: Grune and Stratton.

Gochman, D. S. (1977). Perceived vulnerability and its psychosocial context. *Social Science and Medicine, 11,* 115-120.

Gochman, D. S. (1981). On labels, systems, and motives: Some perspectives on children's health behavior. In *Self-management educational programs for childhood asthma, 2,* Conference Manuscripts. Sponsored by Center for Interdisciplinary Research in Immunologic Diseases, University of California at Los Angeles; National Institute of Allergy and Infectious Diseases; Asthma and Allergy Foundation of America.

Gochman, D. S. (1982). Labels, systems, and motives: Some perspectives for future research [Special issue]. *Health Education Quarterly, 9,* 167-174.

Gochman, D. S. (1985). Family determinants of children's concepts of health and illness. In D. C. Turk & R. D. Kerns (Eds.), *Health, illness, and families: A life-span perspective* (pp. 23-50). New York: Wiley.

Gochman, D. S. (1986). *Youngsters' health cognitions: Cross-sectional and longitudinal analyses.* Louisville, KY: Health Behavior Systems.

Gochman, D. S. (1988a). Assessing children's health concepts. In P. Karoly & C. May (Eds.), *Handbook of child health assessment: Biopsychosocial perspectives* (pp. 332-356). New York: Wiley.

Gochman, D. S. (Ed.). (1988b). *Health behavior: Emerging research perspectives.* New York: Plenum.

Gochman, D. S. (1988c). Health behavior: Plural perspectives. In D. S. Gochman (Ed.), *Health behavior: Emerging research perspectives* (pp. 3-17). New York: Plenum.

Gochman, D. S. (1988d). Health behavior research: Present and future. In D. S. Gochman (Ed.), *Health behavior: Emerging research perspectives* (pp. 409-424). New York: Plenum.

Gochman, D. S., & Saucier, J-F. (1982). Perceived vulnerability in children and adolescents [Special issue]. *Health Education Quarterly, 9,* 46-59.

Hayes-Bautista, D. E. (1978). Chicano patients and medical practitioners: A sociology of knowledges paradigm of lay-professional interaction. *Social Science and Medicine, 12,* 83-90.

Kalnins, I., & Love, R. (1982). Children's concepts of health and illness and implications for health education: An overview [Special issue]. *Health Education Quarterly, 9,* 8-19.

Kolbe, L. J. (1988). The application of health behavior research: Health Education and Health Promotion. In D. S. Gochman (Ed.), *Health behavior: Emerging research perspectives* (pp. 381-396). New York: Plenum.

Lau, R. R., & Hartman, K. A. (1983). Common sense representations of common illnesses. *Health Psychology, 2,* 167-185.

Leventhal, H., Prohaska, T. R., & Hirschman, R. S. (1983). Preventive health behavior across the life-span. In J. C. Rosen & L. J. Solomon (Eds.), *Preventing health risk behaviors and promoting coping with illness,* (Vol. 8, pp. 191-235). Vermont Conference on the Primary Prevention of Psychopathology. Hanover, NH: University Press of New England.

Melamed, B. G., Matthews, K. A., Routh, D. K., & Stabler, B. (Eds.). (1986). Child health psychology [Special issue], *Health Psychology, 5.*

Matarazzo, J. D. (1980). Behavioral health and behavioral medicine: Frontiers for a new health psychology. *American Psychologist, 35,* 807-817.

Matarazzo, J. D. (1984). Behavioral health: A 1990 challenge for the health sciences professions. In J. D. Matarazzo, S. M. Weiss, J. A. Herd, N. E. Miller, & S. M. Weiss (Eds.), *Behavioral health: A handbook of health enhancement and disease prevention* (pp. 3-40). New York: Wiley.

Michela, J. L., & Contento, I. R. (1986). Cognitive, motivational, social, and environmental influences on children's food choices. *Health Psychology, 5,* 209-230.

Nagy, M. H. (1951). Children's ideas on the origin of illness. *Health Education Journal, 9,* 6-12.

Nagy, M. H. (1953). The representation of "germs" by children. *Journal of Genetic Psychology, 83,* 227-240.

Natapoff, J. N. (1982). A developmental analysis of children's ideas of health [Special issue]. *Health Education Quarterly, 9,* 34-45.

Pearlin, L. I., & Schooler, C. (1978). The structure of coping. *Journal of Health and Social Behavior, 19,* 2-21.

Pratt, L. (1976). *Family structure and effective health behavior: The energized family.* Boston: Houghton-Mifflin.

Rashkis, S. R. (1965). Children's understanding of health. *Archives of General Psychiatry, 12,* 10-17.

Roter, D. L. (1988). Reciprocity in the medical encounter. In D. S. Gochman (Ed.), *Health behavior: Emerging research perspectives* (pp. 293-303). New York: Plenum.

Sallis, J. F., & Nader, P. R. (1988). Family determinants of health behavior. In D. S. Gochman (Ed.), *Health behavior: Emerging research perspectives* (pp. 107-124). New York: Plenum.

Schwartz, G. E., & Weiss, S. M. (Eds.). (1978). *Proceedings of the Yale Conference on Behavioral Medicine.* Department of Health, Education and Welfare Publication (NIH Report No. 78-1424).

Simeonsson, R. J., Buckley, L., & Monson, L. (1979). Conceptions of illness causality in hospitalized children. *Journal of Pediatric Psychology, 4,* 77–84.

Stimson, G., & Webb, B. (1975). *Going to see the doctor: The consultation process in general practice.* London: Routledge & Kegan Paul.

Taylor, S. E. (1990). Health psychology: The science and the field. *American Psychologist, 45,* 40–50.

Zastowny, T. R., Kirschenbaum, D. S., & Meng, A. L. (1986). Coping skills training for children: Effects on distress before, during, and after hospitalization for surgery [Special issue]. *Health Psychology, 5,* 231–248.

I

Developmental Trajectories in Behavioral Health

2

Development of Attachment, Health Risks, and Health Control

Colleen Frobose
Elizabeth J. Susman
The Pennsylvania State University

There is a long history of interest, from a psychological and sociological perspective, in risk factors and health behaviors that contribute to the morbidity and mortality of youth. Rarely is a developmental perspective taken regarding risk and health behaviors. The purpose of the three chapters to follow is to place youth risk and health behavior within a developmental perspective.

The physical and psychosocial maturation of the individual over the life span has generally been thought to have a somewhat predictable developmental trajectory. A considerable portion of this development that is particularly salient to health takes place prior to adulthood. Development progresses from the early stages of infant attachment or secure dependency (Fox, chapter 3) to increasing autonomy in childhood and adolescence. The initial responsibility for health-related behaviors is the mother's, but this responsibility is increasingly placed with the child (Iannotti & Bush, chapter 4) and then with the adolescent as development progresses (Irwin & Millstein, chapter 5).

Parallel to increasing autonomy of the child and adolescent is the increase in cognitive capacity that is highly related to health behavior. The infant in the early stages of attachment, with preoperational thinking, has little autonomy in health behavior. The child with slightly less attachment and increased cognitive capacity has slightly more autonomy in health behavior. The adolescent with the capacity for formal operational thinking has sufficient autonomy to engage in both health risk and health-promoting behaviors.

The parallels between the development of cognition and autonomy suggest that they are not unrelated. As explained by Fox as well as in earlier work of Bowlby

(1969), attachment is interwoven with cognition. The strange situation paradigm, often used to measure attachment, is dependent on the ability of the child to cognitively perceive the situation as strange or possibly threatening. In conjunction with temperament and level of attachment, cognitive perception contributes to whether the child will react to the removal of the mother. Individual differences in temperament and cognitive determination of the situation by the child may affect the formation of attachment. Fox makes the point that it is not one factor but the fit of a number of factors that determines attachment.

In relation to health, the fit and subsequent strength of the attachment bond have possible physical and emotional consequences. Secure attachment is proported to be related to emotional health in infants, Fox suggests, because it reflects the trust relationship with the mother. The infant's physical health may also be affected by the ability of the mother to respond to health-related behaviors in the infant, such as cries of pain. In addition, because attachment is a reflection of trust, the subsequent formation of autonomy in the child and adolescent may be affected by the security of the attachment bond.

The relationship between children's health behavior and cognition has rarely been explored. Children are assumed to be attached to their parents and have very little autonomous health behavior (Iannotti & Bush, chapter 4). In health delivery situations, children are often treated as though they do not have the cognitive ability to make health related decisions. Iannotti and Bush make two important points regarding children's health behavior: First, parents convey that some responsibility for decisions regarding health behaviors belongs to the child, and second, children make autonomous decisions related to health behavior. It is thus apparent that many health-related behaviors, such as self-medication, are cognitive decisions that are often made autonomously by the child.

The relation of cognition and autonomous behavior in the adolescent has long been acknowledged by developmental theorists. Recently, the increase in autonomous behavior at the extreme of decision making has been identified as risk-taking behavior. Risk-taking behavior has been explored and linked as a possible although inexplicit unifying concept for a group of adolescent health behaviors that are known to covary (Irwin & Vaughan, 1988; Jessor, 1984). In addition to linking a variety of health-risk behaviors under the overall concept of risk-taking behaviors (e.g., sexual activity, driving habits, and substance use), the cognitive and psychosocial development of children and adolescents is beginning to be integrated into theories of risk-taking behavior.

A review of the literature on risk taking reveals a number of key suppositions that form a framework for a more comprehensive understanding of risk-taking behavior. One key element of risk taking is its intentional nature. This implies a cognitive decision by the adolescent to engage in such a behavior. Earlier literature on risk taking in adults supports this idea, and few would argue that some element of choice is inherent in risk taking. Kogan and Wallach (1964) suggested that all decisions or choices involve an inherent risk. What then distinguishes risk-taking behavior from other volitional behavior?

An inherent aspect of risk taking is the nature of the decision-making process and the reasoning of the decision maker. In risk taking, although the decision is intentional, two scenarios are possible in the decision-making process, either the individual is not cognizant of the risk involved or the individual desires the risk. Both of these scenarios are hypothesized to be taking place in what is currently referred to as risk taking, and both find support in the literature. A developmental perspective, including both cognitive and emotional components, is helpful in the integration of these two scenarios.

The idea that risk is not perceived when engaging in these behaviors is supported by some of the theories of adolescent development (Erikson, 1961; Piaget, 1952). Cognitive development in adolescents, specifically the development of formal operational thinking, may help to explain the nature of risk taking in children and young adolescents. Unable to perceive risks in their own behavior because of concrete operational thinking or inconsistent application of formal operational thinking, children and adolescents are unable to hypothesize outcomes to their behavior. Consequently, they may become victims of accidental injury. This conception is accepted in relation to children because the health-risk behaviors of children are generally not thought of as risk taking since children are not aware of the consequences of their behavior. The question remains, is this the case with the adolescent?

The notion that the adolescent desires the risk also finds support in theories of psychosocial development, primarily theories that incorporate the concept of autonomy. The development of autonomous behavior in the child and the increasing autonomy of the adolescent poses the opportunity to make independent decisions; to test the limits or reactions in a particular situation. It is through autonomous decision making that the adolescent or child may choose the stimulation of a risky decision. Some authors actually attribute risk-taking behavior in adolescents to the formation of autonomy (Irwin & Millstein, 1986; Jessor & Jessor, 1987).

One major theory that has been applied to risk-taking behavior is Jessor and Jessor's (1977) problem-behavior theory. This theory develops the idea that three systems—personality, environment, and behavior—consist of characteristics that contribute to risk-taking behavior. As more of the characteristics become clustered in any one of these systems, the more prone the individual is to problem behavior.

Tonkins (1987) integrated the problem-behavior approach with the epidemiological model. This integrated framework takes into account the two scenarios described previously, the perception or lack of perception of risk and the desired level of risk. The perceived level of risk results from an integration of the perceptual skills, cognition, and motivation of the individual. The desired level of risk results from the motivational state and alternatives available.

In chapter 5, Irwin and Millstein incorporate much of the previous work on risk-taking behavior into a new and comprehensive definition of risk-taking behavior. An interpretation of current morbidity and mortality data in the youth population furthers this definition. Finally, they provide a model for the interrelation of risk-taking phenomenon within the process of cognitive and psychosocial development.

Throughout the following three chapters, it is apparent that the formation of health behavior from infancy through adolescence parallels other developmental processes. Fox's summary of the state of the literature on attachment and the proposal of the idea of goodness of fit begins the trajectory of health behavior processes. Iannotti and Bush further this idea through their explorations of the autonomy of child health behavior. Irwin and Millstein's proposition of a theory of risk-taking behavior and autonomy continue to support the developmental trajectory of health behavior in adolescence. These three chapters provide, for the first time, a developmental theoretical perspective on health behavior in the first two decades of life. At the same time the authors acknowledge the important contributions of developmental processes beyond these periods of the life cycle.

REFERENCES

Bowlby, J. (1969). *Attachment.* New York: Basic Books.

Erikson, E. H. (1968). *Identity, youth and crisis.* New York: Norton.

Irwin, C. E., & Millstein, S. G. (1986). Biopsychosocial correlates of adolescent risk-taking behaviors. *Journal of Adolescent Health Care, 7,* 82-96.

Irwin, C. E., & Vaughan, E. (1988). Psychosocial context of adolescent development. *Journal of Adolescent Health Care, 9,* 11-19.

Jessor, R., & Jessor, S. L. (1977). *Problem behavior and psychological development: A longitudinal study of youth.* New York: Academic.

Jessor, R. (1984). Adolescent development and behavioral health. In J. D. Matarazzo, S. M. Weiss, J. A. Herd, N. E. Miller, & S. M. Weiss (Eds.), *Behavioral Health: A Handbook of health enhancement and disease prevention.* New York: Wiley.

Kogan, N., & Wallach, M. A. (1964). *Risk Taking.* New York: Holt, Reinhart, & Winston.

Piaget, J. (1952). *The origins of intelligence in children.* New York: International Universities Press.

Tonkins, R. S. (1987). Adolescent risk-taking behavior. *Journal of Adolescent Health Care, 8,* 213-220.

3

The Role of Individual Differences in Infant Personality in the Formation of Attachment Relationships

Nathan A. Fox
Institute for Child Study
University of Maryland

INTRODUCTION

The nature of the child's bond to its mother has been of considerable interest to psychologists for many years. Although Freud (1952) articulated a position that placed extreme importance on the experiences of the infant during the first year of life, he did not develop a model of good or bad mothering as subsequent psychoanalytic theorists did (Winnicott, 1975). Nor did he place emphasis on the quality of the relationship between mother and infant. Rather, the infant was a primitive being whose needs and drives had to be met in a satisfactory manner. If the mother or another caregiver could satisfy these needs, then the infant could move through the early stages of psychosexual development to a point at which relations with one figure assumed psychological importance (Freud, 1905). John Bowlby, a trained psychoanalyst, was the first to present a coherent model of the process by which the bond between mother and infant developed and the functions that this bond served (Bowlby, 1969, 1973). He described the importance of the formation of the bond, from its immediate consequences but also from an evolutionary perspective. Bowlby's reasoning took both an ethological and evolutionary perspective. He argued that, with a long period of infancy or immaturity, it becomes necessary for the parent (mother) to protect her immature offspring from predators and danger. Once this period of immaturity ceases, the offspring have the ability to protect themselves within the confines of their environment. Because of this need for protection and the need for the offspring to survive, mother and infant develop an important symbiotic relationship in which infant's signals of distress or fear are noted by the mother, and she, in turn, offers comfort and protection, as well as a secure base from which the young learns to explore the environment. As the infant develops, the system of infant signals and maternal responses grows more complex. However, the basic function of the system remains constant: the infant signals its distress, the mother provides protection and security, and the infant seeks proximity and contact during periods of danger or distress. Bowlby (1969) viewed this goal-corrected partnership, as he called it, prototypical for future relationships with other conspecifics.

Mary Ainsworth adapted Bowlby's model of attachment to the framework of American personality psychology (Ainsworth, 1973). She developed a system by which one can understand individual differences in the development of the attachment bond as well as the consequences of these individual patterns for subsequent personality. Using Ainsworth's paradigm one can assess the quality of the relationship between mother and infant and determine if the pattern of attachment is secure or insecure (Ainsworth, Bell, & Stayton, 1971). She based her notions of security on Bowlby's model in which the "normal" process of attachment includes proximity seeking and contact maintaining by the infant toward the mother during times of danger or stress. Her paradigm, the Strange Situation (Ainsworth & Wittig, 1969), consists of a series of brief separations and reunions in which the level of stress upon the infant increases over the course of the session. Initial separations from mother occur in the presence of an unfamiliar but friendly adult. Subsequent separations occur with no adult present in the room. Ainsworth and her students were interested in the infant's response to these separations and the infant's behavior toward the mother during the reunions.

In her initial development of the Strange Situation paradigm, she observed 52 middle-class families from the Baltimore, Maryland area for a number of times in their homes during the first year of life. Based on these observations, Ainsworth conceptualized and organized individual patterns of interaction between mother and infant into those she believed reflected sensitive and responsive mothering and those she considered insensitive. The sensitive mother responds contingently to her infant's cues or signals. For example, if the infant cries, the mother attempts to determine the nature of the distress and soothe her child. Or the mother responds positively to infant smiles and positive vocalizations. This contingent responding, Ainsworth argued, gives the infant a sense of security and a sense of control over the environment (Ainsworth, 1973). It also gives the infant a sense that in periods of stress or danger it can rely on the mother for protection and comfort. On the other hand, the mother who is insensitive to her infant's cues or distress may elicit one of two patterns in her infant. The infant ignores the mother, withdrawing from social interaction and not seeking the mother's comfort during stress, because the infant has learned that the mother is not available. Or the infant develops an ambivalent relationship with the mother based on the inconsistent pattern of responding previously experienced. This inconsistency leads to a confused response during periods of stress with the infant both seeking proximity and contact but also angry and ambivalent knowing that such contact will not be consistently or sensitively offered.

Ainsworth developed a coding system for behavior in the Strange Situation that has become the heart of current attachment theory (Ainsworth, Blehar, Waters, & Wall, 1978). Two types of insecure patterns are described: the avoidant infant and the ambivalent/angry infant. In addition, there is the infant who seeks proximity and contact with the mother (as it should) but to varying degrees. The infant in the latter category is considered securely attached. Ainsworth, however, decided it was important to distinguish between the degree of proximity and contact seeking that the secure infant exhibits. She divided the secure group into four subcategories (Group 1 through Group 4) based primarily on the degree of contact and proximity exhibited (Group 1 seeks the least, Group 4 the most).

These classifications have become known as the A, B, C typology, derived from behavior in the Strange Situation. The infant classified as A is insecure but avoidant; the infant classified as B is secure (and there are four subcategories within B); and the infant classified as C is insecure and ambivalent in its responses. It should also be noted that within the A and C classifications are two subcategories for each (A1 and A2 or C1 and C2) based primarily on an active/passive dimension in terms of the infant's response.

The reason I provide this much detail on this system is threefold. First, among researchers interested in social development during infancy, the Strange Situation has held an extremely important and almost ubiquitous position for many years (Bretherton, 1985). There are multiple studies of the origins of the different types of attachment classification (A, B, or C) and of the outcomes in personality and cognitive functioning as a function of being an A, B, or C. Second, attachment theorists argue that these differences in insecurity and security reflect the quality of the relationship between mother and infant. That is, within the framework of the Strange Situation, it is the quality of the relationship between the infant and that significant other participating in the paradigm that is measured. So, for example, were infant and father to participate in the Strange Situation, the infant's behavior and subsequent attachment classification would reflect the quality of the bond between father and infant. Indeed, there are numerous studies of infant and father that have been used to describe this relationship (Lamb, 1978). It is also important to note that this paradigm has been used in different cultures with the same understanding as to its meaning and interpretation. Behavior observed in the Strange Situation is a reflection of the quality of the infant's attachment relationship with that significant individual. So, for example, Sagi, Lamb, Lewkowicz, Shoham, Dvir, and Estes (1985) used the Strange Situation to assess the quality of the relationship between an infant and its primary caregiver and an infant and its mother when the infant was raised on an Israeli kibbutz.

A third reason for presenting detail on the Strange Situation is that in recent years this paradigm has come under some criticism. There are a number of excellent reviews that call into question the basis for using the Strange Situation as a measure of attachment quality. Nevertheless, proponents of the system continue to argue, persuasively, that the paradigm is useful and remains a reflection of relationship quality.

Among the challenges to the interpretation of behavior of the Strange Situation are those from researchers interested in infant temperament. There are now many studies that attempt to examine the role of individual differences in infant temperament in Strange Situation behavior (Goldsmith, Bradshaw, & Rieser-Danner, 1986; Vaughn, Lefever, Seifer, & Barglow, 1989; Weber, Levitt, & Clarke, 1986). The focus of this chapter is on this issue. We review two independent sources of evidence that argue that infant temperament plays an important role, not only in the child's behavior in the Strange Situation, but also in the determination of the classification derived from that behavior. The first source of evidence includes research from our laboratory that attempts to examine the role of certain patterns of individual differences on attachment classification. The second source of evidence presented in this chapter involves the results of a meta analysis performed on a series of studies used by attachment researchers as evidence for the lack of influence of infant individual differences in deriving attachment classification from the Strange Situation (Fox, Kimmerly, & Schaffer, 1991). The third and final section of this chapter provides some thoughts about the nature of research needed to understand the interaction of temperament and caregiving.

STUDIES OF TEMPERAMENT AND ATTACHMENT

There have been numerous attempts to examine the relationship between infant temperament and attachment security (e.g., Goldsmith & Alansky, 1987). These studies are grouped into three categories: those that use measures of maternal report of infant temperament, those that examine the factor structure of behavior in the Strange Situation and its relation to infant temperament rather than classification per se, and those that use laboratory measures of temperament in a multimeasure approach to the problem. The findings across studies and these three categories are ambiguous. A number of studies report significant differences in maternal report of infant temperament with respect to attachment classification (Vaughn et al., 1989). Others suggest relationships between maternal report of infant temperament and the pattern of behavior displayed during the Strange Situation (Thompson, Connel, & Bridges, 1988).

There has also been an attempt to outline a compromise position between the temperament and attachment positions (Belsky & Rovine, 1987). Belsky and Rovine argued that infant temperament may account for variance in behavior during the Strange Situation but not predict specific types of attachment classification. In a re-analysis of two data sets they found that measures of infant temperament did not discriminate A versus B versus C children but did differentiate between infants classified as A1 through B2 versus B3 through C2.

There are, of course, a number of possible reasons for the lack of strong temperament predictors of attachment classification. Most studies have only limited sample sizes. Given the distribution of avoidance, security, and resistance in a normal, randomly selected population (Ainsworth et al., 1978), it might be difficult to find significant differences when comparisons are made between attachment categories with small numbers of subjects.

Goldsmith and Alansky (1987) identified 19 studies for which an effect size could be derived. All contained both measures of infant proneness to distress and observation of resistance behavior. Of the 19 studies, 10 rely solely on maternal report data of infant temperament, the remaining 9 contain some type of behavioral observation (either in the infant's home or via the Neonatal Behavioral Assessment Scale [NBAS]) to measure infant proneness to distress. As a result of their meta analysis of these studies Goldsmith and Alansky (1987) concluded that there is a modest association between infant proneness to distress and resistance behavior in the Strange Situation. The authors did not directly assess whether this temperamental characteristic predicts insecure classification.

The infant temperament variables examined and the age at which they are recorded may also contribute to the lack of a strong pattern. Many studies of temperament and attachment use newborn infant performance on the NBAS as a measure of temperament. There are a number of problems with the psychometric properties of the NBAS as well as with its predictive validity (Sameroff, Krafchuk, & Bakow, 1978). In addition, no single set of newborn behavioral characteristics remains stable across the first 12 months of life. On the other hand, one advantage of the NBAS is that it measures reactivity and responsivity during the first days of life. As such it is a window into an as yet unsocialized neonate and provides a "pure" measure of individual differences in temperamental behavior. There are, in fact, a number of studies that find relationships between behavior measured on the NBAS and attachment classification (Grossmann, Grossmann, Spangler, Suess, & Unzer, 1981).

A second measurement issue in this area is the lack of reliable and valid measures of infant temperament. Much of the work in infant temperament utilizes questionnaire data and maternal report. The correlations between factors derived from the different maternal report scales and laboratory measures of infant temperament are modest at best (Rothbart, 1981, 1986). It is also possible that the factors derived from these maternal report scales do not capture the particular dimensions of infant behavior that are related to security or that their meaning to parents may be quite different.

Even with these problems there is agreement that certain patterns of temperament are related to behavior in the Strange Situation. In general, specific dimensions of infant temperament assessed in the laboratory (Gunnar, Mangelsdorf, Kestenbaum, Lang, Larson, & Andreas, in press) or via maternal report (Vaughn et al., 1989) predict crying in the Strange Situation. The pattern of temperamental factors associated with crying includes irritability, negative mood, or difficult temperament. The conclusion of a number of authors is that infants rated as irritable or with difficult temperaments are more likely to display distress during separation (Goldsmith & Alansky, 1987; Weber et al., 1986). Nevertheless, these studies fail to find significant predictors specific to attachment classification.

Recent models of infant temperament stress the importance of individual differences in reactivity. Rothbart (1989; Rothbart & Derryberry, 1981), for example, has outlined an approach to measuring reactivity along dimensions of threshold, latency, and intensity of response. We (Fox, 1989; Fox & Stifter, 1989; Stifter & Fox, 1990), demonstrated that there are stable, individual differences in reactivity during the first year and that these differences are associated with individual differences in autonomic patterning. For example, infant negative affect in response to mildly stressful, novel stimuli and frustration is related to individual differences in vagal tone. The infant with high vagal tone is more reactive. This reactive response may not be similar to the temperamental disposition of irritability or difficult temperament. That is, the infant who reacts intensely to frustration with anger may not necessarily be perceived as an irritable infant or as having negative moods. Indeed, I (Fox, 1989) found that the infant displaying frustrative reactivity in the lab at 5 months is more likely to display positive social behaviors toward strangers and novel events at 14 months compared to the infant who is less reactive to frustration. Irritability and negative mood, on the other hand, may be a class of behaviors that some infants exhibit in response to novelty and challenge. These infants might be perceived as more difficult across situations and may be infants who are more inconsolable and withdrawn later in life (Rubin, LeMare, & Lollis, in press).

The simple dichotomy, then, of reactive versus nonreactive infants and their relationship to behavior in the Strange Situation may not afford a clear understanding of the processes involved in the production of different types of insecurity (avoidance/resistance). For example, one might expect that the infant who responds intensively to frustration with anger is more likely to show avoidance in the Strange Situation, whereas the infant who responds intensively to novelty and mild challenge with negative affect is more likely to exhibit resistance behaviors in the Strange Situation. These differences in infant reactivity may account for variations in behavior in the Strange Situation.

A LONGITUDINAL STUDY OF TEMPERAMENT AND ATTACHMENT

Meaning and Rationale for Psychophysiological Recording

For the past five years we have conducted an ongoing study of the relations between infant reactivity and attachment. The research utilizes behavioral observation of the infant, maternal report of infant temperament, and recording of both peripheral physiological responses that may reflect individual differences in infant reactivity.

The research includes the recording of both peripheral and central measures of physiological activity. At each of the age points in the study we recorded heart rate to examine individual differences in tonic heart rate variability. The notion that individuals differ in their tonic pattern of heart rate and that this pattern may reflect certain personality styles has been articulated by a number of researchers (Eppinger & Hess, 1915; Kagan, 1982; Lacey & Lacey, 1958; Porges, 1976; Wenger, 1941). Most of this research postulates that imbalances in sympathetic or parasympathetic influence on autonomic functioning may affect behavioral reactivity. For example, Kagan (Kagan, Reznick, & Snidman, 1987) demonstrated a relation between measures of heart rate variability and a child's responses to challenging and unfamiliar events. Inhibited, shy behavior is associated with decreased heart rate variability. In our own work (Fox & Gelles, 1984; Stifter, Fox, & Porges, 1989) we found an association between heart rate variability and emotional expressivity. The infant with high vagal tone is more expressive during interactions with its mother. We utilize the vagal tone measure as an index of the coupling of heart rate and respiration and as a measure of parasympathetic influence on the heart (Porges, 1985). The measure reflects the level of parasympathetic influence on heart rate variability and the level of physiological organization of the nervous system (cf. Fox & Porges, 1985).

The use of resting patterns of the Electroencephalogram (EEG) is based on a variety of data suggesting that the pattern of activation in the resting electroencephalogram may be a marker for certain personality differences. For example, Davidson and colleagues (Schaffer, Davidson, & Saron, 1983) selected undergraduate subjects who scored either high or low on the Beck Depression Inventory (BDI) and whose BDI scores were stable across a six-month period. An electroencephalogram was recorded while the subjects sat quietly with either eyes open or eyes closed for a minute baseline period. Analysis of the resting EEG power data revealed that subjects with high and stable scores on the Beck Depression Inventory exhibited greater relative right frontal activation compared to those subjects with low Beck scores. Examination of the individual hemisphere data found that the high Beck subjects displayed greater right-sided and right-frontal activation. Davidson and Fox (1989) recorded EEG activity from 10-month-old female infants prior to the onset of an experimental procedure involving brief maternal separation. Infant affect responses were recorded during the experiment in response to maternal departure. Davidson and Fox (1989) found that those infants who were more likely to cry to maternal separation exhibited greater relative right-frontal activation during the baseline period compared to those infants who did not cry.

One interpretation to these data is that the pattern of frontal EEG asymmetry exhibited by the 10-month-old infants and perhaps also by the adult subjects with high and stable BDI scores reflects an underlying temperamental or personality characteristic. Those infants or adults with greater relative right-frontal activation may have a lower threshold to respond with negative affect to novel and mildly stressful events. Support for this argument is found in data presented by Davidson and colleagues (Finman, Davidson, Colton, Straus, & Kagan, 1989). They reported that children selected for extreme patterns of behavioral inhibition (high degrees of proximity to mother and little interaction with an unfamiliar peer) display greater relative right-frontal activation in their baseline tonic EEG. In this instance, EEG was recorded some four months after the behavioral assessment. It may be, in this case, that the pattern of resting frontal activation reflects a temperamental difference: a threshold to respond with negative affect or withdrawal to novelty or mildly stressful situations.

A number of researchers (Fox & Davidson, 1984; Kinsbourne, 1978) have argued that differences in left- and right-hemisphere activation are associated with tendencies to approach or withdraw toward different stimuli. Thus, individuals with greater right-frontal activation respond with behavioral withdrawal to novelty or stress whereas those with left-frontal activation are presumably more likely to approach. In a series of studies, Fox and Davidson (1987, 1988) have demonstrated the relation between emotion responses reflecting approach or withdrawal and frontal EEG asymmetry. In general, infants exhibited left-frontal asymmetry during emotions associated with approach and right-frontal asymmetry during emotions associated with withdrawal.

Longitudinal Study

The sample for the longitudinal study of temperament and attachment consisted of a group of 80 infants from middle-class homes who were selected randomly from a local hospital nursery at 2 days of age. The major selection criteria included gestational age between 38 and 42 weeks, birth weight between 2,500 and 4,090 grams, vaginal or caesarean delivery, Apgar scores of at least 7 at 1 minute and 8 at 5 minutes, and a normal pediatric examination. Pregnancies were uncomplicated by serious illness, and deliveries did not involve mid or high forceps or general anesthesia. The infants were assessed at 2 days of age, at 5 months of age, and again at 14 months of age. On the average, newborn subjects were tested at 48 hours of age. Sixty-three of these infants were seen in the laboratory at 5 months of age (30 males and 33 females). And 53 returned to the laboratory at 14 months of age (28 males and 25 females).

A description of the procedures administered at the newborn and 5 month age periods is found in Fox (1989) and Stifter & Fox (1990). Briefly, in the newborn period 10 minutes of heart rate was recorded while the infant state was observed. Periods of both quiet and active sleep were recorded. A pacifier withdrawal task (Bell, Weller, & Waldrop, 1971) was administered to the infant when he or she was in a quiet alert state.

At 5 months of age, infants were seen in the laboratory. Five minutes of EKG was recorded while the infant sat on its mother's lap. The infant was then seated in an infant seat, and the mother and an unfamiliar adult female played peek-a-boo with the infant. The infant's mother then gently held her infant's hands down at the side of the infant seat for 2 minutes (or less if the infant cried).

At 14 months infant and mother returned to the lab and again, 5 minutes of heart rate was recorded while the infant sat in a high chair with mother sitting next to it. The infant was videotaped with mother in the Ainsworth and Wittig Strange Situation.

A subset of the infants seen in the Strange Situation was asked to return to the lab for a second visit some two months later. At this second visit, the infant sat in a high chair or in its mothers' laps while 5 minutes of EKG and brain electrical activity (EEG) were recorded.

The distribution of attachment classifications derived from the Strange Situation at 14 months was 13.4% of the children classified as avoidant/insecure (A1/A2), 69.3% classified as securely attached (B1 through B4), and 17.3% classified as anxious/ambivalent/insecure (C1/C2).

The question that we set out to answer with the data collected at the newborn, 5-, and 14-month assessments is: Is there a relationship between newborn and 5-month infant variables and attachment classification at 14 months?

Our approach to answer this question utilized a series of analyses to determine if there were differences in any of the neonatal or 5-month measures. These analyses divided the insecure infants into two categories (avoidant and ambivalent/resistant).

Newborn Measures. There were no differences in birth weight, gestational age, method of delivery (vaginal/caesarean), or method of neonatal feeding (breast/bottle fed) among the infants classified as A, B, or C. There was, however, one significant finding from the delivery variables. Infants subsequently classified as insecure/avoidant (A1/A2) had lower 5-minute Apgar scores compared to the other two groups of infants [$F(2, 49) = 4.35, p < .02$]. A two (cry/no cry) × three (A/B/C) chi-square on the newborn behavior of cry to pacifier withdrawal was nonsignificant. There was no relationship between response to pacifier and subsequent attachment grouping. In addition, there were no significant group differences on the autonomic measures (heart period or vagal tone at the newborn period).

Five-Month Measures. Analyses of variance with attachment group (3 levels) as the independent factor and the 5-month infant behaviors as dependent measures were computed. The only lab/behavioral measure to reveal differences among the groups was 5-month motor arousal [$F(2, 47) = 3.52, p = .04$]. Infants in the B category exhibited lower motor arousal scores than infants in either the A or C categories. None of the other analyses of the 5-month behavioral measures, including the summary scores, produced significant group differences. A two (cry/no cry) × three (A/B/C) chi-square was computed on the response at 5 months to arm restraint. The analysis was nonsignificant.

Analyses of variance with attachment group (three levels) as the independent factor and the IBQ scale scores as dependent measures were computed. There were significant differences among the groups in maternal report of activity level [$F(2, 46) = 5.80, p = .01$]. Infants in the B category were rated by mothers as lowest in activity level whereas infants in the A category were rated as highest in activity level. None of the other scales differentiated among the groups. Analyses of variance with attachment group (three levels) as the independent factor were computed on the 5-month heart period and vagal tone measures. No significant effects were found.

These same analyses were repeated combining the insecure infants into one category (secure vs. insecure). The results of these analyses were similar to those reported when the insecure infants were divided into the A and C categories. There was a trend for differences in newborn vagal tone between secure and insecure infants [$F(1, 43) = 3.02, p < .08$]. Insecure infants had lower vagal tone as newborns. Motor activity [$F(1, 49) = 7.11, p < .01$] and maternal rating of activity level [$F(1, 46) = 7.04, p < .01$] differentiated secure from insecure infants, with insecure infants displaying greater motor arousal and being rated by their mothers as more active. There was also a relationship between crying to pacifier withdrawal at 2 days of age and security. Infants who cried were more likely to be classified as insecure compared to those who did not cry to pacifier withdrawal ($\chi^2 = 4.36, p < .04$).

In an attempt to explore the relationship between behavioral reactivity at 5 months and attachment classification we selected those infants whose scores were in the extreme and examined their attachment classification. Children with negative reactivity scores greater than .5 standard deviation above the mean formed the high reactive group ($n = 10$), and those with scores .5 standard deviation below the mean formed the low reactive group ($n = 10$). Two chi-square analyses were computed; one examining the A/B/C grouping and the second the secure/insecure grouping. The latter analysis was significant (one-tailed Fisher's exact test = .04). All 10 children in the low negative reactivity group at 5 months were classified as secure at 14 months.

We also tested for behavioral and psychophysiological differences among the four subcategories of the secure (B) classification. Spearman's *rho* rank-order correlation coefficients were computed using the newborn and five-month behavioral and physiological variables and summary scores and the subtypes of B1 through B4. Results found subtype differences for the negative reactivity score Rho = $-.43$, $p=.01$, and 5-month vagal tone, Rho = $.44$, $p=.01$. Among the secure infants, those categorized as B1 or B2 exhibited lower negative reactivity scores and lower vagal tone at 5 months compared to those categorized as B3 or B4.

The data display only modest relationships between newborn and 5-month measures and 14-month attachment classification. Indeed, the data differentiate between infants classified as securely or insecurely attached rather than different types of insecurity. There is little discrimination within the insecure group between the two different patterns of behavior elicited in the Strange Situation (avoidance or resistance). Infant reactivity, whether assessed in the laboratory or via maternal report, is associated with subsequent insecurity. Infants rated by their mothers as more active and less able to tolerate frustration at 5 months are found to be more insecure at 14 months. Infants who were more motorically aroused at 5 months in a lab assessment are more likely to be classified as insecure at 14 months. Thus, security of attachment at 14 months is associated with a particular pattern of infant temperament that is observable early in the first half of the first year of life.

However, there were no differences between infants rated as insecure/avoidant versus those rated as insecure/resistant. These are two distinct behavioral patterns of insecurity observed in the Strange Situation. The former are infants who are generally not upset at separation and do not actively greet the mother upon reunion. The latter are infants who are generally highly upset at separation and are not easily calmed during reunion. In fact, they are likely to exhibit anger and resistance to the mother's efforts to soothe them. Given these obvious differences in response to separation and reunion it is likely that indices of early infant reactivity did not discriminate between these two groups.

The data raise the possibility that there is a particular type of infant temperament that in interaction with maternal caregiving style produces a pattern of behavior in the Strange Situation that is classified as insecure. But it seems that whether the infant is classified as avoidant or resistant (A or C) depends more on that pattern of mothering than on infant characteristics. This conclusion is somewhat different from that of other studies of temperament and attachment that find infant predisposition to distress related to crying in the Strange Situation but not to attachment classification. The evidence from our study does not directly support that model. Rather, it says that certain infants are more likely to end up insecure. Their characteristics include high level of motor arousal and activity level and, in general, a high degree of behavioral reactivity. In certain instances (i.e., with a particular type of mothering) they exhibit behavior signifying avoidance whereas with a different pattern of caregiving they exhibit resistant behavior in the Strange Situation. In either case, there is a clear influence of infant temperament on classification of security at 14 months of age.

FURTHER EVIDENCE FOR THE INFLUENCE OF TEMPERAMENT ON ATTACHMENT: THE CASE OF MOTHER–FATHER CONCORDANCE

One piece of evidence for the claim that temperament does not affect attachment classification is the lack of concordance of classification between an infant and its mother and father. These data also argue for the lack of influence of infant temperament on the quality of attachment security and for the use of the Strange Situation as a paradigm from which to derive security of attachment (Main & Weston, 1981; Sroufe, 1985).

There are 11 samples that examine the concordance of infant attachment classification to mother and father (Belsky, Garduque, & Hrncir, 1984; Belsky & Rovine, 1987, 2 samples; Goossens & van IJzendoorn, 1988; Grossmann, Grossmann, Huber, & Wartner, 1981, 2 samples; Lamb, 1978; Lamb, Hwang, Frodi, & Frodi, 1982; Main & Weston, 1981; Owen & Chase-Lansdale, 1982; Sagi et al., 1985). Classification to one parent is dependent upon classification to the other parent in only three of these eleven samples (Goosens & van IJzendoorn, 1988; Lamb, 1978; Owen & Chase-Lansdale, 1982). If individual differences in infant temperament were to influence attachment classification derived from the Strange Situation, one would expect a high degree of concordance between classification of the same infant to mother or father. If temperament were orthogonal to attachment classification (Belsky & Rovine, 1987; Sroufe, 1985; Sroufe & Waters, 1982) and if classification reflected the individual infant–caregiver relationship, the type of classification to mother would be different than the type to father. This argument is based on the organizational view of attachment in which security as derived from the Strange Situation reflects the ongoing relationship that has developed between caregiver and child over the first year of life (Ainsworth et al., 1978; Sroufe & Waters, 1977). Mother and father interact with their infant differently, and the degree to which they are sensitive and responsive to their infant's bids for comfort varies. Were that the case, a child might not have the same attachment classification to both. Indeed, it is possible for a child to be securely attached to one parent and insecurely attached to a second parent. Attachment theorists have argued that the data on discordance of mother/father attachment support these claims. Alternatively, concordance of classification to mother and father may reflect similarity in interactive style between parents. If father and mother were both sensitive and responsive to their infant's cues, one would expect a high degree of identity in classification between parents and infant.

An alternative, temperament position would argue for a high degree of concordance particularly for the two types of insecure patterns of behavior. For many, temperament is regarded as a constitutionally based predisposition that is stable across time and generalizes across situations (Buss & Plomin, 1984; Rothbart & Derryberry, 1981). Thus, for example, there may be individual differences in infant irritability or threshold to respond with distress to novelty that present themselves in the Strange Situation regardless of presence of mother or father. An infant with a low threshold to express negative affect, who is highly irritable, is more likely to be classified as insecure/resistant. Or, an infant highly focused on interaction with toys and objects is more likely to be classified as insecure/avoidant in the Strange Situation (Lewis & Feiring, 1989).

In order to examine these issues we performed a meta analysis of the 11 studies of mother–infant and father–infant attachment (Fox et al., 1991). First we computed a log-linear analysis across the 11 studies to determine the dependence or independence of classification (A/B/C) to mother and father. Following this analysis we broke the 3 × 3 tables (A/B/C × A/B/C) into six 2 × 2 contingency tables. We did so because even with a significant interaction in the 3 × 3 (A/B/C × A/B/C) analysis, with 4 degrees of freedom, it is impossible to specify where the effect originated. We computed the following comparisons between classification with mother and father across studies: (a) secure versus insecure, (b) A versus C, (c) B1 and B2 versus B3 and B4, (d) A1 through B2 versus B3 through C2, (e) A versus B1 and B2, and (f) C versus B3 and B4.

Analysis 1 placed the two types of insecure infants, those classified as A or C, into the insecure category. It examined the possibility of concordance in security or insecurity to both parents. The analysis is interesting from an attachment perspective because it investigates the quality of the relationship a child has with each parent. However, from a temperament perspective, it may confound relationship and disposition because it combines infants who present opposite temperamental patterns (A and C). On the other hand, because most infants in each individual study are classified as secure, one expects high concordance in this analysis.

Analysis 2 examined the relation of ratings of insecurity to either parent by comparing the type of insecurity (avoidance or resistance). Lack of independence here indicates that infants classified as avoidant and insecure to mother are more likely to also be classified as avoidant and insecure to father or that infants classified as resistant and insecure to mother are more likely to be classified as resistant and insecure to father. Significant dependence argues that the two types of insecurity are indeed orthogonal and perhaps represent either different interactional histories, different temperamental styles, or their interaction.

Analysis 3 compared infants in the subcategories of the B classification. The underlying hypothesis is that the four subcategories of security may be dichotomized along a temperamental dimension not unlike Belsky's analysis (Belsky & Rovine, 1987). Significant dependence in this analysis further supports that perspective and argues that within the category of security temperamental differences are evident in the expression of behavior in the Strange Situation.

Analyses 2 and 3 described above are subsets of a grouping first proposed by Belsky, A1 through B2 versus B3 through C2 (Belsky & Rovine, 1987). Belsky argued that temperament plays a role in the overt behaviors of the child in the Strange Situation but does not influence classification per se. Analysis 4 examined differences in classification based on the division proposed by Belsky. Lack of independence in this analysis supports Belsky's dichotomy and argues that styles of behavior in the Strange Situation, rather than classification, have a common basis.

Analyses 5 and 6 were a further attempt to examine the Belsky dichotomy. Belsky and others argued that infants classified as A1 through B2 are less likely to cry than infants classified as B3 through C2. These dispositional differences express themselves in infant behavior during the Strange Situation but do not directly influence classification. For example, B4 infants are as likely to cry as infants classified as C. Analyses 5 and 6 examined the concordance within each half of this dichotomy. Analysis 5 examined the relationship between A versus either B1 or B2. If Belsky and Rovine (1987) are correct, there should not be significant dependence found in this table. Infants within this continuum are as likely to be classified as A (avoidant) as B1 or B2. Similarly, Analysis 6 examined the relationship between C versus either B3 or B4. Again, if the dichotomy based on infant predisposition to cry in response to mild stress that Belsky proposed is correct, there should not be significant dependence found in this latter analysis. Infants should as likely be classified as B3 or B4 as C.

The results of these analyses are presented in Table 3.1. As seen, each of the first four 2 × 2 analyses is significant at the .001 level, indicating concordance in attachment classification between mother and father to the same infant. This concordance holds for the type of insecurity (A vs. C), the type of secure pattern (B1/B2 vs. B3/B4), and for the overall secure versus insecure dichotomy. Analysis 5 is significant at the .05 level but not at the more stringent .001 level. Analysis 6 is significant indicating concordance within the B3 through C2 continuum between mother and father. If an infant is classified as ambivalent/insecure (C), it is likely to be so classified to the other parent rather than classified as B4. The same pattern is not true for the A through B2 continuum. That is, there is no evidence that being classified as A to one parent increases the likelihood of being similarly classified to the second parent as opposed to being classified as B1 or B2.

The results of the meta analyses clearly support a position of dependence of attachment classification to mother and father. They suggest that the assignment of security/insecurity that the child receives as a result of behavior in the Strange Situation is quite similar for both parents. The data also suggest that the type

TABLE 3.1
Results of a Meta Analysis of Mother–Infant and Father–Infant Attachment (Fox et al., 1991).

Comparison	*Average Odds Rates*	*95% Confidence Interval*	*Chi-Square Test of Independence (all df = 1)*	
Secure versus Insecure	1.692	1.218 – 2.351	9.861	p = .002
A versus C	7.791	4.121 – 23.104	13.701	p = .0002
B1 through B2 versus B3 through B4	4.600	2.782 – 7.606	35.394	p = .0001
A1 through B2 versus B3 through C2	3.781	2.675 – 5.344	56.823	p = .0001
A versus B1 and B2	2.073	1.125 – 3.819	5.481	p = .02
C versus B3 and B4	1.970	1.006 – 3.857	3.921	p = .05

of insecurity observed (avoidance or resistance) is similar for both parents. And, they indicate that groups of the subcategories of the secure classification reflect distinct types because classification within the secure infants is similar across mother and father. In addition, within infants who are considered to exhibit similar behaviors in the Strange Situation, perhaps reflecting common disposition (Belsky & Rovine, 1987), there is some evidence for concordance based on classification.

There are a number of alternative explanations for these data. First, it may be argued that the high degree of concordance found across studies supports an argument that the Strange Situation is assessing the working model inherent to the infant (e.g., security) rather than the particular relationship to either parent (Main, Kaplan, & Cassidy, 1985). Hence one expects to find parallels across caregivers in security. This explanation is supported by the pattern of data but may not be totally consonant with attachment theory. A position of attachment researchers is that the Strange Situation reflects the relationship between an individual and the infant and not simply the infant's current working model of security or insecurity (Ainsworth et al., 1978; Sroufe, 1985; Sroufe & Waters, 1977). Attachment security or insecurity is thought to reflect the quality of the relationship with that individual. And, it reflects an organizational system between an individual parent or caregiver and the child (Sroufe & Waters, 1977).

However, if the essence of attachment for the infant is the psychological sense of security or insecurity (e.g., the working model, independent of caregiver) one expects concordance between parents for an individual infant in the type of insecurity (A/C) or concordance in the type of security (B1B2/B3B4). That is, a child is secure or insecure in some basic sense and displays this similarly across individuals.

There are, however, data from a number of sources that find little concordance when additional caregivers such as a day care center teacher (Owen & Chase-Lansdale, 1982) or Israeli kibbutz metapelet (Sagi et al., 1985) are assessed. Were an individual child to be secure in some basic sense, one would expect a high degree of similarity of classification across caregivers. It is, of course, possible that these studies of caregiver/parent concordance have similar problems of small sample size that preclude finding these effects.

A second alternative explanation of these data is that the Strange Situation assesses the history of interaction, the family situation, and environment. Parents may be similar in their caregiving behavior and value systems regarding issues important to secure attachment such as responsivity and sensitivity to infant cues. One parent (a sensitive and responsive one) may serve as a model for the second parent. Or both might learn together to respond sensitively to their infant. The current data thus reflect the fact that the mother and father respond similarly to their infant and, perhaps, share similar views regarding caregiving. Similar patterns of interaction around responsivity and sensitivity to infant cues might result in similar patterns of attachment (Belsky, Rovine, & Taylor, 1984). Although this general explanation is a viable one for the data presented, there are few studies to support it.

There are many studies that find dissimilarity in the manner in which the father and mother interact with their child (Parke, 1978; Parke & Sawin, 1980). For example, Belsky, Gilstrap, and Rovine (1984) conducted observations of the mother, father, and infant when the infant was 1, 3, and 9 months old. The mother was more positively interactive and more responsive with her child at all times of measurement. Other studies find that the mother and father do not share the same values and caregiving expectations regarding their child (Lamb, Hwang, & Broberg, 1989). Along these lines, Bridges, Connell, and Belsky (1988) found that the organization of infant behavior in the Strange Situation varied as a function of the interactive partner. There are differences in the degree to which infant behavior toward either father or mother predicts responses to the stranger in the Strange Situation paradigm. There are, in addition, a number of studies that find a lack of agreement in the mother's and the father's rating of their child's temperament. The mother is more likely to rate her child as difficult particularly if that child is a male whereas the father is less likely to rate the child as difficult in response to identical temperament questionnaires (Frodi, Lamb, Frodi, Hwang, Forsstrom, & Corry, 1982).

There is one report of within-time correlations of maternal and paternal behavior toward an infant. Belsky & Volling (1987) found significant intercorrelations of maternal and paternal responsive behavior at 1, 3, and 9 months of age. Both mother and father are either highly involved or not involved with their infant. At the same time Belsky found consistent negative correlations between stimulation offered by one parent and other behaviors of the second. The more interactive the mother, the less responsive was the father. These within-age correlations begin to address the issue of parental concordance on dimensions important to developing secure attachment. The inconsistency between within-category versus between-category correlations, however, does not allow a clear interpretation of these father–child/mother–child data. Thus, although we cannot discount that the explanation of the high degree of concordance in attachment classification found in the meta analyses is due to concordant interactive behaviors of both mother and father, the supporting and validating studies are yet to be presented.

A third, and perhaps not exclusive, explanation of these data is that the infant's temperament may contribute to variations in classification. Given individual differences in reactivity to novelty and stress (Fox, 1989) or differences in play behavior early in life (Lewis & Feiring, 1989), it is not surprising that the infant responds similarly in the identical situation to both mother and father. There is, in fact, good evidence for the existence of stable individual differences in reactivity during the first year of life.

Fox (1989; Stifter & Fox, 1990) has found stability of infant reactivity to frustrating stimulus situations across the first year of life. An infant who cries in response to mild frustration at 2 days of age is more likely to cry to novel situations at 5 months. It is also more likely to cry in response to maternal separation at 14 months of age and more likely to be classified as insecure/resistant (Calkins & Fox, in press). Lewis and Feiring (1989) found that a child who at 3 months of age is more likely to play with toys compared to people is more likely to show avoidant behavior to its mother at 1 year. It seems plausible, therefore, that an infant who is either more object- and less person-oriented or who is highly reactive and irritable would behave similarly to separation and reunion during the Strange Situation regardless of which caregiver is present. This leads to similar classifications to both mother and father.

PREDISPOSITION IS NOT PREDICTION

In an attempt to clarify their positions, both temperament and attachment researchers emphasize the respective variables in understanding the child's behavior in the Strange Situation. Obviously, the more difficult position to empirically validate is one that emphasizes the interaction of both factors. Such a position necessitates a re-analysis of both the hard-line attachment and temperament cases. In the first place, if the Strange Situation is influenced by infant temperament, then it is no longer the sole paradigm that should be used to assess the attachment bond. The data from the meta analysis of mother/father attachment concordance argue that the Strange Situation is too constrained in its format to clearly provide a look at the quality of the attachment bond. Rather, behavior in this paradigm reflects the interaction of infant temperament and maternal caregiving style. If the product of this interaction is attachment (e.g., security or insecurity), then it becomes necessary to study the process by which different types of temperaments and different caregiving styles interact to form secure or insecure relationships. At the same time, it is clear that temperament is not the sole predictor of behavior in the Strange Situation. This again necessitates a re-evaluation of the focus of temperament research. Temperamental factors are not the only influences on behavior in the Strange Situation (cf. Goldsmith & Alansky, 1987). The data from a number of sources suggest that only a small but significant portion of the variance in behavior during the Strange Situation is the result of individual, temperamental differences among infants (Thompson et al., 1988; Vaughn et al., 1989). However, the data presented in this chapter indicate that these infant characteristics may be important in determining classification.

In first attempting to describe dimensions of individual differences in infant temperament, Thomas and Chess (1977, 1980) underscored the need to examine the *goodness of fit* between infant temperament and parent behavior. There are only a handful of studies (Bates, Maslin, & Frankel, 1985; Crockenberg, 1981) that attempt to directly examine the interaction of infant temperament and maternal behavior in determining security of attachment. More of these studies are clearly necessary. The goal of research should no longer be to demonstrate the importance of infant temperament in determining attachment classification. Rather efforts should be made to understand how the interaction of temperament and caregiver behavior produces the unique and interesting behavior observed over so many studies in the Strange Situation.

ACKNOWLEDGMENT

Support for the research and preparation for this chapter was from a grant from the National Institutes of Health (HD#17899) to Nathan A. Fox.

REFERENCES

Ainsworth, M. D. S. (1973). The development of infant-mother attachment. In B. M. Caldwell & H. N. Ricciuit (Eds.), *Review of child development research* (Vol. 3, pp. 1-94). Chicago: University of Chicago Press.

Ainsworth, M. D. S., Bell, S. M. V., & Stayton, D. J. (1971). Individual differences in Strange-Situation behavior of one-year-olds. In H. R. Schaffer (Ed.), *The origins of human social relations* (pp. 17-58). New York: Academic Press.

Ainsworth, M. D. S., Blehar, M., Waters, E., & Wall, S. (1978). *Patterns of attachment: Psychological behavior in the Strange Situation.* Hillsdale, NJ: Lawrence Erlbaum Associates.

Ainsworth, M. D. S., & Wittig, B. A. (1969). Attachment and exploratory behavior in one-year-olds in a Strange Situation. In B. M. Foss (Ed.), *Determinants of infant behavior IV* (pp. 111-136). London: Methuen.

Bates, J. E., Maslin, C. A., & Frankel, K. A. (1985). Attachment security, mother–child interaction, and temperament as predictors of behavior problem ratings at three years. In I. Bretherton & E. Waters (Eds.), *Growing points of attachment: Theory and research* (pp. 167–193). *Monographs of the Society for Research in Child Development, 50*(1-2, Serial No. 209).

Bell, R. Q., Weller, G. M., & Waldrop, M. F. (1971). Newborn and preschool: Organization of behavior and relations between periods. *Monographs of the Society for Research in Child Development, 36,* (Serial No. 142).

Belsky, J., Garduque, L., & Hrncir, E. (1984). Assessing performance, competence, and executive capacity in infant play: Relations to home environment and security of attachment. *Developmental Psychology, 20,* 406–417.

Belsky, J., Gilstrap, & Rovine, M. (1984). The Pennsylvania Infant and Family Development Project I: Stability and change in mother–infant and father–infant interaction in a family setting at one, three, and nine months. *Child Development, 55,* 692–705.

Belsky, J., & Rovine, M. (1987). Temperament and attachment security in the Strange Situation: An empirical rapprochement. *Child Development, 58,* 787–795.

Belsky, J., Rovine, M., & Taylor, D. G. (1984). The Pennsylvania Infant and Family Development Project: The origins of individual differences in infant–mother attachment: Maternal and infant contributions. *Child Development, 55,* 718–728.

Belsky, J., & Volling, B. L. (1987). Mothering, fathering, and marital interaction in the family triad during infancy: Exploring family system's processes. In P. Berman & F. Pedersen (Eds.), *Men's transition to parenthood.* (pp. 37–63). Hillsdale, NJ: Lawrence Erlbaum Associates.

Bowlby, J. (1969). *Attachment and loss: Vol. 1. Attachment.* New York: Basic Books.

Bowlby, J. (1973). *Attachment and loss: Vol. 2. Separation.* New York: Basic Books.

Bretherton, I. (1985). Attachment theory: Retrospect and prospect. In I. Bretherton & E. Waters (Eds.), *Growing points of attachment theory and research. Monographs of the Society for Research in Child Development 50* (Serial No. 209), 3–38.

Bridges, L. J., Connell, J. P., & Belsky, J. (1988). Similarities and differences in infant–mother and infant–father interaction in the Strange Situation: A component process analysis. *Developmental Psychology, 24,* 92–100.

Buss, A. H., & Plomin, R. (1984). *Temperament: Early developing personality traits.* Hillsdale, NJ: Lawrence Erlbaum Associates.

Calkins, S. D., & Fox, N. A. (in press). Relations among temperament, attachment and behavioral inhibition at 24 months of age. *Child Development.*

Crockenberg, S. B. (1981). Infant irritability, mother responsiveness, and social support influences on the security of infant–mother attachment. *Child Development, 52,* 857–865.

Davidson, R. J., & Fox, N. A. (1989). The relation between tonic EEG asymmetry and ten month old infant emotional responses to separation. *Journal of Abnormal Psychology, 98,* 127–131.

Eppinger, H., & Hess, L. (1915). Vagatonia: A clinical study in vegetative neurology. *Journal of Nervous and Mental Diseases, 20,* 1–93.

Finman, R., Davidson, R. J., Colton, M. B., Straus, A. M., & Kagan, J. (1989). Psychophysiological correlates of inhibition to the unfamiliar in children. *Psychophysiology, 26,* No. 4A., S24.

Fox, N. A. (1989). The psychophysiological correlates of emotional reactivity during the first year of life. *Developmental Psychology, 25,* 364–372.

Fox, N. A., & Davidson, R. J. (1984). Hemispheric substrates of affect: A developmental model. In N. A. Fox & R. J. Davidson (Eds.), *The Psychobiology of affective development* (pp. 353–382). Hillsdale, NJ: Lawrence Erlbaum Associates.

Fox, N. A., & Davidson, R. J. (1987). EEG asymmetry in ten month old infants in response to approach of a stranger and maternal separation. *Developmental Psychology, 23,* 233–240.

Fox, N. A., & Davidson, R. J. (1988). Patterns of brain electrical activity during the expression of discrete emotions in ten month old infants. *Developmental Psychology, 24,* 230–236.

Fox, N. A., & Gelles, M. (1984). Face to face interaction in term and preterm infants. *Infant Mental Health Journal, 5*(4), 192–205.

Fox, N. A., Kimmerly, N. L., & Schaffer, W. D. (1991). Attachment to mother/attachment to father: A meta analysis. *Child Development, 62,* 210–225.

Fox, N. A., & Porges, S. W. (1985). The relationship between neonatal heart period patterns and developmental outcome. *Child Development, 56,* 28–37.

Fox, N. A., & Stifter, C. A. (1989). Biological and behavioral differences in infant reactivity and regulation. In G. A. Kohnstamm, J. E. Bates, & M. K. Rothbart (Eds.), *Temperament in childhood* (pp. 169–183). New York: Wiley.

Freud, S. (1905). *Three essays on the theory of sexuality: Vol. 7. Complete psychological works of Sigmund Freud.* London: Hogarth Press.

Freud, S. (1952). *A general introduction to psychoanalysis.* New York: Washington Square Press.

Frodi, A. M., Lamb, M. E., Frodi, M., Hwang, C., Forsstrom, B., & Corry, T. (1982). Stability and change in parental attitudes following an infant's birth into traditional and non-traditional Swedish families. *Scandinavian Journal of Psychology, 23,* 53–62.

Goldsmith, H. H., & Alansky, J. A. (1987). Maternal and infant temperamental predictors of attachment: A meta-analytic review. *Journal of Consulting and Clinical Psychology, 55,* 805–816.

Goldsmith, H. H., Bradshaw, D., & Rieser-Danner, L. (1986). Temperament as a potential influence on attachment. In J. V. Lerner & R. M. Lerner (Eds.), *Temperament and social interaction during infancy and childhood: New directions for child development* (pp. 5–34). San Francisco: Jossey-Bass.

Goossens, F. A., & van IJzendoorn, M. H. (1988, November). *Quality of infants' attachments to professional caregivers: Relation to parental attachment and day-care characteristics.* Paper presented at the Dutch Conference for Psychologists, Groningen, The Netherlands.

Grossmann, K. E., Grossmann, K., Huber, F., & Wartner, U. (1981). German children's behavior towards their mothers at 12 months and their fathers at 18 months in Ainsworth's Strange Situation. *International Journal of Behavioral Development, 4,* 157–181.

Grossmann, K., Grossmann, K. E., Spangler, G., Suess, G., & Unzer, L. (1981). Maternal sensitivity and newborns' orientation responses related to quality of attachment in northern Germany. In I. Bretherton & E. Waters (Eds.), *Growing points of attachment: Theory and research* (pp. 233–256). *Monographs of the Society for Research in Child Development, 50,* (1-2 Serial No. 209).

Gunnar, M. R., Mangelsdorf, S., Kestenbaum, R., Lang, S., Larson, M., & Andreas, D. (in press). Temperament, attachment, and neuroendocrine reactivity: A systematic approach to the study of stress in normal infants. In D. Cicchetti (Ed.), *Process and psychopathology.* New York: Cambridge University Press.

Kagan, J. (1982). *Psychological research on the human infant: An evaluative summary.* New York: W. T. Grant Foundation.

Kagan, J., Reznick, J. S., & Snidman, N. (1987). The physiology and psychology of behavioral inhibition in children. *Child Development, 58,* 1459–1473.

Kinsbourne, M. (1978). Biological determinants of functional bisymmetry and asymmetry. In M. Kinsbourne (Ed.), *Asymmetrical function of the brain* (pp. 3–13). New York: Cambridge University Press.

Lacey, J. I., & Lacey, B. C. (1958). The relationship of resting autonomic activity to motor impulsivity. *Research Publications Association for Research in Nervous and Mental Disease, 36,* 144–209.

Lamb, M. E. (1978). Qualitative aspects of mother– and father–infant attachments. *Infant Behavior and Development, 1,* 265–276.

Lamb, M. E., Hwang, C., & Broberg, A. (1989). Associations between parental agreement regarding child-rearing and the characteristics of families and children in Sweden. *International Journal of Behavioral Development, 12,* 115–129.

Lamb, M. E., Hwang, C. P., Frodi, A., & Frodi, M. (1982). Security of mother– and father–infant attachment and its relation to sociability with strangers in traditional and non-traditional Swedish families. *Infant Behavior and Development, 5,* 355–367.

Lewis, M., & Feiring, C. (1989). Infant, mother, and mother–infant interaction behavior and subsequent attachment. *Child Development, 60,* 831–837.

Main, M., Kaplan, N., & Cassidy, J. (1985). Security in infancy, childhood, and adulthood: A move to the level of representation. In I. Bretherton & E. Waters (Eds.), *Growing points of attachment: Theory and research. Monographs of the Society for Research in Child Development. 50,* (Serial No. 209) 66–106.

Main, M., & Weston, D. R. (1981). The quality of the toddler's relationship to mother and to father: Related to conflict behavior and the readiness to establish new relationships. *Child Development, 52,* 932–940.

Owen, M. T., & Chase-Lansdale, L. (1982, April). *Similarity between infant–mother and infant–father attachments.* Paper presented at the biennial meeting of the Southwestern Society for Research in Human Development, Galveston, Texas.

Parke, R. D. (1978). Parent–infant interaction: Progress, paradigms, problems. In G. P. Sackett (Ed.), *Observing behavior* (Vol. 1, pp. 9–84). Baltimore, MD: University Park Press.

Parke, R. D., & Sawin, D. B. (1980). The family in early infancy: Social-interactional and attitudinal analyses. In F. A. Pedersen (Ed.), *The father–infant relationship* (pp. 44–70). New York: Praeger Special Studies.

Porges, S. W. (1976). Peripheral and neurochemical parallels of psychopathology: A psychophysiological model relating autonomic imbalance to hyperactivity, psychopathy, and autism. In H. W. Reese (Ed.), *Advances in child development and behavior* (Vol. 11, pp. 35–65). New York: Academic Press.

Porges, S. W. (1985). Method and apparatus for evaluating rhythmic oscillations in aperiodic physiological response systems. Patent No. 4,510,944. Washington, DC: United States Patent Office.

Rothbart, M. K. (1981). Measurement of temperament in infancy. *Child Development, 52,* 569–578.

Rothbart, M. K. (1986). Longitudinal observation of infant temperament. *Developmental Psychology, 22,* 356–365.

Rothbart, M. K. (1989). Temperament and development. In G. A. Kohnstamm, J. E. Bates, & M. K. Rothbart (Eds.), *Temperament in childhood* (pp. 187–248). New York: Wiley.

Rothbart, M. K., & Derryberry, D. (1981). Development of individual differences in temperament. In M. E. Lamb & A. L. Brown (Eds.), *Advances in developmental psychology* (Vol. 1, pp. 37–86). Hillsdale, NJ: Lawrence Erlbaum Associates.

Rubin, K. H., LeMare, L., & Lollis, S. (in press). Social withdrawal in childhood: Developmental pathways to peer rejection. In S. R. Asher & J. Coie (Eds.), *Children's status in the peer group.* New York: Cambridge University Press.

Sagi, A., Lamb, M. E., Lewkowicz, K. S., Shoham, R., Dvir, R., & Estes, D. (1985). Security of infant–mother, father, metapelet attachments among kibbutz-reared Israeli children. In I. Bretherton & E. Waters (Eds.), *Growing points of attachment: Theory and research. Monographs of the Society for Research in Child Development, 50* (1-2, Serial No. 209), 257–275.

Sameroff, A. J., Krafchuk, E. E., & Bakow, H. (1978). Issues in grouping items from the Neonatal Behavioral Assessment Scale. In A. J. Sameroff (Ed.), *Organization and stability of newborn behavior: A commentary on the Brazelton Neonatal Behavior Assessment Scale.* Monographs of the Society for Research in Child Development *43* (Serial No. 177) 46–59.

Schaffer, C. E., Davidson, R. J., & Saron, C. (1983). Frontal and parietal electroencephalogram asymmetries in depressed and non-depressed subjects. *Biological Psychiatry, 18,* 753–762.

Sroufe, L. A. (1985). Attachment classification from the perspective of infant–caregiver relationships and infant temperament. *Child Development, 48,* 1–14.

Sroufe, L. A., & Waters, E. (1977). Attachment as an organizational construct. *Child Development, 48,* 1184–1199.

Sroufe, L. A., & Waters, E. (1982). Issues of temperament and attachment. *American Journal of Orthopsychiatry, 52,* 743–746.

Stifter, C. A., & Fox, N. A. (1990). Behavioral and psychophysiological indices of temperament in infancy. *Developmental Psychology, 26,* 582–588.

Stifter, C. A., Fox, N. A., & Porges, S. W. (1989). The relations between heart rate variability, facial expressivity, and temperament in five and ten month old infants. *Infant Behavior and Development, 12,* 127–138.

Thomas, A., & Chess, S. (1977). *Temperament and development.* New York: Brunner/Mazel.

Thomas, A., & Chess, S. (1980). *The dynamics of psychological development.* New York: Brunner/Mazel.

Thompson, R. A., Connel, J. P., & Bridges, L. J. (1988). Temperament, emotion, and social interactive behavior in the Strange Situation: An analysis of attachment system functioning. *Child Development, 59,* 1102–1110.

Vaughn, B. E., Lefever, G. B., Seifer, R., & Barglow, P. (1989). Attachment behavior, attachment security, and temperament during infancy. *Child Development, 60,* 728–737.

Weber, R. A., Levitt, M. J., & Clarke, M. C. (1986). Individual variation in attachment security and Strange Situation behavior: The role of maternal and infant temperament. *Child Development, 57,* 56–65.

Wenger, M. A. (1941). The measurement of individual differences in autonomic balance. *Psychosomatic Medicine, 3,* 427–434.

Winnicott, D. W. (1975). *Through paediatrics to psychoanalysis.* New York: Basic Books.

4

▼▼▼▼▼▼▼▼

The Development of Autonomy in Children's Health Behaviors

Ronald J. Iannotti
Patricia J. Bush
Georgetown University School of Medicine

Research on the development of autonomy usually focuses on infancy or adolescence. In infancy, autonomy revolves around issues of willfulness or self-control (Erikson, 1968). Whereas Erikson suggests that these issues continue to demand resolution throughout the life cycle, it is in adolescence that autonomy again is a focus of development. In adolescence, autonomy is defined as individuation (Blos, 1979), resistance to control by parents (Kandel & Lesser, 1972) or peers (Berndt, 1979), and self-reliance (Greenberger, 1984). Recent studies of adolescents evaluated each of these elements of autonomy (Small, Eastman, & Cornelius, 1987; Steinberg & Silverberg, 1986; Steinberg, 1987) and found them to be somewhat independent in cause and effect. Whereas self-reliance appears to increase during adolescence, emotional dependency shifts from dependence on parents to dependence on peers (Steinberg & Silverberg, 1986).

In comparison, relatively little is known about the development of autonomous behaviors in childhood. Even less is known about children's self-reliance in dealing with issues of health and illness. Children's conceptions of illness and health differ from those of adults, but illness is recognized as a negative event that interferes with normal life events (Bibace & Walsh, 1980; Natapoff, 1978). Family interactions in response to incidents of illness may provide children with examples of adaptive functioning that generalize to other domains (Parmelee, 1985). Incidents of illness may provide insight into a family's ability to cope or to teach about caring and helping. Yet aside from our work and that of Lois Pratt (1973a, 1973b), there are few studies of children's autonomy in health and illness behaviors.

Responsibility of the patient in health care and maintenance has not received much attention (cf., Maiman, Becker, & Katlic, 1985, 1986), and the role of children in this process is usually not considered. It is common practice for pediatricians to direct their recommendations for treatment to parents, not children. Parents are more likely to be asked about their health beliefs and behaviors and about health beliefs and behaviors of their children. There have been few attempts to examine parental statements regarding health by actually observing family interactions as parents deal with routine issues of health and illness. Also there have been relatively few attempts to question children about their beliefs and behaviors (exceptions include our work and that of Bruhn and Parcel, 1982; Gochman, 1970, 1971, 1972; Gochman & Saucier, 1982; Natapoff, 1978; Perrin & Gerrity, 1981) or to determine the relationship of children's and parents' beliefs and behaviors (in addition to our work, the exceptions are Bruhn and Parcel, 1982; Campbell, 1975a, 1975b; Dielman, Leech, Becker, Rosenstock, & Horvath, 1982; Lau & Klepper, 1988; Mechanic, 1964; Pratt, 1973a).

Much of our work developed from an interest in children's use of medicines and in children's nutrition. Frequency of acute illnesses may decrease with age but still remains quite high through childhood and adolescence, for example, respiratory illnesses average five to seven occurrences per year (Dingle, Badger, & Jordan, 1964). Considering the pervasiveness of medicine use in society, all children can be expected to have been exposed to medicines by personal use or observation and at least by school age to have some beliefs, attitudes, and expectations about them. Moreover, some children, especially children with chronic illnesses such as asthma or diabetes, may have some degree of autonomy in medicine use, and at some age, most individuals begin to take responsibility for their own medicine use. It would be useful to know when this self-reliance begins.

Informal observations of children eating school lunches led Davidson and Kandel (1981) to conclude that traditional dietary measures for children, which relied on mothers' recalls of the nutritional intake of their school-age children, were flawed. Using anthropological methodology, children in various neighborhoods of the District of Columbia were followed during typical days in school, and what they ate and the contexts in which they ate were recorded. The typical eating patterns of children were described as "grazing," and the influence of peers on food choices was noted. It was also observed that much of what children ate was outside the purview of their mothers.

Several studies conducted at Georgetown University (Bush & Davidson, 1982; Bush & Iannotti, 1985, 1988, 1990) and at the National Institute of Mental Health (NIMH) investigated the extent to which young children are expected to take responsibility for their health and how early they report behaviors that indicate self-reliance and responsibility for their own health care. Responsibility was examined in relation to nutrition, medicine use, and preventive health care.

NUTRITION

The Know Your Body Evaluation Project (KYB-EP), an evaluation of the Know Your Body (KYB) health education curriculum in the District of Columbia elementary and junior high schools funded by the National Heart, Lung, and Blood Institute, was conducted by the Laboratory for Children's Health Promotion, Georgetown University School of Medicine, from 1982 to 1987. One component of the dietary data of this project was an assessment of who prepared the food eaten by a sample (sample size ranged from 174 in Year 5 to 289 in Year 2, M = 244) of elementary and middle schoolchildren (Davidson, Bush, Zuckerman, & Horowitz, 1986).

Even in the youngest group (Grades 4-6, M = 11.1 years), well over 80% of the children stated they sometimes cooked for themselves and others at home. All of the children stated that they engaged in some food-related activity including cooking, shopping, or assisting with meal preparation, and almost all reported purchasing a snack at least once every day either at school or from neighboring shops. Autonomy of children in determining their daily nutrient intake is illustrated further in Table 4.1 that presents the percentage of daily calories attributed to different preparers (this includes selection and purchase). In all 5 years, the greatest percentage of daily calories was derived from food prepared or selected by the child. Much the same percentages were found for other dietary measures including fats. Age and socioeconomic status (SES) differences are illustrated in Table 4.2 that shows the percentages for child preparers and selectors only. For two of the years there were significant differences among age groups in Grade by socioeconomic status (SES) analyses of variance (ANOVAs) performed for each year: Year 2, F (2, 271) = 5.49, $p < .01$; Year 3, F (2, 265) = 6.33, $p < .001$. Differences for SES were not as clear. There was lower autonomy for determining food intake in higher SES children in Year 1, F (2, 216) = 5.85, $p < .01$ but the reverse for Year 3, F (2, 265) = 5.61, $p < .01$. Not shown are significant Grade by SES interactions in Year 1, F (4, 216) = 3.77, $p < .01$ and Year 4, F (4, 218) = 4.58, $p < .01$. In these samples, higher SES

TABLE 4.1
Percentage of Total Calories Per Day
Attributed to Child Preparer or Selector of Food

	Grade				
Preparer	*4-6*	*5-7*	*6-8*	*7-9*	*9-10*
Self	43	40	52	50	39
Mother/female relative	35	39	29	18	23
Father/male relative	3	4	3	2	1
Other[a]	19	17	16	30	37

[a]The Other category includes restaurants, meals at school, babysitter's, sibling's, or others' homes.

TABLE 4.2
Percentage of Total Calories Per Day
Attributed to Child Preparer or Selector by Grade and SES

	Grade						
Study	*4*	*5*	*6*	*7*	*8*	*9*	*10*
Year 1	38.9	43.9	47.5				
Year 2*		34.3	40.5	46.6			
Year 3*			44.3	55.3	56.6		
Year 4				48.0	48.3	53.5	
Year 5					38.2	41.0	34.0

	SES		
	Low	*Middle*	*High*
Year 1*	49.8	40.1	38.9
Year 2	41.3	40.2	38.5
Year 3*	47.8	52.4	55.3
Year 4	55.1	48.5	45.5
Year 5	34.3	47.1	38.8

*Significant differences across grade or socioeconomic status (SES), $p < .05$.

children did not demonstrate more dietary autonomy with age. With regard to gender differences, across Grades 6, 7, and 8, older females took more responsibility for their own nutrition ($M = 40.0$, 62.8, and 59.2, respectively), whereas level of responsibility for males was about the same across these grades ($M =$ 48.9, 48.2, and 53.3, respectively), resulting in a Gender by Grade interaction in Year 3, $F\,(2, 265) = 6.91, p < .01$ and a significant Gender effect in Year 5, $F\,(1, 154) = 5.78, p < .05$. It is clear that children have considerable control over their own diets as early as 9 or 10 years of age and that this influence is likely to increase with age. The effect of SES is not as clear, but females play a greater role than males in determining nutrient intake in the adolescent years.

MEDICINE USE

KIDMED is a study of children's knowledge, attitudes, intentions to use, and use of medicines and abusable substances. Funded by the National Institute on Drug Abuse, this project represents a series of cross-sectional and longitudinal studies of elementary and junior high school children that began in 1980 and continues into the 1990s with the third phase, a five-year longitudinal study of approximately 4,000 Grade 4 and Grade 5 children and their friends. Autonomy of medicine use is examined in every phase. Some of the results from the first two phases are presented.

Subjects

Four hundred twenty District of Columbia elementary school children stratified on socioeconomic status, gender, and grade (51% Black, 33% White, 7% Hispanic, and 9% other ethnic groups) participated in the study. Ten boys and 10 girls from each grade, Kindergarten through Grade 6, at each of three schools representing low, middle, and high SES based on 1970 census tract family income data were randomly selected from those returning consent forms. Average age of the 420 children interviewed was 8 years, 10 months. The overall rate of return of consent forms, 72% with .5% refusals, was not related to SES levels. SES levels were validated by comparing the ratios of number of people in the sample households to number of bedrooms. This ratio decreased significantly with increasing SES, $F(2, 417) = 66.9, p < .001$. SES was confounded with ethnicity. In the high, middle, and low SES schools, 10%, 59%, and 81% of the Black children were represented respectively. Caution is therefore necessary in interpreting findings regarding SES and ethnic origin.

Interviews and Reliability

The interview instrument, developed from a pilot study of 60 children (Bush & Davidson, 1982), was administered individually and privately to each child. It included 168 items and took approximately 30 minutes to complete. Questions were read by four trained female interviewers in private rooms at the children's schools. The instrument was divided and the second half administered first to half of the sample; however, subsequent analysis indicated there were no significant order effects. Two figures were used with the instrument, a 4-point unlabeled bar graph to provide a concrete referent for items with Likert-type scales and a picture of a wall of varying height to assess risk taking for injury. Interviewers asked test questions until certain that the child completely understood how to use the bar graph.

A 10% stratified random sample was checked for intercoder reliability on all questions requiring coder judgment or mathematical determination. Of the 10% sample, the mean reliability (agreements/agreements plus disagreements) for objective items was 98% and for subjective responses, 85%. In the following descriptions, means and standard deviations are not reported for standardized scores ($M = 0$).

Sociodemographic Variables

Sociodemographic variables for each child included SES, gender, grade, birth order, family size, and family composition. Grade that was significantly correlated with age, $r = .97$, was used instead of age because it could be assessed more reliably in younger children, and it also may more accurately reflect cognitive maturity. Race was not used in the analysis because it is confounded with SES, a stratification variable, and SES was judged to be a better indicator of differences in children's social, family, and school environments. Family composition reflected presence of both parents, coded as 1, or absence of one or more parents, coded as 0.

Cognitive/Affective Variables

Cognitive variables included Health Locus of Control, Illness and Injury Risk Taking, and Medicine Knowledge.

Health Locus of Control is a 9-item index; each item is answered yes or no. It was adapted from Parcel and Meyer's (1978) 18-item Children's Health Locus of Control Scale based on factor analyses of data collected in this and prior studies (Bush, Parcel, & Davidson, 1983). Responses were scored so that higher scores represent internal control (range 1-9, $M = 5.4 \pm 2.2$ *SD*, Kuder-Richardson [20] = .69).

To measure Illness and Injury Risk Taking, each child was asked four questions adapted from Campbell and Carney (1978):

1. "How often do you drink out of a glass that someone else in your family has used?"
2. "How often do you take a drink from a friend's bottle of pop or lick his or her ice cream cone?"
3. "Suppose you are outside playing and it starts raining a little, do you think you are more likely to come inside right away or stay outside awhile and see if the rain stops?"
4. After giving examples of climbing trees though you might fall, running hard though you might slip, and rough-housing though you might get hurt, "When you're playing, how often do you do something like that even though you know you might get hurt?"

Also, the child was shown a picture of a wall of increasing height with a stick figure on it representing the child and was asked to indicate from which of seven possible locations he or she would jump if he or she were the figure on the wall. The wall varied in height from ground level to 125% of height of the stick figure.

Factor analyses of these five questions indicated that two factors were present: one consisting of the responses to the first two questions was labeled Risking Illness; the other consisting of the response to the fifth question was labeled Risking Injury. For both indices, higher scores indicate greater willingness to take risks. Because the two elements of Risking Illness were measured in different scales, the scores were standardized to a mean of 0 and *SD* of 1 prior to summing. Risking Injury had a range of 0 to 7, $M = 2.9 \pm 2.1$ *SD*.

Medicine Autonomy

Medicine Autonomy was assessed on an 8-item scale developed to measure children's perceptions of their independence in medicine use. The questions in the scale are:

1. "Did you ever get a prescription medicine at the pharmacy, drug store, or clinic for anyone by yourself?" (Scored 0 and not asked of children incorrectly defining prescription.)
2. "Have you ever gone by yourself to buy any pills, medicines, medicines for your skin, vitamins, or tonics?" (Scored 0 and not asked of children who said they never shopped by themselves.)
3. "Did you ever ask anyone to give you a medicine?"
4. "Did you ever get a medicine from somewhere in your house for someone else to take?"
5. "Can you reach them (medicines in your house) by yourself?"
6. For those children who indicated they had taken a nonvitamin medicine "yesterday or today," "Did you ask someone to give it to you?"
7. "Did you get it by yourself from somewhere in the house?"
8. "Did you take it by yourself?"

The Kuder-Richardson reliability coefficient of the 8-item scale was .59 (M = 2.5 $\pm$ 1.5 SD).

Environmental Variables

Alcohol Autonomy and Cigarette Autonomy measured the extent to which a child was involved in alcohol and cigarette use by household members. These scores were the sum of the standardized scores from several items: (a) whether the child had ever served alcohol or brought cigarettes to anyone, (b) whether the child bought cigarettes for anyone, and (c) whether the child lit a cigarette for anyone.

Readiness Variables

Perceived Vulnerability to illness has received considerable attention in the literature (Gochman, 1970, 1971, 1972; Gochman and Saucier, 1982) as a predictor of health behaviors and attitudes. Using the 4-point bar graph to illustrate the choices, not likely at all to very likely, children were asked, "How likely are you to have ______ this year?" for five common health problems: colds, fever, upset stomach, nervousness, and trouble sleeping. Selection of these five health problems was based on pilot data (Bush & Davidson, 1982) indicating that children understand these terms and experience these problems. The score for each health problem was summed to provide a composite score (range = 5–20, M = 12.0 ± 3.6 SD, Cronbach's alpha = .65).

RESULTS OF PHASE I

Although children are generally viewed as passive recipients of medicines, results of this study suggest that children perceive themselves to be quite involved in the medicine use process (see Table 4.3). Across Grades Kindergarten through Grade 7, 80% of the children indicated they had access to medicines in their households, 53% said they sometimes brought medicines to others, 52% said they asked for medicines, 12% said they had bought medicines, and 9% said they had picked up prescription medicines. The last three items indicate autonomous behaviors for children who had taken a medicine in the last 2 days. Considering only those children (40% or 168) who said they had taken a medicine the day before or the day of their interviews, 76% said they had taken it by themselves, 40% said they had gotten it by themselves, and 37% said they had asked someone to give it to them. As expected, perceived independence increased with age for most of these behaviors.

Most of the children could name medicines, most frequently brand names that are taken for common health problems (Bush, Iannotti, & Davidson, 1985). However, knowledge related to medicine efficacy was low, and the majority were confused by drugs as both medicines and abusable substances.

Independent purchase of medicines was related to the neighborhood in which children lived. If the child's neighborhood had grocery and drug stores, children living there were more likely to buy medicines and pick up prescriptions. Neigh-

TABLE 4.3
Frequency of Positive Response to Children's Medicine Autonomy Items in Phase I

	Grade						
Autonomy Items	*K*	*1*	*2*	*3*	*4*	*5*	*6*
Had access to household medicine*	70	75	82	75	83	87	90
Got household medicine for others*	30	40	53	62	60	63	60
Purchased medicine*	2	7	13	5	10	18	30
Picked up prescription*	0	3	3	3	12	12	30
Those Children Who Took Medicine in the Last 2 Days							
Asked for the medicine	22	18	27	18	10	8	8
Got the medicine themselves	3	7	13	7	7	12	15
Took the medicine independently	20	7	23	8	7	12	18

*Significant positive association with grade, $p < .05$.

borhoods around lower SES schools presented more opportunities for children to buy medicines.

Medicine Autonomy showed no Gender or SES effects but significant Age effects were found. The relationship between autonomy and other variables is discussed, but it is worth noting here that, although there were no SES effects, autonomy was related to the number of parents in the home with single parents granting greater autonomy. This is consistent with findings on autonomy in other domains (Steinberg, 1987).

METHODS IN PHASE II

Subjects

Three years later, children in Grade 3 through Grade 7, who were in Kindergarten through Grade 4 in the original sample, were interviewed again. Their primary caretakers, 93% mothers, were also interviewed. Because of the high percentage of mothers interviewed, *mothers* and *primary caretakers* will be used interchangeably. Of the 300 children in Phase II, a Longitudinal Cohort of 142 was from the original Phase I sample. To complete the sample, stratification on the basis of grade, three SES levels, and gender was maintained, and subjects were randomly selected from those returning signed consent forms. There were no significant differences between the Longitudinal Cohort and those who were only in Phase II on the basis of gender, SES, grade, or race. Fifty-six percent of the subjects were Black, 33% White, and the remainder Hispanic or other. The average primary caretaker had 14.5 years of education.

Interviews and Reliability

As in Phase I, students were interviewed privately at their schools, the interview taking about 40 minutes. No sooner than 2 weeks following the student interviews, telephone interviews with the primary caretakers were conducted. Of the total sample, 10% of the primary caretakers could not be located, were not reachable after 10 attempts, or refused to be interviewed. They did not differ from those interviewed on the basis of their children's gender, SES, grade, or race.

Because the students were 3 years older in Phase II, they all were able to understand use of a bar graph with more than 4 points. Therefore, a 6-point bar graph and the wall figure for Risking Injury were used in conjunction with the child's interviews as in Phase I. For the telephone interviews, instead of bar graphs, the primary caretaker was asked to get a piece of paper and a pencil and to number from 1 to 6 across the page. The subject then was asked to write, for example, *not at all likely* under the 1, and *very likely* under the 6, and to respond to questions according to the scale. Test questions were asked until the interviewer was certain that the respondent understood how to use the scale. Instead of the wall of varying heights used in the children's interviews, the primary caretaker was asked to respond in terms of the child's height.

A 10% random sample for each interviewer was recoded to assess intercoder reliability for both the children's and the mothers' interviews. Intercoder reliability (agreements/agreements plus disagreements) over both instruments was 94.6% for items requiring judgment or computation.

Additional Sociodemographic and Affective Variables

The 10-item Rosenberg Self-Esteem Scale (Rosenberg & Simmons, 1972) was used to assess self-esteem. Each item was answered on a scale of 1 *(strongly disagree)* to 6 *(strongly agree)* and recoded so that high scores reflect high self-esteem (range 20–60, $M = 46.99 \pm 7.89$ *SD*). Two questions referring to the frequency of attendance at religious services and the importance of religion were combined to indicate Religiosity (range 1–8, $M = 5.15 \pm 1.84$ *SD*).

Variables for Primary Caretakers' Interviews

Primary caretakers were asked about their own beliefs and behaviors as well as about the beliefs and behaviors of their children. Some of these questions paralleled the attitudes and behaviors being assessed in the children whereas others were designed to obtain information that was either less reliable from children (e.g., mother's education) or reflected beliefs that would be difficult to assess from the child's perspective (e.g., the mother's perception that the child's peers used alcohol).

As an additional measure reflecting SES, mothers were asked the number of years of their education after Kindergarten (range 1–23, $M = 14.4 \pm 3.36$ *SD*).

One of the cognitive/affective measures, Mother's Self-Esteem, paralleled the questions asked of their children (range 21–60, $M = 52.0 \pm 6.84$ *SD*). Mother's Health Locus of Control was assessed with an 11-item index adapted from Wallston, B. S., Wallston, K. A., Kaplan, & Maides (1976). The caretaker indicated agreement or disagreement on the 6-point scale, and scores were recoded so that higher scores reflected internal locus of control (range 18–66, $M = 42.3 \pm 8.03$ *SD*).

A new Adult Risk-Taking Scale was developed to assess Mother's Risk Taking (Bush & Iannotti, 1987). After pilot testing, 25 items were selected for administration to the sample. Principal component factor analyses identified the final 13 items in the scale. The questions concerned

1. driving after drinking or smoking marijuana,
2. driving over the speed limit,
3. walking outside if the streets are icy,
4. checking for fire exits in new places,

5. washing hands before eating,
6. betting money won at gambling,
7. having a yearly physical exam,
8. drinking out of other people's glasses or eating their food,
9. jay-walking,
10. dressing so as not to get wet or cold,
11. reading nutrition information on labels,
12. being a careful person, and
13. being the kind of person who takes risks (range 13-60, $M = 33.2 \pm 10.65$ *SD*, Cronbach's alpha = .77).

Mother's Perceived Vulnerability included the same five questions asked of the children (range 5-30, $M = 15.31 \pm 4.80$ *SD*).

RESULTS OF PHASE II

Areas of exploration relative to children's autonomy in medicine use included taking medicines without asking an adult, accessibility of medicines in the household, medicine purchase, giving medicines to other children without asking an adult, and taking medicines to school (see Table 4.4). Both children and their mothers were asked questions relative to the child's medicine use autonomy.

TABLE 4.4
Frequency of Positive Response to Children's Medicine Autonomy Items in Phase II

	Grade				
Autonomy Items	*3*	*4*	*5*	*6*	*7*
Had access to household meds*	77	90	83	91	100
All household medicines were accessible*	45	59	71	64	78
Asked for the medicine	67	76	72	86	78
Got household medicines for self*	73	86	83	88	89
Got household medicines for self independently*	22	26	33	45	45
Got household medicines for others*	62	64	62	74	71
Got household medicines for others independently*	9	24	24	32	36
Took medicine independently*	23	29	28	48	51
Took medicine independently for headache*	20	22	21	45	45
Took medicine independently for sore throat*	17	26	28	34	33
Gave medicine to another child independently*	9	12	9	22	25
Purchased medicine independently*	14	19	29	32	29
Picked up prescription independently	38	31	34	37	44
Had medicine at school on interview day	6	9	5	12	9

*Significant positive association with grade, $p < .05$.

Except for the general questions about household accessibility, in response to each question in the autonomy series, no child's response was counted as affirmative unless a specific medicine was named, or the child gave the age at which he or she first engaged in the behavior. Relative to taking medicines independently for headaches and sore throats, the response was not counted as affirmative unless the child named a medicine in response to the question inquiring about what the child would do if he or she were home alone and the condition occurred.

Except for asking for medicine, picking up a prescription, and having a medicine at school, children's autonomy in medicine use items were positively related to the children's school grade, but none of the items was related to children's gender or SES. The frequency of positive responses at all grades indicated that children reported considerable autonomy in their access to and use of medicines.

A 12-item Medicine Autonomy Scale was developed as a measure of children's perceptions of their independence in medicine use. Questions in the scale were:

1. "Did you ever get a prescription medicine at the pharmacy, drug store, or clinic for anyone by yourself?" (Scored 0 and not asked of children incorrectly defining prescription.)
2. "Have you ever gone by yourself to buy any pills, medicines, medicines for your skin, vitamins, or tonics?" (Scored 0 and not asked of children who said they never shopped by themselves.)
3. "Did you ever ask anyone to give you a medicine?"
4. "Did you ever give a medicine to another child without asking an adult?"
5. "Can you reach them (medicines in your house) by yourself?"
6. "Do you have a medicine with you at school today?"
7. For those children indicating they had taken a nonvitamin medicine "yesterday or today," "Did you get it by yourself from somewhere in the house?"
8. "Did you take it by yourself?"
9. through 12. Naming a medicine in response to questions that asked the children what they would do if they were home alone, could not reach an adult, and had a headache; or, in the same circumstances, what they would do if they had a sore throat (range 1-12, $M = 4.64 \pm 2.59$ *SD*, Kuder-Richardson reliability coefficient = .75).

Relationships between the Phase I and Phase II Medicine Autonomy Scales and other health-related attitudes and behaviors are shown in Table 4.5. In Phase I, Medicine Autonomy was correlated with grade and family structure (at least one parent absent) as indicated earlier, but it was also correlated with Alcohol Autonomy and Cigarette Autonomy, Health Locus of Control, Risking Injury, Perceived Vulnerability to five common illnesses, and Medicine Knowledge. As predicted, children with asthma, allergies, and other chronic illnesses (approximately 13% of the sample) scored higher on the Medicine Autonomy Scale than

TABLE 4.5
Correlation of Medicine Autonomy Scale With Variables in Phases I and II

	Phase I Scale	*Phase II Scale*	
Variables	*Phase I*[a]	*Phase II*[b]	*Phase I*[c]
Grade	.33**	.29***	.38***
Sex	−.01	.07	.01
SES	−.04	.04	−.05
Birth order	.05	.08	.18*
Family size	−.01	.14*	.24**
Family composition[d]	−.13**	.05	.01
Alcohol autonomy	.11*	.10	.15
Cigarette autonomy	.26***	.21***	.11
CHLC[e]	.15**	.03	.12
Risking illness	.09	.27***	−.03
Risking injury	.22***	.20***	.04
Vulnerability to illness	.12*	.20***	.04
Chronic illness	.13**	.05	.03
Medicine knowledge	.26***	.13*	.04
Self-esteem	NA	−.14*	NA
Religiosity	NA	−.01	NA
Alcohol availability	NA	.19***	NA
Phase I autonomy	NA	NA	.17*

[a]$n = 420$. [b]$n = 300$. [c]This column presents the correlation of Phase I variables with the Phase II Medicine Autonomy Scale, $n = 142$. [d]For Family Composition, presence of both parents was coded as 1 and absence of one or more parents was coded as 0. [e]Children's Health Locus of Control.
*$p < .05$; **$p < .01$; ***$p < .001$.

other children ($r = .13, p < .05$). The significant correlations found with Health Locus of Control, Cigarette Autonomy, and Alcohol Autonomy were also expected.

In Phase II, which had a smaller but older sample, many of the relationships were replicated. However, the expanded autonomy scale was correlated with family size, Risking Illness, and Alcohol Availability but, contrary to expectations, negatively related to Self-Esteem. Correlations with family structure, Alcohol Autonomy, Health Locus of Control, and chronic illness were no longer statistically significant. Chronic illness may no longer be significant because most children have some autonomy with regard to medicines by this age.

The Longitudinal Cohort of Phase II ($N = 142$) had participated in Phase I as well. Correlations between Phase I variables and Phase II Medicine Autonomy in the Longitudinal Cohort are shown in the third column of Table 4.5. Aside from the Phase I autonomy scale, the significant correlates were three demographic variables. Stepwise regression analyses shown in Table 4.6 further demonstrate the importance of grade (or age) in the autonomy behaviors reported by the children. In all three regressions, Phase I, Phase II, and the Longitudinal Cohort, grade was the best single predictor of Medicine Autonomy. Health attitudes and

TABLE 4.6
Regression Analyses Predicting Children's Medicine Autonomy

Variable	*Partial R^2*	R^2	*Beta*
Regression of Phase I Autonomy Scale on Phase I Variables (n = 420)			
Grade	.09	.09	.23***
Cigarette autonomy	.06	.15	.22**
Risking injury	.04	.18	.17*
Regression of Phase II Autonomy Scale on Phase II Variables (n = 300)			
Grade	.07	.07	.26***
Risking illness	.04	.11	.11**
Self-esteem	.03	.14	−.12**
Family size	.02	.16	.14*
Alcohol availability	.01	.17	.13*
Regression of Phase II Autonomy Scale on Phase I Variables (n = 142)			
Grade	.15	.15	.42***
Alcohol autonomy	.05	.20	.21**
Family size	.04	.23	.18*

Note: Partial R^2s do not always sum to R^2 because of rounding.
*$p < .05$; **$p < .01$; ***$p < .001$

behaviors which were related to age and which were correlated with autonomy in the univariate analyses did not appear in the regression equation once grade entered. In Phase I, the two other significant predictors were autonomy of cigarette use and risk taking with regard to injury. In Phase II, Risking Illness, Self-Esteem (negative regression coefficient), family size, and Alcohol Availability were significant predictors. In the Longitudinal Cohort, Alcohol Autonomy, which was not significant in the univariate analysis, entered the equation.

Personal attitude or behavior differences do not appear to account for individual differences in Medicine Autonomy. Aside from age-related and family-related variables, only risk taking and self-esteem contributed to the prediction of autonomy. There is strong evidence that autonomy in health behaviors develops at an early age and increases with maturity. Home environment, that is, family size, family structure, and parental behavior (providing access to and opportunities to participate in the consumption of abusable substances), contribute to autonomy as well.

Mother's Reports

There was the possibility that children were not reliable reporters of their own autonomy behaviors. They may have inflated their independence in order to appear more mature. Mothers did not always agree with their children's perceptions of themselves as autonomous medicine users. Mothers' responses to questions

TABLE 4.7
Age at Which Mothers and Children
Indicate Onset of Medicine Autonomy Behaviors

	Mothers		Children	
Behavior	*N*[a]	*Mean Age*	*N*[a]	*Mean Age*
Shopped by self*	228	8.0	232	8.8
Bought medicines	32	9.7	72	9.8
Bought prescription medicines	51	10.2	75	9.2
Took medicines independently	49	9.1	95	9.1
Got medicines for another child	10	8.8	43	9.2
Took medicines for headache without asking an adult	29	10.5		
Used a topical medicine without asking an adult	112	9.1		
Age children are old enough to take medicine without asking	245	12.7		
Asked for medicines			189	6.5
Got medicine for self			239	8.3
Got medicine for others			177	8.3
Got medicine for self without permission			96	9.1
Got medicine for others without permission			68	9.4

[a]*N* indicates number of mothers and children who reported an age when event first occurred.
*Mothers and children differed significantly in ages reported, $p < .05$.

about their children's independent use and the children's responses to similar questions are shown in Table 4.7. Mean age is indicated for those mothers or children who said the child had already performed the behavior. Where similar questions were asked of mother and child, the ages were not significantly different except for shopping alone where the children actually reported a higher age of first occurrence. One point worth noting is that for children at every age, mothers reported they thought children in general can take medicines without asking at approximately 12 years of age even when their own younger children had already done so.

Disagreement between mothers and children is evident in the proportions of mothers and children who indicated that the child has already performed one of these autonomous behaviors (see Table 4.8). Children's responses, in the first column, indicate that they generally perceived themselves to have access to medicines and reported that they had taken medicines for some common health problems or had given medicine to another child. Mother's responses, in the second column, indicate substantial agreement regarding access in the home but disagreement with (or a failure to report) the child's self-administration of medicines (as noted in the percentages in the third column). There was significant but weak agreement between mothers and children (as shown in Table 4.9).

Although one may argue that the parents were probably more accurate in their self-reports, it is worth noting the last two questions from Table 4.8. When children were asked whether they had any medicines with them on the day they were

TABLE 4.8
Percentage of Children's and Mothers' Positive Responses and Agreement on Children's Medicine Autonomy Items

Autonomy Items	*Child*	*Mother*	*Agreement*[a]
Had access to household medicines	87.6%	88.0%	88.8%
All household medicines were accessible	63.1	74.1	78.2
Took medicine independently	35.7	18.0	29.9
Took medicine independently for headache	24.9	14.5	28.4
Took medicine independently for sore throat	26.6	12.7	21.7
Used topical medicine independently	NA	45.5	NA
Gave medicine to another child	15.3	3.3	4.4
Purchased medicines independently	24.7	12.3	25.7
Picked up prescription independently	36.7	17.7	30.0
Had medicine at school on interview day	8.3	NA	NA
Took medicines to school	NA	21.7	NA

[a]Agreement between mothers and children as a percentage of the number of children responding affirmatively.

interviewed, 25 said they had one or more with them and specified which medicines they were. Medicines that the children indicated they had brought to school the day of the interview were: Actifed, *Allerest,* allergy liquid, *aspirin* (mentioned by 2 children), *asthma medicine* (2), bee pollen tablet, calamine lotion, *Clearasil, Cleocin, cough drops* (3), *cough syrup, erythromycin, Midol, Nice, nose spray,* Orajel, *pain killer,* phenobarbitol, Preventos, *Ritalin,* Robitussin, *skin medicine, throat lozenges, Tridesilon* and *Tylenol* (3). Several weeks later, mothers were asked if their children *ever* took medicines to school. Sixteen of the mothers

TABLE 4.9
Kappa Statistic for Agreement Between Mothers and Children on Medicine Autonomy Items

		Grade		
Autonomy Items	*Overall*	*3–4*	*5–6*	*7*
Had access to household medicines	.07	.04	.06	–[a]
All household medicines were accessible	.09*	–.05	.24**	.09
Took medicine independently	.21***	.01	.23**	.26
Took medicine independently for headache	.21***	.07	.26**	.26
Took medicine independently for sore throat	.14**	.04	.07	.47**
Gave medicine to another child independently	.02	.13	–.03	–[a]
Purchased medicine independently	.21***	.18*	.26**	.25
Picked up prescription independently	.22***	.06	.30**	.45**
Took medicines to school[b]	.05	.02	.12	.11

[a]Zero cell obviates use of *Kappa* statistic; agreement approaching 100%.
[b]Based on number of children responding affirmatively.
Kappa $*p \leq .05$; $**p \leq .01$; $***p \leq .001$

of these 25 children said their children *never* took medicines to school. Those medicines italicized were mentioned by children whose mothers said they never took medicines to school. Seven of the children had two medicines with them and in at least one case (Robitussin and Actifed) the medicines contained synergistic ingredients that could affect the child's behavior. Other medicines could have caused problems if taken by other children or if taken too frequently.

Although there is considerable disagreement between mother and child, and the evidence would suggest that the children may be the more reliable reporters, the results of one final analysis is interesting. An autonomy of medicine use scale was created based on the mother's responses to the eight autonomy items. Mother's responses for questions about her child and the three demographic variables, SES, gender, and grade, were entered into a stepwise regression analysis. The regression equation, accounting for 20% of the variance of the mother's perceived autonomy for her child, included many of the same variables as the child's regression equation: grade, risk taking, and SES (in this case it may have represented the environment because mother's education did not enter the equation). In an attempt to better understand the processes by which mothers may foster the development of autonomy and self-reliance for health behaviors, the results of a pilot study that indicated that mothers do indeed convey attitudes regarding the child's responsibility for health care and illness are interesting.

EARLY CHILDHOOD

Over 150 two-year-olds and their mothers participated in a study of child-rearing patterns in normal and depressed mothers at the National Institute of Mental Health.[1] Although drawn from a diverse economic, racial, and ethnic population, the sample was primarily middle class. Mother and child visited the laboratory on at least two separate occasions and spent approximately 2½ hours each visit in a comfortably furnished apartment-like setting consisting of two living rooms, a kitchenette, and a bathroom. These visits included opportunities for naps, eating snacks or a meal, and a variety of other standard situations designed to simulate the normal occurrences in a family's day.

Each of these sessions was videotaped. Naturally occurring incidents of minor illness were identified in a subsample of 18 of these children while they were visiting the lab. In these episodes, the child demonstrated symptoms of minor illness such as a cold, cough, or stomach virus. Sessions in which the child did not display symptoms were also identified. Although one purpose of this study was to compare the behavior of mother and child during episodes of illness with their behavior when the child was relatively symptom free, these sessions indicate

[1]This project represents the work of a number of collaborators including Arthur Parmelee, Marian Radke-Yarrow, and Leon Kuczynski.

the potential influence of mothers on their children's health beliefs and behaviors.

Mother's behaviors were examined for: references to illness, discussion of the child's physical needs, recommendations for health behaviors, and attributions of responsibility for the child's health or illness. The frequency over two sessions of mother's recommendations regarding health behaviors is shown in Table 4.10. Recommendations regarding nutrition were most frequent, with one mother making 128 recommendations, such as, "People don't get dessert if they haven't had a nutritious meal," and "That's for after we've had our body building food." Personal hygiene, the next most frequent area of recommendation, included statements like "Boy, oh boy, are your teeth dirty. When's the last time you brushed your teeth?" Mothers frequently recommended that their children take a nap or rest and occasionally provided the rationale that the rest would help them feel better. The typical mother did not make any recommendations regarding exercise, fitness, or medications.

Mothers may encourage or discourage a sense of autonomy and personal control in the early years of childhood. As shown in Table 4.10, mothers were equally likely to place responsibility for illness or for health care with her child as with herself. Although neither of these statements had high frequencies, at least 50% of the mothers made one statement regarding attributions of responsibility in each of three different categories, child, mother, or another person. For example, "Do you want to hurt yourself?" "You're gonna fall down and hurt your head." "Let me pull your bloomers down so you don't have an accident." "The doctor will help you." The frequency of statements of responsibility attributed to the mother, another person, or chance were significantly correlated, but attributions to the child were not significantly correlated with the other categories. This suggests

TABLE 4.10
Mothers' Statements Regarding Their Children's Health Behaviors

	Recommendations			
Topic	*Frequency*	*Minimum*	*Median*	*Maximum*
Hygiene	12.3	2	9.5	31
Nutrition	14.9	0	7.5	128
Sleep/rest	9.3	0	6	28
Fitness	.3	0	0	1
Medicines	.6	0	0	4
Other (injury)	4.7	0	4	14
	Attributions of Responsibility or Cause			
Cause/Control	*Frequency*	*Minimum*	*Median*	*Maximum*
Child	2.9	0	2	11
Mother	2.9	0	1	14
Other person	1.3	0	1	5
Chance	.1	0	0	1

that, although there is no difference in the group means, individual mothers differentially attribute control to the child or themselves.

It appears that in the child's early formative years, before language skills have matured, messages about health behaviors and responsibility for health care are offered by the mother. Unfortunately, the impact of these statements on the child's beliefs and behaviors have not been examined. It might be best to view this work as a pilot study of mothers' potential influence on children's health behaviors and the function of families in health education.

CONCLUSIONS

From the observations of mother and child at two years of age, one could conclude that mothers devote considerable effort to teaching their children about health and illness. Mothers vary considerably in style, with some mothers emphasizing the child's control of health and illness and others emphasizing their own control. These interactions may have an influence on the child's beliefs and attitudes regarding health and may relate to those specific behaviors under the parent's direct supervision.

Autonomous health behaviors of older children relate to autonomy in other domains, certainly autonomy with regard to abusable substances. Older children also show similar patterns of autonomy in adolescence, significant correlations with health locus of control, and family structure (Pratt, 1973a; Small et al., 1987; Steinberg, 1987; Steinberg & Silverberg, 1986). However, the predictive model for these behaviors is still quite weak. Aside from age and environmental factors permitting independence and access to and opportunities for practicing autonomous behaviors, there are no consistent individual characteristics evident in the research with school-age children.

By the time children reach school, they are discriminating among different health problems and different remedies. Children are clearly engaged in health care and treatment. Results of the assessment of dietary intake are relevant to efforts to prevent cardiovascular disease (Newman et al., 1986; Stone, 1985) because it is the ingestion of calories and fats for which children appear to have the greatest control. Levels of perceived autonomy found in these studies suggest that health professionals should address children when prescribing and dispensing medicines, and that children, as well as their mothers, might be the focus of compliance efforts and research. Other intervention strategies should also be directed to children.

Further research is needed to validate the children's reports of autonomous behaviors. Better measures of children's health attitudes and perceptions at this age are also needed.

Clearly research that reaches beyond the school into the homes and the other social influences on children's health behaviors is needed to build the base for developmental theory and effective health education programs. A study of parental and preschool/day-care influences on patterns of nutrition and exercise in young children is being conducted at Georgetown University. Homes and day-care centers are visited to observe the child's behaviors in different settings and the social interactions that affect these behaviors. Studies like these shed further light on the processes of development involved in children's autonomy in health behaviors.

ACKNOWLEDGMENTS

Portions of this research were supported by grants from the National Institute of Drug Abuse, DA02686, National Heart, Lung and Blood Institute, HL30610, HL35621, and the John D. and Catherine T. MacArthur Foundation.

REFERENCES

Berndt, T. J. (1979). Developmental changes in conformity to peers and parents. *Developmental Psychology, 15,* 608-616.

Bibace, R., & Walsh, M. (1980). Development of children's concepts of illness. *Pediatrics, 66,* 913-917.

Blos, P. (1979). *The adolescent passage.* New York: International Universities Press.

Bruhn, J. G., & Parcel, G. S. (1982). Preschool health education program (PHEP): An analysis of baseline data. *Health Education Quarterly, 9,* 116-129.

Bush, P. J., & Davidson, F. R. (1982). Medicines and "drugs": What do children think? *Health Education Quarterly, 9,* 209-224.

Bush, P. J., & Iannotti, R. J. (1985). The development of children's health orientations and behaviors: Lessons for substance use prevention. In C. L. Jones & B. J. Battjes (Eds.), *Etiology of drug abuse: Implications for prevention* (pp. 45-74). (DHHS Publication No. ADM 85-1335). Washington, DC: U.S. Government Printing Office.

Bush, P. J., & Iannotti, R. J. (1987, August). *Development of an adult risk-taking scale.* Paper presented at the meeting of the American Psychological Association, New York. (ERIC Document Reproduction Service No. ED 290 779)

Bush, P. J., & Iannotti, R. J. (1988). Origins and stability of children's health beliefs relative to medicine use. *Social Science and Medicine, 27,* 345-352.

Bush, P. J., & Iannotti, R. J. (1990). A children's health belief model. *Medical Care, 28,* 69-86.

Bush, P. J., Iannotti, R. J., & Davidson, F. R. (1985). A longitudinal study of children and medicines. In D. D. Breimer & P. Speiser (Eds.), *Topics in pharmaceutical sciences 1985* (pp. 391-403). Amsterdam: Elsevier Science Publishers.

Bush, P. J., Parcel, G. S., & Davidson, F. R. (1982, August). *Reliability of a shortened children's health locus of control scale.* Poster presented at the meeting of the American Psychological Association, Washington, DC. (ERIC Document Reproduction Service No. ED 223 354)

Campbell, J. G. (1975a). Attribution of illness: Another double standard. *Journal of Health and Social Behavior, 16,* 114-126.

Campbell, J. G. (1975b). Illness is a point of view: The development of children's concepts of illness. *Child Development, 46,* 92-100.

Campbell, J. G., & Carney, C. (1978). Socialization to health-relevant risk taking: Contributions of status-defining characteristics, maternal values and standards. Unpublished manuscript.

Davidson, F. R., Bush, P. J., Zuckerman, A. E., & Horowitz, C. J. (1986). *Who's feeding the children?: Sources of nutrients in urban school children's diets (Know Your Body Evaluation Project).* Paper presented at the meeting of the Society for Nutrition Education, Chicago, IL.

Davidson, F. R., & Kandel, R. F. (1981). The individualization of food habits. *Journal of the American Dietetic Association, 72,* 341-348.

Dielman, T. E., Leech, S. L., Becker, M. H., Rosenstock, I. M., & Horvath, W. J. (1982). Parental and child health beliefs and behaviors. *Health Education Quarterly, 9,* 156-173.

Dingle, J. H., Badger, B. F., & Jordan, W. S. (1964). *Illness in the home: A study of 25,000 illnesses in a group of Cleveland families.* Cleveland: The Press of Western Reserve University.

Erikson, E. H. (1968). *Identity, youth and crisis.* New York: Norton.

Gochman, D. S. (1970). Children's perceptions of vulnerability to illness and accidents. *Public Health Reports, 85,* 69-73.

Gochman, D. S. (1971). Some correlates of children's health beliefs and potential health behavior. *Journal of Health and Social Behavior, 12,* 148-154.

Gochman, D. S. (1972). Consistency in children's perceptions of vulnerability to health problems. *Health Services Reports, 87,* 282-288.

Gochman, D. S., & Saucier, J.-F. (1982). Perceived vulnerability in children and adolescents. *Health Education Quarterly, 9,* 142–155.

Greenberger, E. (1984). Defining psychosocial maturity in adolescence. In P. Karoly & J. Steffen (Eds.), *Adolescent behavior disorders: Foundations and contemporary concerns* (pp. 54-81). Lexington, MA: Heath.

Kandel, D., & Lesser, G. S. (1972). *Youth in two worlds.* San Francisco: Jossey-Bass.

Lau, R. R., & Klepper, S. (1988). The development of illness orientations in children ages 6 through 12. *Journal of Health and Social Behavior, 29,* 149-168.

Maiman, L. A., Becker, M. H., & Katlic, A. W. (1985). How mothers treat their children's physical symptoms. *Journal of Community Health, 10,* 136-155.

Maiman, L. A., Becker, M. H., & Katlic, A. W. (1986). Correlates of mothers' use of medications for their children. *Social Science and Medicine, 22,* 41-51.

Mechanic, D. (1964). The influence of mothers on their children's health attitudes and behavior. *Pediatrics, 33,* 444-453.

Natapoff, J. (1978). Children's views of health: A developmental study. *American Journal of Public Health, 68,* 995-1,000.

Newman, W. P., Freedman, D. S., Voors, A. W., Gard, P. D., Srinivasan, S. R., Cresanta, J. L., Williamson, G. D., Webber, L. S., & Berenson, G. S. (1986). Relation of serum lipoprotein levels and systolic blood pressure to early atherosclerosis. *New England Journal of Medicine, 314,* 138-144.

Parcel, G. S., & Meyer, M. (1978). Development of an instrument to measure children's health locus of control. *Health Education Monographs, 6,* 149-159.

Parmelee, A. H. (1985). Children's illnesses: Their beneficial effects on behavioral development. *Child Development, 57,* 1-10.

Perrin, E. C., & Gerrity, P. S. (1981). There's a demon in your belly. *Pediatrics, 67,* 841-849.

Pratt, L. (1973a). Child learning methods and children's health behavior. *Journal of Health & Social Behavior, 14,* 61-69.

Pratt, L. (1973b). The significance of the family medication. *Journal of Comparative Family Studies, 4,* 13-35.

Rosenberg, M., & Simmons, R. G. (1972). Black and white self-esteem: The urban school child. *American Sociological Association Rose Monograph Series.*

Small, S. A., Eastman, G., & Cornelius, S. (1987, April). *Adolescent autonomy and parental stress.* Paper presented at the meeting of the Society for Research in Child Development, Baltimore, MD.

Steinberg, L. (1987, April). *Emotional autonomy, parental permissiveness, and adolescents' susceptibility to antisocial peer pressure.* Paper presented at the meeting of the Society for Research in Child Development, Baltimore, MD.

Steinberg, L., & Silverberg, S. B. (1986). The vicissitudes of autonomy in early adolescence. *Child Development, 57,* 841-851.
Stone, E. J. (1985). School-based health research funded by the National Heart, Lung, and Blood Institute. *Journal of School Health, 55,* 168-174.
Wallston, B. S., Wallston, K. A., Kaplan, G. D., & Maides, S. A. (1976). Development and validation of the health locus of control scale. *Journal of Consulting and Clinical Psychology, 44,* 580–585.

5

Risk-Taking Behaviors and Biopsychosocial Development During Adolescence

Charles E. Irwin, Jr.
Susan G. Millstein
University of California, San Francisco

INTRODUCTION

Adolescents continue to be portrayed as a homogeneous and healthy group (Irwin, 1990a). They represent a segment of the population having the least contact with the health care system that is often interpreted as absence of need (National Center for Health Statistics [NCHS], 1983, 1984, 1990a). Indeed, most adolescents experience no major health disorders or debilitating conditions as reflected in health status indicators most commonly used for adults and children (Irwin, 1987; Newacheck, 1989). These health status indicators are measures that utilize quantifiable mortality and morbidity outcomes that are best reflected in mortality rates, hospital discharge rates from acute care facilities, conditions cited in visits to office-based physician practices, and prevalence of specific infectious diseases or disabling conditions (Gans, Blyth, Elster, Gaveras, 1990; Irwin, Brindis, Brodt, Bennett, & Rodriguez, 1991; Irwin & Vaughan, 1988). Others (including a popular assumption in the lay press) argue that the health problems experienced by adolescents result from their own risk-taking behaviors that often begin with adolescents' perceptions of invulnerability.

This chapter presents our definition of risk taking; reviews national data on mortality and morbidity using traditional outcome measures, morbidity data on three specific risk behaviors, and covariation of these risk behaviors; provides an overview of the contribution of biopsychosocial development to the onset of risk behaviors; and discusses a model of risk-taking behavior. In the final section, we present some preliminary data on a longitudinal project on risk taking.

RISK-TAKING BEHAVIOR: DEFINITION

Morbidity and mortality patterns of adolescence show some interesting properties: The behaviors responsible for these patterns begin during early adolescence; the behaviors are prevalent in all socioeconomic and racial groups; significant gender differences in prevalence rates emerge; and there is a major increase in mortality from early to late adolescence. Unlike childhood, the morbidity and mortality patterns of adolescence are behaviorally generated and remain that way through the 4th decade of life (U.S. Preventive Services Task Force, 1989).

The behaviors associated with the major mortalities and morbidities of adolescents share a common theme: risk taking. Young people with limited or no experience engage in potentially destructive behaviors with anticipation of benefit and without understanding the immediate or long-term consequences of their actions (Greydanus, 1987; Irwin, 1989, 1990a, 1990b). Even though some risk taking is necessary in the normal developmental process, often the short- and long-term results of risk taking are disastrous (Baumrind, 1987). In the past researchers have included the following behaviors under this generic construct: eating disorders, homicide, mountain climbing, reckless vehicle use, sexual activity, substance use, suicide, and skydiving. These behaviors are associated with a wide range of negative and positive precursors and outcomes. By using our definition of risk taking, issues emerge regarding which behaviors one includes under this broad category. Inherent in the risk-taking terminology is an implication that the behavior has a volitional quality in which the outcome remains uncertain. There is a possibility of a negative health outcome. We include three behaviors in our definition: motor/recreational vehicle use, sexual activity, and substance use. The behaviors included in our definition have an "exploratory" quality to them (Irwin, 1987; Irwin & Vaughan, 1988). These risk behaviors result from an interaction between the biopsychosocial processes of the organism (the adolescent) and the environment. Adolescents may also be utilizing these behaviors as a method to assess their own biopsychosocial functioning.

MORTALITY

Prior to 1980, adolescence (10 to 20 years old) was the only age cohort in the United State to experience a rise in mortality from 1960–1979 (*Healthy people*, 1979). Since 1980, the age specific mortality rate for adolescence has remained high with a less rapid decline than other age cohorts of the population. Mortality rates for the second decade of life in 1987 differ markedly by age, gender, and race. Younger adolescents (10 to 14 years old) have a rate of 26.9 per 100,000 compared to a rate of 84.6 per 100,000 for older adolescents (15 to 19 years old) (NCHS, 1990a). This increase in mortality by over 200% within the second decade is the largest increase in any two consecutive 5-year age cohorts over the entire life span. Accidents (or unintentional injuries) still account for the majority of adolescent deaths. Fifty-five percent of the deaths are attributed to injuries involving motor vehicles and, to a lesser extent, injuries involving other off-road bicycles, falls, and drownings (NCHS, 1990a). The second leading cause of death for this age group during the 1980s is suicide, with homicide a close third. Injuries from violence, suicide, and homicide account for over 70% of deaths in the second decade of life. The death rates for males are more than twice that for females with 71% of the deaths occurring in males. The difference between males and females becomes more pronounced as they progress through the second decade. For adolescents age 10 to 14 the mortality rate for males is 67% higher than for females whereas for older adolescents age 15 to 19 the rate is over 150% grater (Irwin et al., 1991; NCHS, 1990a). The patterns of mortality in the second decade of life are clearly determined by males. Race is an additional important factor in determining the etiology of death. Black adolescents are more likely to die from homicide than White adolescents. Older Black adolescent males have a rate of mortality from homicide at 50 per 100,000 compared to a rate of 14.8 per 100,000 for White males (NCHS, 1990a).

MORBIDITY

Indicators used to assess morbidity are less well-defined than those used for mortality profiles. Several measures of morbidity have recently been used in combination to build a health profile of populations. These measures include: the prevalence of various diseases and illnesses, the number of acute conditions including unintentional and intentional injuries, and measures of disability (Irwin, 1987; Irwin & Vaughan, 1988). Once again, these measures suggest a relatively healthy adolescent population, although in some domains morbidity is still significant.

Hospital discharge rates for the adolescent population point to some interesting changes during the second decade of life. For males, the rate increases by 53% (from 433 per 10,000 for 13-year-olds to 821 per 10,000 for 18-year-olds), and for females (excluding pregnancy) the rate increases by 43% (from 367 per 10,000 for 13-year-olds to 846 per 10,000 for 18-year-olds) (Graves, 1988; Irwin, 1986). Trauma and poisonings (which includes substance use and abuse) account for the single largest category of hospitalization if one excludes pregnancy (Irwin, 1986).

In the area of infectious diseases (a measure of morbidity for all age groups), sexually transmitted diseases represent a significant negative outcome of sexual activity during adolescence (Bell & Holmes, 1984). Because not all sexually transmitted diseases are reportable and because this number is dependent on a report being made, any number has to represent a minimum of true prevalence rates. The 1988 rates for *Neisseria gonorrhoea* in adolescents are 65 per 100,000 for early adolescents and 1,073 per 100,000 for older adolescents (Centers for Disease

Control [CDC], 1990b; Irwin & Shafer, 1991). Significant gender differences currently exist. During adolescence the reported prevalence of gonorrhea is much greater among females than males. During early adolescence the rate is more than three times higher in females than males whereas during late adolescence, the reported rate is still more than 50% higher. The fact is noteworthy because for all other age groups, the reported prevalence of gonorrhea is substantially higher among males than females. Gender differences may result from access to health care services with teen-age girls having greater access to health services for reproductive or other health problems. Males may represent a huge undetected reservoir of sexually transmittable diseases. Another explanation may be that in order to get similar prevalence rates by gender, we would need to utilize a 2- to 3-year age gradient difference since females tend to have sexual intercourse with males at least 2 years older than themselves in late adolescence. This age difference may be even greater in early adolescence. Beyond the behavioral and access to services explanation for the higher rates in females, there appears to be gender specific risk factors including the site of infection (ectocervix), easier access to the organisms during infectious disease specimen collection in females and efficiency of transmission of organisms (*Chlamydia trachomatis* and *Neisseria gonorrhoeae*) to females. All adolescent population-based prevalence rates should be multiplied by a factor of 2 because a maximum of 50% of the population is sexually active (Aral, Schaffer, Mosher, & Cates, 1988; Cates, 1990; Shafer & Sweet, 1990).

Both morbidity and mortality patterns are reflective of three behaviors that have their onset in early adolescence: sexual activity, motor/recreational vehicle use, and the role of substance use in its contribution to mortality in the area of motor vehicle use and utilization of health services. Another way to assess morbidity within adolescence is to look at behaviors with high prevalence rates and considerable potential for negative outcomes. Utilizing this approach, once again three behaviors emerge which account for greater than 50% of the morbidity in the second decade: motor/recreational vehicle use, sexual activity, and substance use. The prevalence of these three behaviors and their patterns of covariation are reviewed.

RISK-TAKING BEHAVIORS: SINGLE BEHAVIORS

Over the past decade a small group of investigators have suggested that risk behaviors do not occur in isolation but tend to covary within individuals. More is known about specific single behaviors and the factors associated with their onset, maintenance, and negative outcomes. Before we look at the interrelationships of the behaviors, we review what we know about the single specific behaviors under consideration.

Motor and Recreational Vehicle Use

Unintentional injuries (or accidents) continue to head the list of premature mortality in the United States. Unintentional injuries not only cause the largest number of deaths in adolescents, but the resultant nonfatal injuries account for the largest number of hospital days among males and females. Injuries also account for a significant number of ambulatory visits: 16.1% and 12.5% for younger and older adolescents, respectively (NCHS, 1989a, 1989b). Morbidity and mortality data cite speed, time of day, and lack of experience as contributing factors. Jonah has concluded that risky driving habits may be a more significant cause of these accidents than driving experience or exposure (Jonah, 1985). Included in these risky driving habits are speeding, tailgating, nonuse of seat belts, and driving under the influence of alcohol and other drugs.

As early as 10 years of age, Lewis and Lewis (1984) demonstrated that 22% of the fifth graders reported placing themselves at risk for personal injury. Our own work supports this finding with approximately 29.5% in the middle school and 37.5% in the senior high school engaging in physically risky activities such as physical fights, skateboarding, and bicycling dangerous (Millstein et al., in press).

Within all the injury literature, male gender emerges as the most critical factor. Males are particularly vulnerable beginning in the first year of life (NCHS, 1990a).

Sexual Behavior

The most recent data on sexual activity during adolescence comes from the National Survey of Family Growth (NSFG), Cycle IV, and the National Survey of Adolescent Males (Centers for Disease Control [CDC], 1991; Forrest & Singh, 1990; NCHS, 1990b; Sonenstein, Pleck, & Ku, 1989; Pleck, Sonenstein, & Swain, 1988). The incidence of sexual activity has increased dramatically from 1971 to the late 1980s in both younger and older age cohorts of adolescents. In 1988, by age 15, 24% of Black females, 26% of White females and males, and 69% of Black males have experienced coitus at least once. By age 19, 83% of Black females, 76% of White females, 86% of White males, and 98% of Black males have had coitus at least once. White adolescent females report more frequent intercourse with more partners than their age-related Black cohorts (CDC, 1991; Pratt, 1990; Sonenstein et al., 1989). Although specific data on Hispanic adolescents is not reported in the 1988 survey, previous research in 1982 documents that patterns of sexual activity among Hispanic youth fall between that of Black and White youth. For example, among females aged 15–19, 59% of Black females had initiated sexual activity compared to 50% of Hispanics and 44% of Whites (Hayes, 1987).

Since 1970, there have been five national surveys documenting sexual activity (1970, 1975, 1980, 1985, and 1988). The most dramatic increase in the proportion of sexually active females has occurred in the 3-year period, 1985–1988 (CDC, 1991). One third of the increase in premarital sexual experience among adolescent women for the entire 18-year period spanning 1970–1988 occurred in one 3-year period, 1985–1988.

Age appears to be a significant factor in the adoption of contraceptive use among sexually active adolescents. For adolescents as a whole, the percentage of sexually active adolescents who have ever used contraceptives jumped from 58% to 83% between the ages of 15 to 16 and reached 91% by age 19. By race and ethnicity, sexually active Black adolescents have the highest percentage of sexually active adolescents who have ever used contraception at the youngest ages. At age 15, 71% of Black adolescents have used contraceptives compared to 58% of Whites and only 10% of Hispanics. By age 19, 83% of Black females, 94% of Whites, and 81% of Hispanics have initiated contraceptive use.

Although patterns of contraceptive choice change over the life course of an adolescent, a key factor in their adoption and utilization within the adolescent's sexual relationship appears to be related to their initial utilization at the point of sexual debut. In a recent national survey (Kahn, Rindfuss, & Guilkey, 1990) only about one half of Whites and one third of Blacks use a method of contraception at first intercourse. Only a small proportion of adolescents (19% of Whites and 13% of Blacks) became contraceptive users during the next two months, thus the slow rate of subsequent adoption of a method leaves a large group of adolescents continuing high risk of an unintended pregnancy (Kahn et al., 1990).

The 1988 data provide a further look at the sexual behaviors of young women during their adolescence. Among 15- to 24-year-old women who began coitus before age 18, 75% had 2 or more partners, and 45% reported having had 4 or more partners. Among those women who became sexually active after age 19, only 20% reported having had more than 1 partner and 1% 4 or more partners. When one controls for duration of sexual activity and limits it to less than 24 months, 45% of 15- to 17-year-olds have had 2 or more partners compared with 40% of 18- to 19-year-olds and 26% of those greater than 20 years of age (CDC, 1991). Little is known about sexual behaviors other than coitus in adolescents (Brooks-Gunn & Furstenberg, 1989, 1990).

Substance Use and Abuse

Johnston and his colleagues have documented the trends of substance use over the past decade among high school seniors through cross-sectional epidemiological studies using retrospective measures of substance use during the past year and month. The most recent data continue to point to high rates of use with alcohol and tobacco-related substances.

In 1989 the lifetime prevalence use of alcohol and cigarettes was 91% and 66%, respectively, for high school seniors (Johnston, O'Malley, & Bachman, 1990). Four percent of high school seniors report daily use of alcohol and 33% report having had at least 5 drinks in a row at one sitting in the last 2 weeks.

Nineteen percent report daily use of cigarettes. The National Household Survey data for 1988 indicate that 26% of eighth graders and 38% of tenth graders report having had 5 or more drinks on at least one occasion in the 2 weeks prior to the National Household Survey (National Institute on Drug Abuse [NIDA], 1989).

Marijuana remains the most popular illicit drug for adolescents. Data from the high school survey report lifetime prevalence rates of marijuana use dropping from its peak of 60% in 1979–80 to 44% in 1989. Rates of cocaine use remain at 4.7% for crack and 8.5% for other cocaine. Heroin use is rare among adolescents with approximately 1% of adolescents reporting ever using it (Johnston, O'Malley, & Bachman, 1989a, 1989b, 1990). The problem with the data on substance use is that the highest risk adolescents do not participate in these high school surveys that require attendance in the 12th grade of high schools on the day the surveys are done; therefore, all the current surveys probably underestimate the use of substances in adolescents (Irwin, 1990b).

The 1988 NIDA National Household Survey substantiates the high rates of substance use in adolescence with the following lifetime prevalence rates of 12- to 17-year-olds: alcohol 50.2%, cigarettes 42.3%, cocaine 3.4%, and marijuana 17.4%. These rates are lower than the rates in the 1970s. However, the decreasing rates witnessed in the early 1980s have stopped. This may reflect earlier initiation of use (NIDA, 1989).

The mean age of onset of cigarettes, alcohol, and marijuana are 12.0, 12.5 and 14.0 years, respectively (Irwin & Ryan, 1989; Johnston, O'Malley, & Bachman, 1989a). Kandel and her colleagues further pointed out the importance of early adolescence as a period of vulnerability by providing longitudinal data on sequences and progression of youth and predictors of progression in a sample of 1,300 New York residents. Alcohol use began early with 20% of their cohort having ever used alcohol by age 10, over half by age 14, and 80% by age 18. The onset of cigarette smoking was similar to alcohol until age 15, after which the onset decreased. Marijuana initiation was most likely to occur at age 13 and to peak at age 18, with a 20% prevalence of use (Yamaguchi & Kandel, 1984a, 1984b). Chewing tobacco or smokeless tobacco has recently appeared as the newest substance for adolescents. Current data point to the use of this substance primarily by adolescent males with an onset in Grade 7, and some studies point to a prevalence rate of 23.1% by Grade 10 (Connolly et al., 1986; Hunter, Croft, & Burke, 1986).

Additional support for the early onset of substance use comes from the initial phases of our longitudinal study on risk. This study involves 1,500 adolescents in grades 6 through 10 (ages 10–16). The overall rates of use of alcohol, cigarettes, and marijuana were 48%, 32%, 42%, respectively. In the middle school sample (ages 10–14), the rates for alcohol, cigarettes, and marijuana were 23%, 20%, and 17%, respectively (Millstein et al., in press). Gender and grade level were significant factors in the use of both alcohol and cigarettes. Alcohol use increased by age and was more prevalent in males. Cigarette use increased by age and was more prevalent in females. Marijuana remained the same across gender and grade (Irwin & Millstein, in press).

RISK-TAKING BEHAVIORS: COVARIATION OF RISK BEHAVIORS

A number of investigators have suggested that certain risk-taking behaviors do not occur in isolation but tend to covary within individuals. The most comprehensive work on the covariation of risk behaviors is by Jessor and Jessor who have provided compelling evidence for a syndrome of problem behaviors that includes cigarette smoking, alcohol use, marijuana use, premature sexual activity, and other problem behaviors (Jessor & Jessor, 1977). Before exploring the mechanisms of the interrelations, we review what is currently known about the covariation of substance use, sexual activity, and vehicle use.

Vehicle Use and Substance Use

The co-occurrence of alcohol and motor vehicle injuries is well established. In approximately half of the motor vehicle fatalities involving an adolescent driver, the driver has a blood alcohol level above .10% (CDC, 1983, 1990a; Mayhew, Donelson, & Beirness, 1986). Beyond the well-established relationship of alcohol and motor vehicle injuries, data are emerging to support the relationship of alcohol use to other injuries. The CDC has reported a higher than expected frequency of high blood alcohol levels in individuals coming to emergency rooms for burns, drownings, etc. (CDC, 1983). In another study by Friedman (1985), who looked at adolescent deaths in San Francisco County, data on blood alcohol concentrations were available on 20 adolescents. Four of these adolescents died while using bicycles or skateboards, and all four had blood alcohol levels greater than .10%.

Our own data point to the association of substance use and vehicle use. Fourteen percent of our entire sample reported having used a bicycle or skateboard under the influence of alcohol or other drugs. Among adolescents in the middle school setting (ages 10 to 14), 7.7% admitted using recreational vehicles under the influence: In high school students, the rate was 19.5% (Millstein et al., in press). These data underestimate the percentage of risky users because they reflect the percentage among the sample as a whole and not just among users of these vehicles. With regard to motor vehicle use, riding with a driver under the influence was reported by 36.9% of the middle school students and 58% of the high school students. It is probable that many of the impaired drivers are parents of the adolescent, especially among the younger adolescents. Driving a car under the influence of alcohol or other drugs was reported by 6.8% of the entire sample. Within the high school sample, 9.4% reported this behavior. Once again, these percentages underestimate the problem because the sample is primarily composed of adolescents who are not eligible for driving (Millstein et al., in press). Even though conventional wisdom supports the concept that substances other than alcohol are involved in recreational and motor vehicle injury, there are no definite outcome data to support this assumption.

Substance Use/Abuse Patterns

Within the area of substance use itself, there are certain patterns of covariation that deserve mention. Although many adolescents experiment with certain substances and do not proceed on to other substances, there are some established patterns of initiation and associations. Covington (1981) has shown that adolescents who experiment with cigarette smoking are more likely to experiment with other drugs. In his sample of students in grades 6 through 10, 69%–87% of smokers had tried marijuana compared with only 3%–17% of nonsmokers.

Yamaguchi and Kandel (1984a, 1984b) provided prospective longitudinal data on the interrelations in use of substances and gender differences in these patterns. The critical difference in their sample is that cigarettes or alcohol can precede marijuana use in females whereas with males alcohol generally precedes marijuana use. Marijuana use is also an important precursor of use of other illicit drugs. Kandel and Logan (1984) further examined the role of personal antecedent variables and found that substance use by one's friends in adolescence and early onset of substance use were the best predictors of subsequent substance use. The trajectory of use patterns was validated further by Newcomb and Bentler (1986) in a longitudinal study in Los Angeles with alcohol use in the preceding year being an important predictor of marijuana use and marijuana use in the preceding year being an important predictor of cocaine use in the following year.

Sexual Behavior, Substance Use, and Other Risk Behaviors

Associations among sexual activity and other risk behaviors are not as well documented as the area of injuries and substance use where outcome data such as motor vehicle deaths and hospitalization for injuries are more quantifiable outcome measures. With the emergence of acquired immune deficiency syndrome (AIDS), there is a greater focus on this area of covariation (Miller, Turner, & Moses, 1990). Research indicates that adolescents who are having sex are also engaging in other risk behaviors. Zabin (1984) looked at the association of cigarette smoking and sexual behavior in a sample of 1,200 female teenagers attending 32 contraception clinics. Within this sample that had a 25% prevalence rate of cigarette smoking, there was an association between onset of coitus at an early age and less effective use of contraceptives with cigarette use (Zabin, 1984). Zabin and colleagues have also shown that at each age sexually active teens are significantly higher on a substance use index than virgins (Zabin, Hardy, Smith, & Hirsch, 1986).

Jessor and Jessor (1977) documented the association between early sexual activity and use of marijuana, cigarettes, and alcohol. With drinking status as a marker for at-risk youth, they found 80% of their subjects were marijuana users, and better than 50% had initiated coitus.

Analyses from the National Longitudinal Survey of the Labor Market Experience of Youth show the strong correlation between prior substance use and sexual initiation by age 16 (Mott & Haurin, 1987; Rosenbaum & Kandel, 1990). Even when such covariates as race, religion, parental education, family structure, and personality (including delinquency and school characteristics) are controlled for, there is still a strong association of drug use and sexual behavior. Early sex is 1.4 times more frequent for boys who have used alcohol or cigarettes or both than for boys who did not report any prior drug use. It is 2.7 times more frequent for boys who have used marijuana and 3.4 times more frequent for boys who have used other illicit drugs. For females, the association is even stronger with 1.8, 3.5, and 4.9 times more frequent use of alcohol or cigarettes, marijuana, and illicit drugs, respectively, for female users than for nonusers. The association is stronger for Whites and Hispanics than for Blacks (Rosenbaum & Kandel, 1990). Additional analyses done by Kandel and Davies (in press) on the entire National Longitudinal Survey of the Labor Market Experience of Youth sample from 1984 find that sexual activity is the most important predictor of cocaine involvement. Among the 93% of males and 86% of females who were sexually experienced, the earlier sex was initiated, the greater the incidence of subsequent cocaine use. Additional data from the National Survey of Youth indicate that early alcohol use in females is more predictive of early sexual activity than in males (Mott & Haurin, 1987).

Additional studies to document the relationship between substance use and sexual activity are highlighted below. Elliott and Morse (1989) reanalyzed data from the 1976–80 waves of the National Youth Survey (a national probability sample of 2,360 adolescents aged 11 to 17 at the time of the first interview in 1976). Among males in the survey, the percentage of those who were sexually active increased with increasing involvement in substance use: 10% with no history of substance use, 23% with a history of alcohol use only, 48% with a history of combined alcohol and marijuana, and 72% with a history of multiple illicit drugs. In these analyses, Elliot and Morse attempted to establish the temporal sequence of sexual activity and substance use. They found that males and females tended to initiate substance use prior to sexual activity: 5 times as many females and 2.25 times as many males initiated substance use prior to sexual activity rather than initiating sexual activity prior to substance use.

Beyond the covariation of substance use and sexual activity, other behaviors covary with sexual activity (Ensminger, 1987). Miller and Simon (1974) studied the relationship of sexual intercourse with other adolescent behaviors in a random stratified sample of 2,064 White adolescents aged 14 to 17 living in Illinois households. Sexual intercourse was once again associated with drug use in their data. In males more than females, sexual intercourse was also related to delinquent activity. Additionally, they found that adolescents who have had sexual intercourse are less likely to aspire to advanced education and less likely to report being very religious. Studies done in other countries also support the covariation. Epstein and Tamir (1984) found that initiation of sexual intercourse in males was clearly related to cigarette smoking and dropping out of school. Using smoking status as an indicator condition, 64% of those males who began smoking had intercourse compared to 20% of males who did not smoke. In the female cohort, 38.5% of smokers initiated intercourse compared to 13% of nonsmokers.

In our own data on risk-taking behaviors and intention to become sexually active during the next year, we have found that the number of risk behaviors (e.g., substance use, cigarette use, dangerous vehicle use, etc.) reported by White females correlates positively with their intention to become sexually active (Irwin & Millstein, in press; Kegeles et al., 1987). Among the entire sample, sexually active youth engaged in significantly more risk behaviors than confirmed virgins. There is no significant difference between the sexually active teens and those in transition in the number of risks engaged in for any of the subjects. Among White adolescents, males and females in transition had engaged in significantly more risk behaviors than the confirmed virgins. Among females, engaging in risk behaviors is predictive of intentions to become sexually active for Whites, but only age is associated with sexual activity intentions for Blacks. This relationship does not hold up in Black females. A factor analysis of our cross-sectional data on risk behaviors demonstrates an interrelationship of substance use and other physical risk behaviors in males but not in females (Irwin & Millstein, in press).

Other factors associated with intention to initiate sexual behaviors include knowledge of transmission, beliefs and attitudes regarding sexually transmitted diseases/human immunodeficiency virus (STD/HIV) and the adolescent's personal vulnerability for STD, and peer influences including perceptions of peer norms. Among urban high school students surveyed as a part of a STD/HIV intervention project (mean age 14.6 years), nonsexually active students who anticipated commencing sexual activity over the next 12 months were found to be less anxious about acquiring STD and HIV, perceived that peers do not believe in preventive health behaviors, including condom use with sexual intercourse, and engaged in more risk behaviors as reflected by the increased use of alcohol and drugs (Shafer & Boyer, 1990).

Summary of Covariation Section

With the mean age of onset of cigarette and alcohol use being 12 years, it is not surprising that alcohol and cigarette use often precede or are associated with vehicle use, sexual behavior, and other substances. Substance use and lack of conventional lifestyle including delinquency are clearly related to sexual activity. Prior use of substances, both licit and illicit, significantly increases the risk of early sexual activity among adolescents. Early sexual activity increases the likelihood of involvement with cocaine, a substance for which the age of initiation is typically much later than that reported for initiation of sexual intercourse. The strong covariation of substance use and dangerous vehicle use and/or sexual intercourse may actually occur secondary to the disinhibitory effect of alcohol and other substances.

Gender differences in the increase and onset of behaviors may be associated with testosterone. Udry and his colleagues (Udry, 1985; Udry & Talbert, 1988) pointed out the critical role of testosterone in males in the onset of risk behaviors and the mediating effect of androgens for females.

Even though the research on covariation establishes some of the mechanisms by which the behaviors are interrelated, there remains little work in the area of motivation for initiation and perception of the actual risk from the perspective of the adolescent. The intervention and prevention programs attempt to educate teens about the risk without a careful understanding of why adolescents actually choose to engage in risk behaviors with the probability of negative outcomes. Recently completed analyses of our longitudinal data regarding expected outcomes of certain risk behaviors show that adolescents are making choices based on positive expectations of outcomes of sexual and fighting behaviors. In the area of substance use, adolescents make choices based on different expected outcomes. They do not expect negative outcomes. These differences of expected outcomes may be critical for developing interventions. Motivations regarding the various behaviors have yet to be explored. Investigators are now focusing on the possible mechanisms responsible for the interrelationships of the behaviors and the positive and negative health outcomes (Baumrind, 1987; Donovan & Jessor, 1985; Irwin & Millstein, 1987, 1991, in press; Udry, 1988).

MECHANISMS OF COVARIATION

Even though some of the behaviors are interrelated, few investigators have attempted to develop a theoretical framework for consideration of the mechanisms. Jessor has proposed the problem behavior theory as a mechanism to explain the interrelationships (Jessor & Jessor, 1977). Udry and his colleagues (Udry, 1985, 1988; Udry & Billy, 1987; Udry & Talbert, 1988; Udry, Talbert, & Morris, 1986) provided important data on the importance of gonadal steroids (e.g., testosterone) in the initiation of coitus in males and heterosocial behavior in females. Beyond the work by Udry and his colleagues, few investigators have attempted to integrate both biological and psychosocial factors in developing theories to explain onset of risk behaviors during adolescence.

We maintain that risk taking during adolescence is a part of the developmental process of adolescence and that a careful understanding of the process of development itself may give clues to the mechanisms that explain the onset and maintenance of the behaviors. If one examines the data on behaviors for prevalence, age of onset, gender distribution, and covariation of the three behaviors and the nature of factors that generate these behaviors, certain issues regarding development emerge. First, there appears to be a developmental trajectory with certain behaviors preceding other behaviors. For example, substance use (either alcohol or generally cigarettes) occurs in early adolescence. Other investigators have proposed that there may be a developmental trajectory regarding risk behaviors with one behavior preceding another behavior (Irwin & Vaughan, 1988). As Yamaguchi and Kandel (1984a, 1984b) demonstrated, one substance may precede another substance, and there is a definite progression through different substances with males and females having somewhat different trajectories. Recently, Rosenbaum and Kandel (1990) maintained that one behavior may not be the functional equivalent of another behavior but may actually constitute a risk factor for a subsequent behavior. In our longitudinal analyses of onset of risk behaviors in a middle school population, there appears to be a developmental trajectory with substance use preceding the onset of sexual behavior (Irwin, Millstein, Adler, & Turner, 1988).

A slight variation of this theme is the development of deviant behavior as discussed by Robins and Wish (1977). They argued that the initiation of one behavior is in part a function of past deviant behaviors and also makes more probable the initiation of additional deviant behaviors. They further suggested that differences between subcultures regarding the ages that are considered appropriate for various activities may be a key to value differences between the subcultures as well. In studying St. Louis Black males born in the 1930s, alcohol use was found to be one of the strongest antecedents to precocious sexual activity (Robins & Wish, 1977).

Second, the behaviors do not occur in isolation. Adolescents who engage in one risk behavior are more likely to engage in other risk-taking activities if the onset of the behavior occurs chronologically early in adolescence. Jessor and Jessor (1977) affirmed a group of adolescent problem behaviors that includes precocious sexual activity, cigarette smoking, assertiveness, nonconventionality, marijuana use, and alcohol use. Their problem behavior theory describes a proneness to engage in certain deviant behaviors. Jessor and colleagues utilize three systems to define problem behavior: the personality, the perceived environment, and the behavior. Within the personality constructs, high value on independence and low expectation for academic goals are both conceptualized as favorable to problem behavior. Within the perceived environment system, low support and control from significant others and approval for and models for engaging in problem behavior are the important constructs. Within the behavior system, the degree of involvement in other problem behavior and the degree of involvement in conventional behaviors (e.g., school performance and church attendance) are expected to predict problem behavior. Early transition to sexual intercourse is related to the personality and perceived environment scales (Jessor, Costa, Jessor, & Donovan, 1983; Jessor & Jessor, 1975). In adolescence, early sexual experience, problem drinking, delinquency, and illicit drug use represent a claim on more adult status or a transition in development, and engaging in such behaviors at a time that is considered too early constitutes a departure from norms. Recently, some investigators have argued that the concept of a single general tendency to explain a variety of risk behaviors accounts for some but not all of the meaningful variance to explain risk behaviors (Osgood, 1989; Osgood, Johnston, O'Malley, & Bachman, 1988).

Third, there appears to be gender specific differences among the three behaviors. For example, White males and females initiate sex at about the same time, however, more males report using substances except cigarettes. Black males and females differ on their initiation of sex and substance use.

Fourth, peers and family play critical roles in the onset and maintenance of the behaviors. Important predictors of substance use are family members (including siblings) and peer participation in substance use. Recent data further supports this finding for sexual activity with regard to peers (Billy & Udry, 1985; Smith, Udry, & Morris, 1985).

BIOPSYCHOSOCIAL DEVELOPMENT

Adolescence is a time of dramatic biological, psychosocial, and environmental change (Hamburg & Hamburg, 1975; Lerner, 1987; Petersen, 1988; Simmons & Blyth, 1987). Before we present our model, we highlight the critical contributing factors of biological and psychosocial change to onset of risk behaviors.

Biological Development During Adolescence

Biological development, characterized by the rapid hormonal, physiological, and somatic changes of puberty, is dramatic and interwoven with the other aspects of maturation. With the exception of sexual differentiation during fetal growth and hormonal changes during senescence, there is no other period in the life-span development in which such significant hormonal and biological change takes place. The age of onset and duration of these changes have broad and different ranges both between and within genders.

The range of pubertal onset for females is 8 to 13 years of age, with completion at 13 to 18 years of age (Marshall & Tanner, 1969). For males, the onset is 9.5 to 13.5 years, with completion at 13.5 to 19 years of age (Marshall & Tanner, 1970). The earlier onset of puberty in females may account for some of the gender differences in the onset of certain behaviors.

Psychosocial Significance of Puberty

Psychosocially, the onset of puberty is accompanied by changes in family interactions, parental feelings, peer relationships and expectations, patterns of intimacy, changes in self-esteem, heterosocial interests, and educational achievements

cognitive ability to reason abstractly and consider cause and effect relationships, he or she also has had little experience in applying these skills to decisions in a more autonomous manner. For the young adolescent, this translates into a belief in the power and possibilities of though itself, in which possibility is secondary to reality. One effect of this cognitive immaturity is what Elkind calls cognitive egocentrism, which includes the inability to recognize one's similarities with other people (Elkind, 1967). If the adolescent believes that he or she is not subject to the same laws of chance as others, perceptions of invulnerability result, affecting the adolescents' perceptions of the risk associated with specific behaviors (Millstein, in press).

As one examines the specific cognitive changes and psychosocial changes and biological changes that characterize the adolescent period, the emergence of risk taking is not surprising. With the developmental tasks and biological change providing the push and cognitive abilities being immature accompanied with lack of experience with the behaviors, the adolescent period is a critical developmental period in the life cycle for the onset of life-long risky behaviors and the associated negative outcomes.

ETIOLOGY OF INTEREST IN LINKAGE OF BEHAVIORS WITH MATURATION, BOTH BIOLOGICAL AND PSYCHOLOGICAL

Careful analyses of the mortality and morbidity data of adolescence, the interrelationships of these behaviors responsible for the negative outcomes, age of onset, gender differences, and some important early clinical observations lead to an observation of the behaviors as a group and what might be the common underlying mechanisms driving the behaviors.

Our clinical observations over the past decade are consistent with the literature. Many of our patients with behavioral problems associated with their medical problems developed earlier or later than their age related peers. This asynchrony appears to be a contributing factor to the etiology of their problems. Earlier developing girls were brought to our clinical setting by their mothers because of "acting out problems" within their families. Later developing males were also brought by their parents with concerns about their development and often their sons' dissatisfaction with school. Another group of patients at the Pediatric Endocrinology Clinic were the females with precocious puberty. These females were having difficulty in school, difficulty in functioning within their homes, and, in particular, were seeking out older young people as friends. The problems with adolescent females who have precocious puberty are well documented (Sonis, Comite, & Blue, 1985).

The greatest effects of timing of puberty are in the following areas: self-conceptions (body image and self-esteem), developmental needs (heterosexual relationships, peer affiliation, and family independence), school performance (academic performance and problem behaviors), and environmental responses (peer, parental, and teacher expectations). These effects vary by gender, the pubertal status of the adolescent and how it relates to that of his or her peers, definitions of maturational timing, and the specific risk behavior under investigation (for extensive discussion, see Brooks-Gunn, 1989; Brooks-Gunn et al., 1985; Irwin & Millstein, 1986; Steinberg, 1987). In general, the most negative effects are reported for early maturing females (Brooks-Gunn, 1989). Some recent work shows that the effects of early maturation may be detrimental for both sexes, with early maturation in males being associated with the early initiation of sexual activity (Irwin et al., 1989; Westney et al., 1984).

For risk-taking behaviors to be both interrelated and developmentally driven, one needs to bring together two areas of research that have until recently been considered separately: (a) the relationship of biological development to psychosocial functioning during adolescence; and (b) the relationship of risk-taking behaviors to psychosocial correlates of these behaviors. The first section of this chapter reviewed the mortality and morbidity data of adolescence emphasizing the negative outcomes. The second section reviewed the covariation literature and introduced the known mechanisms by which the behaviors are interrelated. The third section emphasized the issues of biopsychosocial maturation and the effect of pubertal maturation. The fourth section highlighted how these risk behaviors fulfill many developmental needs which have their onset throughout adolescence.

BIOPSYCHOSOCIAL MODELS OF RISK-TAKING BEHAVIOR

In the past decade, biopsychosocial models (Irwin & Millstein, 1986; Jessor & Jessor, 1977; Udry, 1988) have been proposed that integrate adolescent developmental principles with risk factors for the development of risk-taking behaviors. Jessor and Jessor have proposed a problem behavior framework arising from an interaction of factors within and among each of these systems: the personality system, the perceived environment, and the behavior system (Jessor, 1984; Jessor & Jessor, 1977). This model was discussed earlier in the chapter. More recently, Udry (1988) proposed a model for males that includes the effects of sex hormones. Specifically, considering five behaviors (got drunk, smoked cigarettes, cut school, had sex, and used marijuana), levels of free testosterone add significant variance to a social model. In girls, there are no specific biological effects. Udry has found a link between testosterone and sexual behavior that appears to be mediated through the social environment (Udry & Billy, 1987; Udry, Talbert, & Morris, 1986). Increasing levels of testosterone give rise to increased heterosocial interest and masturbatory activity but not actual coital behavior. Other models draw heavily from the concept of sensation seeking as a personality trait that correlates with risk behaviors (Daitzman & Zuckerman, 1980; Zuckerman, 1986) and the perception of risk constructs (Slovic, 1987).

The causal model as depicted in Fig. 5.1 integrates biological maturation and psychosocial functioning (Irwin & Millstein, 1986; see Irwin & Millstein, in press-b, and Irwin & Ryan, 1989, for extensive discussion of model). The model draws heavily on the previous work of Jessor and Jessor, the biological effects demonstrated by Udry, and integrates our knowledge about the psychosocial effects of pubertal maturational timing. The model states that biological maturation during adolescence has specific psychosocial sequelae. Specifically, timing of biological maturation directly influences four areas of psychosocial functioning: (a) cognitive scope, (b) self-perceptions, (c) perceptions of the social environment, and (d) personal values. Each broad area of psychosocial functioning has components that play a larger role in initiation and maintenance of risk behaviors. These areas are expanded in Fig. 5.1. In younger adolescents, who are at the height of cognitive egocentrism, these effects are especially strong.

These four factors influence two additional mediating factors, peer group selection and perceptions of risk. The behavior and standards of the peer group are powerful motivators for adolescents. Risk perception, although it has not been studied extensively in adolescents, is expected to be affected by peer norms, cognitive capacity, and self-perceptions, particularly self-esteem. Recently, data from

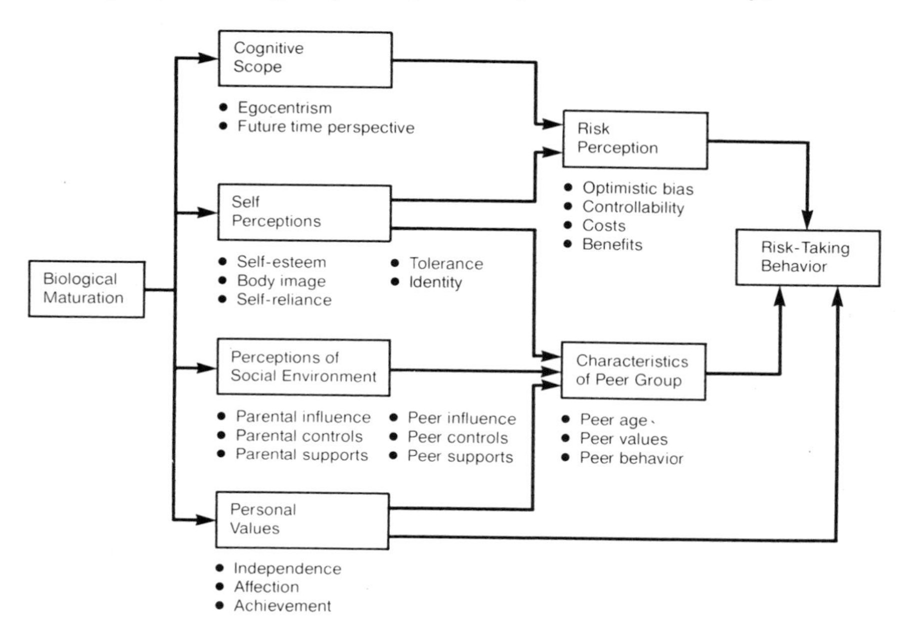

FIG. 5.1. Causal model of adolescent risk-taking behavior. Adapted and modified from Irwin & Millstein (1986).

Johnston and his colleagues in the annual surveys of substance use provide insight into the importance of risk perception. Over the past decade as the high school seniors have viewed marijuana as being more risky to their health, there has been a significant decrease in marijuana use (Johnston, O'Malley, & Bachman, 1989a, 1989b). The adolescent's peer group influences risk-taking behavior both in its effects on risk perceptions and directly in providing opportunities for risk-taking behavior. The influence of personal values on risk taking occurs as a function of its effects on peer group choice with some direct effects as well.

The specific way in which pubertal timing affects the adolescent depends on a number of factors such as gender and age. For example, the effects of early pubertal maturation in males is positive with negative health outcomes in the area of sexual activity. In females, the effects of early pubertal maturation are negative in both the psychological and health outcome arenas. In males, the effect of late development is negative psychosocially with positive health outcomes. In females, the outcomes are both positive in psychosocial functioning and health. The efficacy of this model to explain adolescent risk taking is currently being explored in an extensive longitudinal study of adolescents.

GENERAL OVERVIEW OF CURRENT RESEARCH

A series of longitudinal studies is currently being used to test the model. The initial sample (Phase 1) consists of 1,636 adolescents from one middle school (881) and two high schools (755) in an urban bay area community. Phase 1 identifies the base rates of the risk-taking behaviors in the entire sample and an appropriate cohort of adolescents based on self-report measures of maturation (Irwin, Millstein, Adler, Kegeles, & Cohn, 1986). These data are reported in two publications (Irwin & Millstein, in press; Millstein et al., in press). The final phase (Phase 3) of the longitudinal study consists of a cohort of 200 adolescents who were part of all three phases. In the longitudinal phases (Phase 2 and Phase 3) of the project, two critical qualitative components of the study are (a) the meaning of maturation interview and (b) the concepts of risk interview.

From the self-report data in the schools, it is clear that the self-report measures of maturation in the male population are not accurate reflections of the young people's actual status; however, the bias is in a predicted direction. For males, a much higher percentage reported that they were early developers in middle school than is expected. In high school, a much higher percentage stated they were late developers than expected. For females, there was a bias in the direction of normal to late developers in all classes. The predicted distribution should be Early, 20%; Normal, 60%; and Late, 20% based on an algorithm. Table 5.1 highlights the distribution and the above reported discrepancies.

To understand how timing of pubertal maturation interacts with risk and resultant behavior, it is not enough to know where the young person is in terms of

TABLE 5.1
Percent of Adolescents Classifying Themselves as Early/Normal/Late Developers Based on Self-Staging

	Grade Level in School					
	6	*7*	*8*	*9*	*10*	*Total*
Males (N = 571)						
Early (%)	55	45	36	32	38	38
Normal (%)	28	27	36	17	25	25
Late (%)	(NA)	2	12	51	26	26
Unknown (%)	17	27	15	0	11	11
Females (N = 590)						
Early (%)	6	8	5	13	9	8
Normal (%)	51	64	76	70	56	63
Late (%)	16	3	4	18	35	18
Unknown (%)	27	25	16	0	0	11

NA—Not applicable in Grade 6.

maturation. One needs to also have an understanding of the meaning of maturation to the young person. The meaning of maturation interview queries adolescents about where they currently are in maturation and then probes the following areas: sources of information, social support, affective response from friends, perceived advantages and disadvantages of their own rates of maturation and other rates of maturation.

From our early work on risk taking it is clear that adolescents recognize the negative aspects of risk-taking behaviors, however, they are also able to identify developmental changes in risk as a function of age (Millstein & Irwin, 1985). Of 11 behaviors ranging from taking drugs to not exercising, they ranked them as *at least somewhat risky* to *extremely risky* on a 5-point scale. Older adolescents perceive significantly less risk across the 11 behaviors than do younger adolescents. There are some interesting anticipated changes of risk with age. In the area of sexual activity and smoking cigarettes, adolescents anticipate less risk when older. In the area of not seeing a physician and not exercising, they anticipate more risk when older. In the areas of driving and drinking, driving fast, reckless vehicle use, and drug use, they anticipate no changes with age: the risk will be the same as they get older (Irwin & Millstein, in press). The concepts of risk interview is an in-depth qualitative assessment of the positive and negative expectations assigned to risk, both prospectively and after engagement.

Several of the early analyses focus on the relationship between onset of risk behaviors and the attributions assigned to risk behaviors. Throughout this chapter, data has been provided on morbidity, covariation, and biopsychosocial development. Recent analyses testing the model point out the importance of expectations of outcomes of risk behaviors and the social environment. Positive attributions regarding sexual activity and fighting predict their onset, whereas less negative attributions predict substance abuse behaviors (Irwin et al., 1988). Preliminary analyses of the social environment point out that adolescents in nontraditional families have a greater tendency to initiate substance use related behaviors earlier, however, the effects of emotional detachment (Ryan & Lynch, 1989; Steinberg & Silverberg, 1986) are powerful predictors of initiation and maintenance of risk behaviors (Turner, Irwin, & Millstein, 1989, 1991). Throughout the studies, intention to initiate a behavior remains a critical factor in determining whether adolescents will engage in a behavior in the following year (Irwin et al., 1988) that further confirms the volitional nature of these behaviors.

CONCLUSION

Risk behaviors are not unique to adolescence. The major health-damaging behaviors initiated during adolescence continue into adulthood. These same behaviors are responsible for the major morbidities and mortalities through the fourth decade of life. The major biopsychosocial changes that are interactive and may be additive are unique to adolescence.

Over the past decade, there has been a significant movement away from studying single behaviors to studying multiple behaviors and their covariation. With this movement, there is a tendency to focus on the sociodemographics of risk behaviors. Irwin (in press), Millstein (1989) and others (e.g., Baumrind, 1987, 1991) suggested that there is little information on the functional role of risk taking for adolescents and the meaning and natural history of risk taking as adolescents enter adulthood.

ACKNOWLEDGMENTS

The preparation of this manuscript and initial data collection for the longitudinal study were supported in part by grants from the Bureau of Maternal and Child Health, Department of Health and Human Services (MCJ 000978 and MCJ 060564), William T. Grant Foundation, and the San Francisco Node of the Research Network of the Health Promoting and Damaging Behaviors of the John D. and Catherine T. MacArthur Foundation. The authors thank Ms. Dulce Padilla for her assistance with the preparation of this manuscript.

REFERENCES

Aral, S. O., Schaffer, J. E., Mosher, W. D., & Cates, W. (1988). Gonorrhea rates: What denominator is most appropriate? *American Journal of Public Health, 78*, 702–703.

Baumrind, D. (1987). A developmental perspective on adolescent risk taking in contemporary America. In C. E. Irwin, Jr. (Ed.), *New directions for child development: Vol. 37. Adolescent social behavior and health* (pp. 91–126). San Francisco: Jossey-Bass.

Baumrind, D. (1991). The influence of parenting style on adolescent competence and substance use. *Journal of Early Adolescence, 11*, 56–95.

Bell, T. A., & Holmes, K. K. (1984). Age-specific risks of syphilis, gonorrhea and hospitalized pelvic inflammatory disease in sexually experienced hospitalized U.S. women. *Sexually Transmitted Diseases, 11*,, 291–295.

Billy, J. O. G., & Udry, J. R. (1985). The influence of male and female best friends on adolescent sexual behavior. *Adolescence, 20*, 21–32.

Blyth, D. A., Simmons, R. G., Bulcroft, R., Felt, D., Van Cleave, E. F., & Bush, D. M. (1981). The effects of physical development on self-esteem and satisfaction with body image for early adolescent males. In R. G. Simmons (Ed.), *Research in community and mental health* (Vol. 2, pp. 43–73). Greenwich, CT: JAI Press.

Brooks-Gunn, J. (1988). Antecedents to and consequences of variations in girls' maturational timing. *Journal of Adolescent Health Care, 9*, 1–9.

Brooks-Gunn, J. (1989). Pubertal processes and the early adolescent transition. In W. Damon (Ed.), *Child development today and tomorrow* (pp. 155–176). San Francisco: Jossey-Bass.

Brooks-Gunn, J., & Furstenberg, F. F., Jr. (1989). Adolescent sexual behavior. *American Psychologist, 44*, 249–257.

Brooks-Gunn, J., & Furstenberg, F. F., Jr. (1990). Coming of age in the era of AIDS: Puberty, sexuality and contraception. *The Millbank Quarterly, 68*, 59–84.

Brooks-Gunn, J., Petersen, A. C., & Eichorn, D. (1985). The timing of maturation and psychosocial functioning in adolescence. *Journal of Youth and Adolescence, 14*(3,4).

Cates, W., Jr. (1990). The epidemiology and control of sexually transmitted diseases in adolescents. *Adolescent Medicine: State of the Art Reviews, 1*, 409–428.

Centers for Disease Control. (1983). Alcohol as a risk factor for injuries—United States. *Morbidity & Mortality Weekly Report, 32*, 61–62.

Centers for Disease Control. (1990a). Current trends: Alcohol-related traffic fatalities—United States, 1982–1989. *Morbidity & Mortality Weekly Report, 39*, 889–891.

Centers for Disease Control. (1990b). [Sexually transmitted diseases, 1950–1988]. Unpublished raw data.

Centers for Disease Control. (1991). Current trends: Premarital sexual experience among adolescent women—United States, 1970–1988. *Morbidity & Mortality Weekly Report, 39*, 929–932.

Clausen, J. A. (1975). The social meaning of differential physical and sexual maturation. In S. E. Dragastin & G. H. Elder, Jr. (Eds.), *Adolescence in the life cycle*. New York: Halstead.

Connolly, G. N., Winn, D. M., Hecht, S. S., Henningfield, J. E., Walker, B., Jr., & Hoffman, D. (1986). The reemergence of smokeless tobacco. *New England Journal of Medicine, 314*, 1,020–1,027.

Covington, M. V. (1981). Strategies for smoking prevention and resistance among young adolescents. *Journal of Early Adolescence, 1*, 349–356.

Daitzman, R., & Zuckerman, M. (1980). Disinhibitory sensation seeking, personality and gonadal hormones. *Personality and Individual Differences, 1*, 103–110.

Donovan, J. E., & Jessor, R. (1985). Structure of problem behavior in adolescence and young adulthood. *Journal of Consulting Clinical Psychology, 53*, 890–904.

Eichorn, D. H., Clausen, J. A., Haan, N., Honzik, M. P., & Mussen, P. H. (Eds.). (1981). *Present and past in middle life*. New York: Academic Press.

Elkind, D. (1967). Egocentrism in adolescence. *Child Development, 38*, 1,025–1,034.

Elliott, D. S., & Morse, B. J. (1989). Delinquency and drug use as risk factors in teenage sexual activity. *Youth and Society, 21*, 32–60.

Ensminger, M. E. (1987). Adolescent sexual behavior as it relates to other transition behaviors in youth. In S. L. Hofferth & C. D. Hayes (Eds.), *Risking the future* (Vol. II, pp. 36–55). Washington, DC: National Academy of Science.

Epstein, L., & Tamir, A. (1982). Health related behavior of adolescents: Change over time. *Journal of Adolescent Health Care, 5*, 91–95.

Faust, M. S. (1969). Developmental maturity as a determinant of prestige in adolescent girls. *Child Development, 40*, 137–154.

Forrest, J. D., & Singh, S. (1990). The sexual and reproduction behavior of American women, 1982–1988. *Family Planning Perspectives, 22*, 206–214.

Friedman, I. M. (1985). Alcohol and unnatural deaths in San Francisco youths. *Pediatrics, 76*, 191–193.

Gans, J. E., Blyth, D. A., Elster, A. B., & Gaveras, L. L. (1990). *America's adolescents: How healthy are they? Profiles of adolescent health series* (Vol. 1). Chicago: American Medical Association.

Graves, E. J. (1988). *Summary: National hospital discharge survey* (DHHS Publication No. PHS 90-1250). Washington, DC: U.S. Government Printing Office.

Greydanus, D. E. (1987). Risk-taking behaviors in adolescence. *Journal of the American Medical Association, 258*, 2,110.

Hamburg, B. A., & Hamburg, D. A. (1975). Stressful transitions of adolescence: Endocrine and psychosocial aspects. In *Society, stress and disease: Childhood and adolescence* (pp. 93–107). London: Oxford University Press.

Hayes, C. D. (1987). *Risking the future: Adolescent sexuality, pregnancy and childbearing* (Vol. I). Washington, DC: National Academy Press.

Hayes, C. D., & Hofferth, S. L. (1987). *Risking the future: Adolescent sexuality, pregnancy and childbearing* (Vol. II). Washington, DC: National Academy Press.

Healthy people: The Surgeon General's report on health promotion and disease prevention, 1979 (DHEW Publication No. PHS 79-55071). Washington, DC: U.S. Government Printing Office.

Hunter, S. M., Croft, J. B., & Burke, G. L. (1986). Longitudinal patterns of cigarette smoking and smokeless tobacco use in youth: The Bogalusa heart study. *American Journal of Public Health, 76*, 193–195.

Irwin, C. E., Jr. (1986). Why adolescent medicine? *Journal of Adolescent Health Care, 7*, 1S–12S.

Irwin, C. E., Jr. (Ed.). (1987). *New directions for child development: Vol. 37. Adolescent social behavior and health.* San Francisco: Jossey-Bass.

Irwin, C. E., Jr. (1989). Risk-taking behaviors in the adolescent patient: Are they impulsive? *Pediatric Annuals, 18*, 122–134.

Irwin, C. E., Jr. (1990a). Risk taking during adolescence. In M. Green & R. J. Haggerty (Eds.), *Ambulatory pediatrics IV* (pp. 24–26). Philadelphia: Saunders.

Irwin, C. E., Jr. (1990b). The theoretical concept of at-risk adolescents. *Adolescent Medicine: State of the Art Reviews, 1*, 1–14.

Irwin, C. E., Jr. (in press). Adolescents and risk taking: How are they related? In N. Bell & R. Bell (Eds.), *Risk taking in the life cycle*. Lubbock, TX: Texas Tech University Press.

Irwin, C. E., Jr., Brindis, C., Brodt, S., Bennett, T., & Rodriguez, R. (1991). *The health of America's youth: Current trends in adolescent health status and utilization of health services*. Washington, DC: Department of Health and Human Services, Bureau of Maternal and Child Health.

Irwin, C. E., Jr., & Millstein, S. G. (1986). Biopsychosocial correlates of risk-taking behaviors during adolescence: Can the physician intervene? *Journal of Adolescent Health Care, 7*, 82S–96S.

Irwin, C. E., Jr., & Millstein, S. G. (1987). The meaning of alcohol use in early adolescents. *Pediatric Research, 21*, 175A.

Irwin, C. E., Jr., & Millstein, S. G. (in press). Correlates and predictors of risk-taking behaviors during adolescence. In L. P. Lipsitt & L. L. Mitnick (Eds.), *Self-regulating and risk-taking behavior: Causes and consequences*. Norwood, NJ: Ables.

Irwin, C. E., Jr., & Millstein, S. G. (1991). Risk-taking behaviors during adolescence. In R. Lerner, A. Petersen, & J. Brooks-Gunn (Eds.), *The encyclopedia of adolescence* (pp. 934–943). New York: Garland.

Irwin, C. E., Jr., Millstein, S. G., Adler, N. E., Kegeles, S. M., & Cohn, L. (1986). *The utility of the teen health risk appraisal in early adolescents*. Paper presented at the annual meeting of the Society for Prospective Medicine, San Francisco, CA.

Irwin, C. E., Jr., Millstein, S. G., Adler, N. E., & Turner, R. (1988). Predictors of risk-taking behaviors in early adolescents. *Pediatric Research, 23*, 201A.

Irwin, C. E., Jr., Millstein, S. G., Adler, N. E., & Turner, R. (1989). Pubertal timing and adolescent risk taking: Are they correlated? *Pediatric Research, 25*, 8A.

Irwin, C. E., Jr., & Ryan, S. A. (1989). Problem behaviors of adolescence. *Pediatric Review, 10*, 235–246.

Irwin, C. E., Jr., & Shafer, M. A. (1991, February). *Adolescent sexuality: The problem of negative outcomes of a normative behavior*. Paper presented at the meeting of the Cornell University Medical College Seventh Annual Conference on Health Policy, Ithaca, NY.

Irwin, C. E., Jr., Shafer, M. A., & Millstein, S. G. (1985). Pubertal development in adolescent females: A marker for early sexual debut. *Pediatric Research, 19*, 112A.

Irwin, C. E., Jr., & Vaughan, E. (1988). Psychosocial context of adolescent development: Study group report. *Journal of Adolescent Health Care, 9*(Suppl.), 11–20.

Jessor, R. (1984). Adolescent development and behavioral health. In J. D. Matarazzo, S. M. Weiss, J. A. Herd, N. E. Miller, & S. M. Weiss (Eds.), *Behavioral health: A handbook of health enhancement and disease prevention* (pp. 69–90). New York: Wiley.

Jessor, R., Costa, F., Jessor, S. L., & Donovan, J. E. (1983). Time of first intercourse: A prospective study. *Journal of Personality and Social Psychology, 44*, 608–626.

Jessor, R., & Jessor, S. L. (1977). *Problem behavior and psychological development: A longitudinal study of youth*. New York: Academic Press.

Jessor, S. L., & Jessor, R. (1975). Transition from virginity to nonvirginity: A social-psychological study over time. *Developmental Psychology, 11*, 473–484.

Johnston, L. D., O'Malley, P. M., & Bachman, J. G. (1989a). *Drug use, drinking and smoking: National survey results from high school, college and young adult populations* (DHHS Publication No. ADM 89-1638). Washington, DC: U.S. Government Printing Office.

Johnston, L. D., O'Malley, P. M., & Bachman, J. G. (1989b). *Illicit drug use, smoking and drinking by America's high school students, college students and young adults* (DHHS Publication No. ADM 89-1602). Washington, DC: U.S. Government Printing Office.

Johnston, L. D., O'Malley, P. M., & Bachman, J. G. (1990). [Monitoring the future: Substance use data, 1989]. Unpublished raw data.

Jonah, B. (1985). Adolescent risk and risk-taking behavior among young drivers: Relevant research. *Proceedings of a Conference on Adolescent Risk-Taking Behaviors* (pp. 26–38). Vancouver, British Columbia, Canada: University of British Columbia, Department of Pediatrics.

Kahn, J. R., Rindfuss, R. R., & Guilkey, D. K. (1990). Adolescent contraceptive method choices. *Demography, 27*, 323–335.

Kandel, D. B., & Davies, M. (in press). Cocaine use in a national sample of U.S. youth (NLSY): Epidemiology, predictors and ethnic patterns. In C. Schade & S. Scholer (Eds.), *The epidemiology of cocaine use and abuse* (Research Monograph). Rockville, MD: National Institute on Drug Abuse.

Kandel, D. B., & Logan, J. A. (1984). Patterns of drug use from adolescence to young adulthood: I. Periods of risk for initiation, continued use and discontinuation. *American Journal of Public Health, 74*, 660–666.

Kegeles, S. M., Millstein, S. G., Adler, N. E., Irwin, C. E., Jr., Cohn, L., & Dolcini, P. (1987). The transition to sexual activity and its relationship to other risk behaviors. *Journal of Adolescent Health Care, 8*, 303.

Lerner, R. (1987). A life span perspective for early adolescence. In R. Lerner & T. Foch (Eds.), *Biological-psychological interactions in early adolescence* (pp. 9–34). Hillsdale, NJ: Lawrence Erlbaum Associates.

Lewis, C. E., & Lewis, M. A. (1984). Peer pressure and risk-taking behaviors in children. *American Journal of Public Health, 74*, 580–584.

Marshall, W. A., & Tanner, J. M. (1969). Variations in the pattern of pubertal changes in girls. *Archives of Diseases in Childhood, 44*, 291–303.

Marshall, W. A., & Tanner, J. M. (1970). Variations in the pattern of pubertal changes in boys. *Archives of Diseases in Childhood, 45*, 13–23.

Mayhew, D. R., Donelson, A. C., & Beirness, D. J. (1986). Youth, alcohol and relative risk of crash involvement. *Accident Analysis and Prevention, 18*, 273–287.

McNeil, D., & Livson, N. (1963). Maturation rate and body build in women. *Child Development, 34,* 25–32.

Miller, H. G., Turner, C. F., & Moses, L. E. (1990). *AIDS: The second decade*. Washington, DC: National Academy Press.

Miller, P. Y., & Simon, W. (1974). Adolescent sexual behavior: Context and change. *Social Problems, 22,* 58–76.

Millstein, S. G. (1989). Adolescent health: Challenges for behavioral scientists. *American Psychologist, 44,* 837–842.

Millstein, S. G. (in press). Perceptual, attributional and affective processes of vulnerability through the life span. In *Current issues and new directions in risk-taking research and intervention*. Lubbock, TX: Texas Tech University Press.

Millstein, S. G., & Irwin, C. E., Jr. (1985). Adolescents' assessments of behavioral risk: Sex differences and maturation effects. *Pediatric Research, 19,* 112A.

Millstein, S. G., & Irwin, C. E., Jr. (1988). Accident-related behavior in adolescents: A biopsychosocial view. *Alcohol, Drugs and Driving, 4,* 21–30.

Millstein, S. G., Irwin, C. E., Jr., Adler, N. E., Cohn, L., Kegeles, S. M., & Dolcini, P. (in press). Health risk behaviors and health concerns among young adolescents. *Pediatrics.*

Mott, F. L., & Haurin, R. J. (1987, April/May). *The interrelatedness of age at first intercourse, early pregnancy and drug use among American adolescents: Preliminary results from the National Longitudinal Survey of Youth Labor Market Experience*. Paper presented at the meeting of Population Association of America, Chicago, IL.

Mott, F. L., & Haurin, R. J. (1988). Linkages between sexual activity and alcohol and drug use among American adolescents. *Family Planning Perspectives, 20,* 128–136.

National Center for Health Statistics. (1983, September 14). Utilization of short-stay hospitals by adolescents: United States, 1980. *Advance Data, 93,* 1–5.

National Center for Health Statistics. (1984, September 28). Health care of adolescents by office-based physicians: National ambulatory medical care survey, 1980–81. *Advance Data, 99,* 1–8.

National Center for Health Statistics. (1989a). Ambulatory medical care rendered in physician's offices: United States, 1975. *Vital Health Statistics, 16*(12), 1–11.

National Center for Health Statistics. (1989b). Ambulatory medical care rendered in pediatrician's offices during 1975. *Vital Health Statistics, 16*(13), 1–7.

National Center for Health Statistics. (1990a). *Vital statistics of the United States, 1987: Vol. II. Mortality: Part A* (DHHS Publication No. PHS 90-1101). Washington, DC: U.S. Government Printing Office.

National Center for Health Statistics. (1990b). Wanted and unwanted childbearing in the United States, 1973–88. *Advance Data, 189,* 1–8.

National Institute on Drug Abuse. (1989). *National household survey on drug abuse, 1988 population estimates* (DHHS Publication No. ADM 89-1636). Washington, DC: U.S. Government Printing Office.

Newacheck, P. W. (1989). Adolescents with special health needs: Prevalence, severity, and access to health services. *Pediatrics, 84,* 872–881.

Newcomb, M. D., & Bentler, P. M. (1986). Cocaine use among adolescents: Longitudinal associates with social content, psychopathology and use of other substances. *Addictive Behavior, 11,* 263–270.

Osgood, D. W. (1989). *Covariation of risk behaviors during adolescence*. Paper prepared for the Office of Technology Assessment, U.S. Congress Study on Adolescent Health Behavior.

Osgood, D. W., Johnston, L. D., O'Malley, P. M., & Bachman, J. G. (1988). The generality of deviance in late adolescence and early adulthood. *American Sociological Review, 53,* 81–93.

Petersen, A. C. (1988). Adolescent development. In M. R. Fosenzweig & L. W. Portere (Eds.), *Annual Review of Psychology, 39,* 583–607.

Petersen, A. C., Tobin-Richards, M., & Boxer, A. (1983). Puberty: Its measurement and its meaning. *Journal of Early Adolescence, 3,* 47–62.

Pleck, J. H., Sonenstein, F. L., & Swain, S. O. (1988). Adolescent males' sexual behavior and contraceptive use: Implications for male responsibility. *Journal of Adolescent Research, 3*, 275-284.

Pratt, W. (1990). [National survey of family growth. Cycles III and IV for 1988]. Unpublished tabulations.

Robins, L. N., & Wish, E. (1977). Childhood deviance as a developmental process: A study of 223 urban black men from birth to 18. *Social Forces, 56*, 448-473.

Rosenbaum, E., & Kandel, D. B. (1990). Early onset of sexual behavior and drug involvement. *Journal of Marriage and the Family, 52*, 783-798.

Ryan, R. M., & Lynch, J. H. (1989). Emotional autonomy versus detachment: Revisiting the vicissitudes of adolescence and young adulthood. *Child Development, 650*, 340-357.

Ryan, S. A., Millstein, S. G., & Irwin, C. E., Jr. (1988). Pubertal concerns in young adolescents. *Journal of Adolescent Health Care, 9*, 267.

Schlossberger, N., Irwin, C. E., Jr., Turner, R., & Millstein, S. G. (1990). Validity of self-report of pubertal maturation in early adolescents. *Pediatric Research, 27*, 7A.

Shafer, M. A., & Boyer, C. (1990, May). *Psychosocial correlates of risk for STD/AIDS among urban high school students*. Paper presented at the Society for Pediatric Research Annual Meeting, Anaheim, CA.

Shafer, M. A., & Sweet, R. L. (1990). Pelvic inflammatory disease in adolescent females. *Adolescent Medicine: State of the Art Reviews, 1*, 545-564.

Shafer, M. A., Sweet, R. L., Ohm-Smith, M. J., Shalwitz, J., Beck, A., & Schachter, J. (1985). The microbiology of the lower genital tract of post-menarchal adolescent females: Differences by sexual activity, contraception, and presence of non-specific vaginitis. *Journal of Pediatrics, 107*, 974.

Shore, L. (1984). Experience of puberty development. *Social Science and Medicine, 19*, 461-465.

Simmons, R. G., & Blyth, D. A. (1987). *Moving into adolescence: The impact of pubertal change and school context*. New York: Aldive Press.

Slovic, P. (1964). Assessment of risk-taking behavior. *Psychological Bulletin, 61*, 220-236.

Slovic, P. (1987). Perceptiosn of risk. *Science, 236*, 280-285.

Smith, E. A., Udry, J. R., & Morris, N. M. (1985). Pubertal development and friends: A biosocial explanation of adolescent sexual behavior. *Journal of Health and Social Behavior, 26*, 183-192.

Sonenstein, F. L., Pleck, J. H., & Ku, L. C. (1989). Sexual activity, condom use and AIDS awareness among adolescent males. *Family Planning Perspectives, 21*, 152-158.

Sonis, W. A., Comite, F., & Blue, J. (1985). Behavior problems and social competence in girls with true precocious puberty. *Journal of Pediatrics, 106*, 156-160.

Steinberg, L. D. (1987). The impact of puberty on family relations: Effects of pubertal status and pubertal timing. *Developmental Psychology, 23*, 451-460.

Steinberg, L., & Silverberg, S. B. (1986). The vicissitudes of autonomy in early adolescence. *Child Development, 57*, 841-851.

Susman, E. J., Inoff-Germain, G., Nottelmann, E. D., Loriaux, D. L., Cutler, G. B., Jr., & Chrousos, G. P. (1987). Hormones, emotional dispositions and aggressive attributes in young adolescents. *Child Development, 58*, 1,114-1,134.

Susman, E. J., Nottelmann, E. D., Inoff-Germain, G., Dorn, L. D., & Chrousos, G. P. (1987). Hormonal influences on aspects of psychological development during adolescence. *Journal of Adolescent Health Care, 8*, 492.

Turner, R., Irwin, C. E., Jr., & Millstein, S. G. (1989). Effects of family structure, emotional autonomy and parental permissiveness on adolescent risk behaviors. *Journal of Adolescent Health Care, 10*, 250.

Turner, R., Irwin, C. E., Jr., & Millstein, S. G. (1991). Family structure, family processes and experimenting with substances during adolescence. *Journal of Research on Adolescence, 1*, 93–106.

Udry, J. R. (1985). Androgenic hormones motivate serum sexual behavior in boys. *Fertility and Sterility, 43*, 90-94.

Udry, J. R. (1988). Biological predispositions and social control in adolescent sexual behavior. *American Sociological Review, 53*, 709-722.

Udry, J. R., & Billy, J. O. (1987). Initiation of coitus in early adolescence. *American Sociological Review, 52*, 841-855.

Udry, J. R., & Talbert, L. M. (1988). Sex hormone effects on personality at puberty. *Journal of Personality and Social Psychology, 51*, 291-295.

Udry, J. R., Talbert, L. M., & Morris, N. M. (1986). Biosocial foundations for adolescent female sexuality. *Demography, 23*, 217-227.

U.S. Preventive Services Task Force. (1989). *Guide to clinical preventive services. An assessment of the effectiveness of 169 interventions*. Baltimore, MD: Williams & Wilkins.

Westney, Q. E., Jenkins, R. R., Butts, J. D., & Williams, I. (1984). Sexual development and behavior in Black adolescents. *Adolescence, 19*, 558–568.

Yamaguchi, K., & Kandel, D. B. (1984a). Patterns of drug use from adolescence to young adulthood: II. Sequences of progression. *American Journal of Public Health, 74*, 668-672.

Yamaguchi, K., & Kandel, D. B. (1984b). Patterns of drug use from adolescence to young adulthood: III. Predictors of progression. *American Journal of Public Health, 74*, 673.

Zabin, L. S. (1984). The association between smoking and sexual behavior among teens in U.S. contraceptive clinics. *American Journal of Public Health, 74*, 261-263.

Zabin, L. S., Hardy, J. B., Smith, E. A., & Hirsch, M. B. (1986). Substance use and its relation to sexual activity among inner-city adolescents. *Journal of Adolescent Health Care, 7*, 320-331.

Zuckerman, M. (1986). Sensation seeking and the endogenous deficit theory of drug abuse. In S. I. Szara (Ed.), *Neurobiology of behavioral control in drug abuse* (DHHS Publication No. ADM 87-1506). Washington, DC: U.S. Government Printing Office.

Developmental Processes and Disease

6

Disease Processes and Behavior

William J. Ray
The Pennsylvania State University

In this century, an ever increasing complex model has evolved concerning the relationship between disease and an individual's psychosocial development. Differentiations are made between disease, illness, and illness behaviors, as well as positive life style changes that promote health. For example, some authors (Kaplan & Bush, 1982) speak of *well years* in order to emphasize how positive factors lead to qualitative life changes as well as absence of disease. Even within the concept of disease, there are attempts to understand the manner in which the level of psychological development impacts the ability to understand disease processes. This trend is clearly demonstrated in the Ingersoll, Orr, Vance, and Golden paper in this volume in which the level of cognitive development is suggested to be directly related to how one controls the disease processes. However, the field of health and behavior has taken some time to come to such conclusions.

Many of the current views on disease processes and behavior are, in fact, reactions to the view of the last century in which disease was seen as the resultant of an external agent acting upon the person to produce cellular or organ pathology. One initial reaction to this view developed under the name *psychosomatic medicine*. Psychosomatic medicine attempts to move the level of analysis from that of a cellular or diseased organ level to that of the total person. One outcome of this approach is to seek possible links to disease through an examination of emotional processing. Given that psychodynamic thought was one of the few areas that had studied emotional processes, its perspective shaped much of early psychosomatic thought. For example, within a psychodynamic frame of reference, specific medical disorders are viewed as maladaptive responses to internal conflict (Alexander, 1950). Within this information is the understanding that specific emotions or conflicts are expressed in different physiological systems. Thus, it is suggested that particular types of conflicts (e.g., guilt) influence people with particular types of personalities (e.g., passive) to result in a particular disorder. Although such a specificity theory has not proven to be fruitful as the Ingersoll et al. paper in this volume points out in relation to diabetes, this perspective has proven useful in directing attention historically toward the interactive role emotional factors play in relation to sickness and disease. In fact, there is a return to an understanding of the person-situation interaction in relation to specific pathophysiology, as in the case of Type-A behavior patterns and the role of anger. The greatest difficulty of the early psychosomatic approach is the lack of methodological sophistication that indirectly leads professionals to seek alternative explanations of disease processes including considerations of environmental factors as causal influences in disease.

This new theoretical shift emphasizes illness more as a response to environmental stress and less as a reflection of internal psychological conflicts (Hinkle, 1967; Lipowski, 1977). Within this tradition emerged the behavioral medicine movement and its recognition of the changing nature of Western mortality and longevity over the century with the transition from germ-orientated disorders (e.g., tuberculosis) to environmentally influenced disorders (e.g., smoking and cancer or diet and hypertension). Likewise, the traditional disorders (e.g., arthritis, ulcers, asthma, and hypertension) are expanded to include a variety of problems (e.g., cancer, eating disorders, and cardiovascular problems). Further work seeks to involve the functioning of the endocrine and immune systems in disease processes as their function is influenced by environmental factors, especially in relation to stress.

As recent work progresses, there is a return to include internal organismic processes including emotions, cognitions, and behavioral factors, as well as environmental factors. As the field progresses, the theoretical perspectives evolve to include the development of new fields such as pediatric psychology (Routh, 1988; Tuma, 1982) and the study of children's knowledge concerning their bodies, their illnesses, and their health (Eiser, 1985). In addition, clinical studies do not seek to limit the particular disorder studied nor does the theoretical framework limit itself to simple causal models. The present view emphasizes the multicausation of pathology across a variety of levels.

The papers in this volume continue this tradition and add a new dimension to the understanding of health and disease. This new dimension includes the perspective of developmental processes. For example, both papers on diabetes emphasize either cognitive or ego development as an important consideration for understanding how adolescents respond to their illness. Hauser and colleagues use a model proposing that ego development moves from less to greater: (a) internalization of rules of social intercourse, (b) cognitive complexity, (c) tolerance of ambiguity, and (d) objectivity.

Ingersoll and colleagues utilize the model described by Harvey, Hunt, and Schroder for assessing levels of cognitive maturity. In this model individuals are seen as moving through four stages in which they are described as authoritarian at Stage 1, negativistic at Stage 2, internally integrated at Stage 3, and environmentally independent at Stage 4. Overall, both the model used by Hauser and that used by Ingersoll suggest that as one matures there is a movement from a simple or concrete level to a more complex one. From this perspective, diabetes control, for example, is greatly influenced by one's cognitive and ego development. Of course, the more traditional question of how the disease influences cognitive and ego development must also be considered.

The work by Lozoff on iron deficiency anemia attempts to understand how one particular disorder impacts cognition and emotional development of infants. In her work, iron deficient infants were found to have lower mental test scores as well as to show abnormal affective behavior. However, as she examined this relationship further, she reported that the relationship of iron deficiency and mental test scores is not a simple relationship, but the iron deficiency has an impact on emotion and behavior that influences how the children were tested. The complexity of this research consistently points to the difficulty in adopting a simple causal model to direct research in infant health and development.

One of the next challenges in the field of health and behavior is to better understand the adolescent in relation to disease processes and behavior. In general, a greater proportion of adolescents as compared to children present for the treatment of psychophysiological disorders. This fact has prompted several researchers to suggest that adolescence is a period of risk for such problems (Aro, 1987; Hoffman, 1983; Humphries, 1982; Mechanic, 1983). Adolescence is a time of increased stress due to social and physical changes, and, with increasing introspective ability, many adolescents become preoccupied with physical changes and bodily appearance and function. Such stress appears to predispose adolescents to increased risk for psychophysiological symptoms (Brunswick & Merzel, 1986; Mechanic, 1983).

Recent research indicates that the key risk factor associated with adolescent problems is puberty. For example, somatic complaints increased significantly after puberty in a sample of 90 normal individuals (Rauste-von Wright & von Wright, 1981). Hamburg (1974) has argued that because of psychophysiological pubertal changes, early adolescence is more stressful than later adolescence. This may account for the fact that when assessed again at ages 15 and 18, such complaints had decreased significantly from their height at age 13.

The gender differences in disease processes present an additional challenge. Prior to puberty, most studies suggest that such symptoms are equally prevalent among boys and girls (Rauste-von Wright & von Wright, 1981; Shapiro & Rosenfeld, 1987). Following puberty, the rates for males either decrease or continue unchanged whereas females report such symptoms much more frequently. This gender difference pattern and rates are similar to those found in adult populations.

In one review of 13 studies of various psychophysiological disorders, it is found that adolescent females are four times as likely to report such problems than adolescent males (Shapiro & Rosenfeld, 1987). In addition, females appeared to show greater constancy in symptoms over the period from age 11 to 18 (Rauste-von Wright & von Wright, 1981). This gender difference may be related to greater life stress perception because females report higher levels of perceived life stress (Aro, 1987). Significantly, when equated for levels of perceived life stress and relationship problems, boys report as many somatic symptoms as do girls.

Since life stress appears related to psychophysiological symptoms, several researchers have explored the importance of peer and family support during adolescence in reducing such symptoms. Walker and Greene (1987) demonstrated that peer support is especially important. As negative life events increase, males with low peer support report more symptoms whereas males with high peer support appear to be unaffected. Among females, those with low peer support report high levels of symptoms regardless of current life stress. These authors speculate that lack of peer support may constitute a significant stressor in its own right. Overall, peer support appears to act as a buffer against psychophysiological problems. Similar results were obtained for family cohesion.

Overall, the current trend is to view disease processes and behavior within a broad context of health and behavior involving a theoretical orientation based on a variety of disciplines. One consistent trend is an emphasis on environmental and stress-related factors as well as emotional responding, including interpersonal relationships. Newer work, as represented in this volume emphasizes the level of cognitive and emotional development and its relation to disease processes and behavior. However, neither a unified theoretical approach nor a disorder-related classification system designed specifically for adolescents has yet to emerge.

REFERENCES

Alexander, F. (1950). *Psychosomatic Medicine*. New York: Norton.

Aro, H. (1987). Life stress and psychosomatic symptoms among 14- to 16-year old Finnish adolescents. *Psychological Medicine, 17*, 19–201.

Brunswick, A. F., & Merzel, C. R. (1980). Biopsychosocial and epidemiologic perspectives on adolescent health. In N. A. Krasnegor, J. D. Arasteh, & M. R. Cataldo (Eds.), *Child health behavior: A behavioral pediatrics perspective.* (pp. 94–112). New York: Wiley.

Eiser, C. (1985). *The psychology of childhood illness*. New York: Springer-Verlag.

Hamburg, B. A. (1974). Early adolescence: A specific and stressful stage of the life cycle. In G. Coelho, D. Hamburg, & J. Adams (Eds.), *Coping and adaptation* (pp. 101–124). New York: Basic Books.

Harvey, O. J., Hunt, D. E., & Schroder, H. M. (1961). *Conceptual systems and personality organization*. New York: Wiley.

Hinkle, L. E. (1967). Ecological observations of the relations of physical illness, mental illness, and the social environment. *Psychosomatic Medicine, 23*, 298.

Hoffman, A. (1983). *Adolescent Medicine*. Menlo Park, CA: Addison-Wesley.

Humphries, C. L. (1982). Psychosomatic problems in adolescent medicine. In R. Blum (Ed.), *Adolescent health care: Clinical issues* (pp. 267–270). New York: Academic Press.

Kaplan, R. M., & Bush, J. W. (1982). Health-related quality of life measurement for evaluation research and policy analysis. *Health Psychology, 1*, 61–80.

Lipowski, Z. J. (1977). Psychosomatic medicine: Current trends and clinical applications. In Z. Lipowski, D. Lipsitt, & P. Whybrow (Eds.), *Psychosomatic medicine: Current trends and clinical applications.* New York: Oxford University Press.

Mechanic, D. (1983). Adolescent health and illness behavior: Review of the literature and a new hypothesis for the study of stress. *Journal of Human Stress 9*, 4–13.

Rauste-von Wright, M., & von Wright, J. (1981). A longitudinal study of psychosomatic systems in healthy 11–18 year-old girls and boys. *Journal of Psychosomatic Research, 25*, 525–534.

Routh, D. (Ed). (1988). *Handbook of pediatric psychology*. New York: Guilford Press.

Shapiro, E. G., & Rosenfeld, A. A. (1987). *The somatizing child: Diagnosis and treatment of conversion and somatization disorders*. New York: Springer-Verlag.

Tuma, J. M. (Ed.). (1982). *Handbook for the practice of pediatric psychology*. New York: Wiley-Interscience.

Walker, L. S., & Greene, J. W. (1987). Negative life events, psychosocial resources, and psychophysiological symptoms in adolescence. *Journal of Clinical Child Psychology, 16*, 29–36.

7

Iron Deficiency Anemia and Infant Behavior

Betsy Lozoff
Case Western Reserve University
School of Medicine
Rainbow Babies and Children's Hospital
Cleveland, OH

The issue of emotion and cognition in infancy is approached by considering the relationship between infants' behavior and their scores on developmental tests. After illustrations of the importance of this relationship from research on iron deficiency anemia, more general questions and hypotheses about the emotion and cognition interface in infancy are presented.

ILLUSTRATIONS FROM STUDIES ON IRON DEFICIENCY ANEMIA

Iron deficiency anemia is the most commonly recognized form of nutritional deficiency in developing countries as well as in affluent societies and has a peak prevalence among infants (Dallman & Siimes, 1979). Several recent studies find that infants with iron deficiency anemia test lower on mental and motor developmental measures than controls (Lozoff, 1988). Some of the major results of our research, conducted in collaboration with Central American investigators, are highlighted, because they provide the background for relating behavioral disturbances to anemic infants' lower developmental test scores.

Our study in Guatemala, in collaboration with the Institute of Nutrition of Central America and Panama, compares the development of anemic infants with a nonanemic control group (Lozoff, Brittenham, Viteri, Wolf, & Urrutia, 1982a). Participants were recruited in door-to-door screening from a socioeconomically homogeneous, impoverished section of Guatemala City. Infants with hemoglobin

(Hb) values $\leq$ 10.5 gm/dl and at least 2 of 3 measures of iron status in the deficient range constituted the iron deficient anemic group. Those with hemoglobin values $\geq$ 12 gm/dl constituted the nonanemic group. Any infant with acute or chronic illness, birth complications, prematurity, congenital anomalies, Hb levels $\leq$ 6 gm/dl, known malnutrition, or developmental delay was excluded. The Bayley Scales of Infant Development (Bayley, 1969) were administered by a Guatemalan tester, who was unaware of hematologic status, before and after short-term oral iron or placebo treatment. Twenty-eight iron-deficient anemic infants and 40 nonanemic control babies met all study criteria. The iron-deficient anemic babies have significantly lower mental test scores, an average of 14 points below nonanemic controls. There is an age effect such that the mean mental scores of anemic infants under 19 months of age are normal, but older anemic infants have an average mental score of 73 (Lozoff, Brittenham, Viteri, Wolf, & Urrutia, 1982b). The anemic group also has a significant 9 point deficit on the motor scale, without age effects. No differences in family background, birth history, or growth were found to explain the anemic group's poor performance.

Our next study, conducted in Costa Rica in collaboration with the Hospital Nacional de Ninos, is designed to determine the degree of iron deficiency that adversely affects developmental test performance and includes the full range of iron deficiency, from complete iron sufficiency to anemia (Lozoff et al., 1987). Once again the study involves an entire community. The community was urban, generally homogeneous, lower-middle class and literate, with parents averaging 8 years of education. The 191, 12- to 23-month-old infants who participated in the study were carefully screened to exclude those with problems that might adversely affect development. All infants were singletons, born at term without perinatal complications or congenital anomalies. They had no known developmental delays, were free of acute and chronic illnesses, and appeared normal on physical examination by an experienced pediatrician. These stringent criteria were successful in eliminating children with low Bayley Scores: mean Mental Development Index (MDI) and Psychomotor Development Index (PDI) scores were 103 and 110, respectively, and there was only one mental and one motor score more than 2 SD below the U.S. norm. Those infants with moderate iron deficiency anemia have mental scores 8 points below the other groups of infants, and those with mild or moderate anemia average 10 points lower in motor scores. Infants with biochemical evidence of iron deficiency but no anemia do not have lower scores.

Results from a new study by Walter and colleagues (Walter, deAndraca, Chadud, & Perales, 1989) in Chile are very similar to those obtained in the Costa Rican study. There are lower mental and motor test scores among infants with iron deficiency anemia and no lower test scores among infants with lesser degrees of iron lack. In sum, all studies to date with careful definition of iron status and nonanemic control groups find clinically and statistically lower mental test scores among anemic infants, and three of the four that assess motor development observe lower motor test scores as well (Lozoff, 1988).

These observations present a further question: Why do the iron-deficient anemic babies have lower scores? Although it is possible that the anemic infants simply can not do test items due to limitations in their cognitive capacities, it is at least as likely that some aspect(s) of their behavior interfere with optimal performance on the Bayley Scales. For instance, their performance may be impaired by irritability or fussiness or by inattentiveness. The fruitfulness of a behavioral explanation is suggested by several observations (Lozoff, 1988; Lozoff & Brittenham, 1985):

1. Some anemic babies are clinically described as apathetic, distractible, and irritable, behaviors noted to improve within days of iron therapy.
2. Behavior abnormalities are reported in controlled studies of iron-deficient laboratory animals and human infants.
3. Iron plays an essential role in the metabolism of central nervous system neurotransmitters that influence emotional responses and states of alertness and arousal.

Despite these clinical and theoretical reasons to expect behavioral explanations for poor developmental test performance in iron deficiency anemia, the hypothesized relationship between behavior and developmental test scores is difficult to assess adequately. Documenting alterations in behavior is hindered by the paucity of standardized measures of noncognitive behavior in infancy. Therefore, the research described in this section often consists of initial exploratory efforts.

To determine if behavioral disturbance accounts for the poor developmental test performance of the iron-deficient anemic infants in the Guatemalan study, the relationship between abnormal ratings on the Infant Behavior Record (IBR), the third component of the Bayley Scales, and the scores on the Mental and Motor Scales was assessed (Lozoff, Wolf, Urrutia, & Viteri, 1985). The IBR, although a standard element of the Bayley Scales, generates no summary scores. Instead, the IBR employs 30 separate rating scales to describe an infant's behavior during developmental testing. We used a new approach to IBR analysis (Wolf & Lozoff, 1985) in combination with recent factor analytic work (Matheny, 1980) to identify affective and task orientation behaviors that could be suspected as abnormal, because they are poorly adaptive in the test situation and are observed in only a small proportion of infants in two large normative U.S. samples. These new approaches to IBR analysis are combined to generate summary scores, one that characterizes an infant's affect during testing and another that describes orientation to tasks. Infants are considered abnormal in affect if their IBR ratings include at least two of the following behavior patterns: withdrawal from or hesitance with the examiner, increased fearfulness, unhappiness all or part of the session, easy fatigability or restlessness, and increased body tension. Infants are considered abnormal in task orientation if their IBR ratings include at least two of the following: brief interest in objects, little directed effort or persistence in reaching a goal, short attention span, and lack of reaction to the usual test stimuli.

A significantly greater proportion of anemic than nonanemic infants (36% versus 13%) show abnormal affective behavior. The anemic group is no different from the nonanemic group in task orientation. Abnormal affective behavior is closely related to poor mental test scores in iron-deficient anemic infants in every age group, not just in the oldest group. Regardless of age, anemic infants with abnormal affect score low on the Bayley mental scale (MDI/M, = 66), whereas those with normal affect have mental test scores (MDI/M, = 97) that are normal by U.S. standards and comparable to the nonanemic group's mean (MDI/M, = 100). An examination of the individual IBR scales indicates that a greater proportion of anemic than nonanemic infants is withdrawn or hesitant with the tester, excessively fearful, tense, and unreactive to test materials. The few infants with more severe anemia (Hb levels below 9 gm/dl) all show pervasive behavioral disturbances and have low motor as well as mental scores. On readministration of the Bayley Scales after one week, the behavior of the anemic infants is generally rated as improved, regardless of iron or placebo treatment.

These results suggest several hypotheses about the developmental test score findings of the various infant studies:

1. The analysis indicates that poor developmental test performance may not be a consistent manifestation of iron deficiency in infancy but may rather be observed only in a subset of babies who display behavioral disturbances.
2. The study also suggests that there may be some hemoglobin level at which the severity of anemia itself, in addition to iron deficiency, impairs behavior and developmental test performance. Such results indicate that behavioral alterations may become more apparent at lower hemoglobin levels, perhaps reflecting changes in energy and activity, as well as affect.
3. Finally, the study provides a potential explanation for the rapid improvement in test scores that some researchers have observed (Oski & Honig, 1978; Oski, Honig, Helu, & Howanitz, 1983; Walter, Kovalskys, & Stekel, 1983).

If the performance of iron-deficient infants on an initial Bayley test is less than optimal, because they are more bothered, frightened, or stressed by the test situation than controls, their scores on the second test might improve as a result of feeling more comfortable with the tester and test situation. Such an effect might not be observed among controls, if they are not particularly uncomfortable during the initial testing. This explanation, which could account for improved test scores in iron-deficient infants without implicating iron therapy, is supported by the observation in the Guatemalan study that infants who improved in affect, regardless of iron or placebo treatment, increased their test scores.

The methods for analyzing the infants' behavior during developmental testing are new in the Guatemalan study. Therefore, the results cannot be directly compared to those in other studies. Nonetheless, other investigators who made IBR ratings have reported altered behavior patterns among iron-deficient infants (Lozoff, 1988).

It is possible that such behavioral characteristics directly interfere with developmental test performance and thus, result in low test scores. It is also possible that infant irritability, restlessness, and the like limit developmental test performance indirectly by means of their effect on caregivers. As a result of their babies' behavioral disturbances, the caregivers of anemic infants may be less responsive and stimulating than the caregivers of nonanemic infants. Since a number of studies in the child development literature (Beckwith, 1976; Belsky, 1981) find that children of unresponsive and unstimulating mothers often have a poorer developmental outcome, compromised interactional patterns between anemic infants and their caregivers might provide another explanation for the low test scores of the iron-deficient anemic infants. To assess these possibilities, we analyzed the behavior of iron-deficient anemic infants and their mothers from a videotaped free play session in our study in Guatemala (Lozoff, Klein, & Prabucki, 1986).

The resultant analyses provide little support for the hypothesis that anemic infants experience unresponsive patterns of mother–infant interaction. The results of quantitative coding of behavior during play indicate that the anemic infants in the Guatemalan study were not more irritable or distractible than nonanemic controls, nor were their mothers less responsive or stimulating. However, the anemic and nonanemic groups consistently differ from one another on measures of the spatial relations between mothers and infants. Anemic infants initiated and maintained more body contact with their mothers than did nonanemic babies: 71% of the anemic group were high in body contact, compared to 29% of the control group. Furthermore, the mothers of anemic infants spent less time at a distance from them, were less likely to break close contact, and more likely to reestablish close contact if the baby moved away.

We hypothesized that the close contact observed between anemic infants and their mothers during play was a manifestation of disturbance in affect, energy, or activity. Such close contact might also be a relatively effective compensatory mechanism that enabled the anemic infants to play without the more marked behavioral disturbances that were noted during developmental testing. A brief observation of behavior in a playroom does not necessarily reflect levels of cognitive stimulation in the home. Nonetheless, it seems that disturbed behavior, rather than unstimulating patterns of mother–infant interaction, contributed to poor developmental test performance in the anemic group. Faced with a structured test situation and the tester, a stranger who expected the babies to perform without help from their mothers, some of the anemic infants displayed more obvious behavioral dysfunction and did poorly on the test.

Detailed behavioral analyses thus generated several specific hypotheses:

1. that iron deficiency alters affective behavior;

2. that altered affect impairs developmental test performance; and
3. that mothers and infants may minimize behavioral disturbances and their consequences by maintaining close contact with each other.

These analyses also suggest that it may be important to study such aspects of behavior as activity, attention, and affect, in addition to specific cognitive processes.

We are now examining the variety of factors that may influence developmental test scores in the new Costa Rican study. Such factors might include socioeconomic background, home environment, parental IQ, experiences in the neonatal period, age and sex of the child, growth and nutritional status, behavior toward the test and tester, and so forth. In preliminary analyses, we used exploratory path analysis and structural modeling techniques to identify influences on mental and motor test scores in this group of infants (Lozoff, Wolf, & Jimenez, 1987). Exploratory path analysis and structural modeling are multivariate statistical techniques to describe relationships among a number of variables. Structural modeling, in this case LISREL, is specifically suited to determining causal relationships and confirming hypothesized models. In the present study, however, the techniques were not used to determine causality or confirm hypotheses, but rather for variable reduction. We wanted to group potential influences on test scores on conceptual grounds. Yet no comprehensive theory of developmental test performance was available to guide our analysis, because none has been proposed that takes into account such factors as the child's social milieu, nutritional status, and behavior. We know that such factors are important but do not have specific hypotheses about their interrelationships in influencing developmental test scores. Therefore, we grouped the variables in terms of their remote to immediate influence on the test. For example, a mother's education is usually prior in time to the child's diet, and the child's diet precedes current nutritional status. The seven conceptual groupings and their constituent variables included:

1. family background; maternal IQ, maternal education, and maternal age;
2. neonatal status; birth weight, cesarean delivery, and Apgars at 1 minute and 5 minutes;
3. age and sex;
4. home environment; father absence, grandparents in the home, and the Home Observation Measurement of the Environment (HOME) scale;
5. diet; age at weaning from the breast and intake of cow's milk;
6. current physiologic status; weight/length percentile, iron deficiency anemia, and lead level; and
7. testing factors; mother's presence and infant behavior ratings.

The next step of data analysis was to examine the correlation matrix of the entire set of variables and eliminate those variables not correlated with any other variable at a significance level less than or equal to .05. A series of multiple regression analyses was then performed to select those variables with either direct or indirect relationship with mental or motor test scores. The next stage was to assess the models of direct and indirect effects using the chi-square goodness of fit measure from LISREL. Lastly, the models whose goodness of fit were not appreciably altered by the addition of further parameters were selected as the final, most parsimonious models. We offer the models that emerged for further testing, well aware that random factors or peculiarities of our population may account for some of the specific relationships observed.

The LISREL goodness of fit measures indicate a good fit of the data to the model for both mental and motor scores. The most powerful influences on MDI scores are the infant's age (path coefficient $= -.59$, $p = .0001$) and behavior during the test as rated on the Bayley Infant Behavior Record (path coefficient $= -.31$, $p = .0001$), followed by birth weight ($p = .03$) and iron deficiency anemia ($p = .07$). All indirect effects on MDI are mediated by iron deficiency anemia and include maternal IQ, HOME scale, sex, amount of cow's milk, and age at weaning from the breast. In contrast to some U.S. studies, no association is observed between MDI and lead levels, all of which are below 25 μg/dL. PDI scores are influenced by iron deficiency anemia ($p = .0008$) and the infant's behavior ($p = .04$). Indirect effects on PDI are again mediated by iron deficiency anemia.

GENERAL QUESTIONS AND HYPOTHESES ABOUT THE EMOTION/COGNITION INTERFACE

It should be noted that the findings reported here are based on data from a developing country. Therefore, the results may be most relevant to disadvantaged populations in the United States among whom iron deficiency anemia continues to be a common health problem. However, because the majority of the world's children in fact live in developing countries, research with these children may generate questions about child development that would be overlooked if normative studies continue to focus, as in the past, primarily on middle-class groups in industrialized countries.

Issues raised by research in less advantaged populations can be illustrated by considering the strong association in the present study between age and MDI scores—the older the infant, the lower the mental test scores. In the standardization of the Bayley Scales, mean scores do not change with age. Yet in disadvantaged populations in the United States (Brown & Halperin, 1971; Egeland & Sroufe, 1981; Escalona, 1982), Chile (Lira & Rodriguez, 1981), Guatemala (Lozoff, Brittenham, Viteri, Wolf, & Urrutia, 1982b), the Caribbean (Powell & Grantham-McGregor, 1985), and Costa Rica (Lozoff et al., 1987), mental scores are noted to decline substantially during the second year of life. These studies remind us that the interpretation of test scores must consider the cultural context and also raise questions, as yet not entirely answered, about the factors explaining the decline in scores.

In contrast, the relationship between infant behavior and test scores has been observed in a number of U.S. studies. It is consistently noted that the more sociable infants score higher on developmental tests (Bayley & Schaefer, 1964; Lamb, Garn, & Keating, 1981; Lamb, Garn, & Keating, 1982; Lamb, 1982; Stevenson & Lamb, 1979). The first issue in interpreting this observation is whether or not the measurements of behavior are independent of the scores. In most studies, as in the present one, the Bayley Infant Behavior Record is the measure of behavior. Because it is completed by the tester, the behavioral ratings and the test scores are not independent. However, there is one study in the literature, by Stevenson and Lamb (1979), in which behavior ratings were made by a hidden observer. A substantial correlation—of the order of .50—between infant sociability and mental test scores was still observed.

These observations raise the question as to whether the behaviorally disturbed infant is actually less competent or simply performing less well (Lamb, 1982). One hypothesis is that more sociable infants do better on developmental assessments because of their willingness to interact and cooperate with the tester. That is, they perform better without necessarily being more competent. A second hypothesis is that such infants invite more stimulation from caregivers and that, over time, the supplementary stimulation facilitates their development and they in fact become more competent. We hope to assess these alternatives, at least in part, in future analyses of our data. Because we have videotapes of the infants during mental and motor testing and during play, before treatment and after one week, we have information on the babies' affect and abilities in different contexts and with different degrees of familiarity with the test and tester.

The analyses presented here generate a number of questions about influences on developmental test scores. The studies also identify two factors often not measured systematically in developmental assessments—iron deficiency anemia and infant behavior during the test—that seem to exert powerful influences on both mental and motor test scores.

ACKNOWLEDGMENT

This research was supported in part by a grant from the National Institutes of Health, No. R22 HD14122.

REFERENCES

Bayley, N. (1969). *Bayley scales of infant development*. New York: Psychological Corporation.

Bayley, N., & Schaefer, E. S. (1964). Correlations of maternal and child behaviors with the development of mental abilities: Data from the Berkeley Growth Study. *Monographs of the Society for Research in Child Development 29* (6, Serial No. 97).

Beckwith, L. (1976). Caregiver-infant interaction and the development of the high risk infant. In T. D. Tjossem (Ed.), *Intervention strategies for high risk infants and young children* (pp. 119–139). Baltimore: University Park Press.

Belsky, J. (1981). Early human experience: A family perspective. *Developmental Psychology, 17*, 3–23.

Brown, R. E., & Halperin, F. (1971). The variable pattern of mental development of rural black children. *Clinical Pediatrics, 10*, 404–409.

Dallman, P. R., & Siimes, M. A. (1979). *Iron deficiency in infancy and childhood*. Report for the International Nutritional Anemia Consultative Group. New York: The Nutrition Foundation.

Egeland, B., & Sroufe, L. A. (1981). Developmental sequelae of maltreatment in infancy. In R. Rizley & D. Cicchetti (Eds.), *New directions for child development: Developmental perspectives in child maltreatment* (pp. 77–92). San Francisco: Jossey-Bass.

Escalona, S. K. (1982). Babies at double hazard: Early development of infants at biologic and social risk. *Pediatrics, 70*, 670–676.

Lamb, M. E. (1982). Individual differences in infant sociability: Their origins and implications for cognitive development. *Advances in Child Development and Behavior, 16*, 213–239.

Lamb, M. E., Garn, S. M., & Keating, M. T. (1981). Correlations between sociability and cognitive performance among eight-month-olds. *Child Development, 52*, 711–713.

Lamb, M. E., Garn, S. M., & Keating, M. T. (1982). Correlations between sociability and motor performance scores in eight-month-olds. *Infant Behavior and Development, 5*, 97–101.

Lira, M. I., & Rodriguez, S. (1981). Psychomotor performance of Chilean infants from low socioeconomic level during their second year of life. *Infant Mental Health Journal, 2*, 44–47.

Lozoff, B. (1988). Behavioral alterations in iron deficiency. *Advances in Pediatrics, 35*, 331–360.

Lozoff, B., & Brittenham, G. M. (1985). Behavioral aspects of iron deficiency. *Progress in Hematology, 14*, 23–53.

Lozoff, B., Brittenham, G. M., Viteri, F. E., Wolf, A. W., & Urrutia, J. J. (1982a). The effects of short-term oral iron therapy on developmental deficits in iron-deficient anemic infants. *Journal of Pediatrics, 100*, 351–357.

Lozoff, B., Brittenham, G. M., Viteri, F. E., Wolf, A. W., & Urrutia, J. J. (1982b). Developmental deficits in iron-deficient infants: Effects of age and severity of iron lack. *Journal of Pediatrics, 101*, 948–952.

Lozoff, B., Brittenham, G. M., Wolf, A. W., McClish, D. K., Kuhnert, P. M., Jimenez, E., Jimenez, R., Mora, L. A., Gomez, I., & Krauskoph, D. (1987). Iron deficiency anemia and iron therapy: Effects on infant developmental test performance. *Pediatrics, 79*, 981–995.

Lozoff, B., Klein, N. K., & Prabucki, K. M. (1986). Iron-deficient anemic infants at play. *Journal of Developmental and Behavioral Pediatrics, 7*, 152–158.

Lozoff, B., Wolf, A. W., & Jimenez, E. (1987). Influences on infant developmental test scores. *Journal of Developmental and Behavioral Pediatrics, 8*, 119.

Lozoff, B., Wolf, A., Urrutia, J. J., & Viteri, F. E. (1985). Abnormal behavior and low developmental test scores in iron-deficient anemic infants. *Journal of Developmental and Behavioral Pediatrics, 6*, 69–75.

Matheny, A. P., Jr. (1980). Bayley's Infant Behavior Record: Behavioral components and twin analyses. *Child Development, 51*, 1157–1167.

Oski, F. A., & Honig, A. S. (1978). The effects of therapy on the developmental scores of iron deficient infants. *Journal of Pediatrics, 92*, 21–25.

Oski, F. A., Honig, A. S., Helu, B., & Howanitz, P. (1983). Effect of iron therapy on behavior performance in nonanemic, iron-deficient infants. *Pediatrics, 71*, 877–880.

Powell, C. A., & Grantham-McGregor, S. (1985). The ecology of nutritional status and development in young children in Kingston, Jamaica. *American Journal of Clinical Nutrition, 41*, 1322–1331.

Stevenson, M. B., & Lamb, M. E. (1979). Effects of infant sociability and the caretaking environment on infant cognitive performance. *Child Development, 50*, 340-349.

Walter, T., deAndraca, I., Chadud, P., & Perales, C. G. (1989). Adverse effect of iron deficiency anemia on infant psychomotor development. *Pediatrics, 84*, 7-17.

Walter, T., Kovalskys, J., & Stekel, A. (1983). Effect of mild iron deficiency on infant mental development scores. *Journal of Pediatrics, 102*, 519-522.

Wolf, A. W., & Lozoff, B. (1985). A clinically interpretable method for analyzing the Bayley Infant Behavior Record. *Journal of Pediatric Psychology, 10*, 199-214.

8

Cognitive Maturity, Stressful Events, and Metabolic Control Among Diabetic Adolescents

Gary M. Ingersoll
Indiana University

Donald P. Orr
Indiana University Medical Center

Michael D. Vance
Family Support Center, Omaha, NE

Michael P. Golden
University of Washington

Insulin dependent diabetes mellitus (IDDM) is a unique chronic illness in that its successful management depends upon the active participation and cooperation of the patient in his or her treatment program. Compliance with the diabetic regimen is necessary for avoidance of long-term complications of the disease that include blindness, kidney failure, and cardiovascular problems. Compliance, however, includes monitoring complex interactions and variations in diet, exercise, and insulin regulation. As such, compliance with a diabetes regimen requires complex information processing strategies.

As a group, adolescents with IDDM are in less good metabolic control than younger children or young adults (Daneman, Wolfson, Becker, & Drash, 1981). It is tempting to attribute these differences in metabolic control to developmental physiologic differences linked to puberty. Indeed, there is some evidence to suggest that increased insulin resistance is associated with puberty (Amiel, Sherwin, Simonson, Lauritano, & Tamborlane, 1986; Bloch, Clemons, & Sperling, 1987; Mann & Johnston, 1984). However, the requirements of positive diabetes management may also be in direct conflict with salient elements of adolescent psychosocial and cognitive development. The degree to which psychosocial elements of the adolescent transition affect adolescents' abilities to manage their disease remains an important and not well-documented domain. Our analyses focus on the effects of level of cognitive maturity and stressful life events on control behaviors and adequacy of metabolic control among adolescents with IDDM. The paradigm used to examine psychosocial factors and diabetes generalizes to other adolescents who deal with chronic conditions.

The manner in which adolescents and children with IDDM think about their illness plays a direct role in their willingness and capacity to deal with it. A variety of researchers have reviewed the correspondence between children's and adolescents' level of cognitive maturity and their concepts of body, illness, or wellness (Bibace & Walsh, 1979; Eiser, 1985). More central to our hypothesized link between level of cognitive social maturity and metabolic control is the recognition that cognitive structures serve as information processing filters through which individuals organize and respond to their world. Conceptual systems theory (Harvey, Hunt, & Schroeder, 1961; Schroeder, Driver, & Streufert, 1967; Hunt & Sullivan, 1974) integrates elements of developmental, cognitive, and social psychology into a generalized model in which individuals are described as progressing from simple, concrete, and self-centered thinking to complex, abstract, and multi-perspective thinking. Individuals respond to and interact with their social and psychological world in ways consistent with their network of concepts. Adolescents at early levels of cognitive social maturity, for example, are unlikely to recognize links between current behaviors and long-range outcomes; they are more motivated by egocentric, hedonic needs. Hence, it is reasonable to speculate that they would be much less likely to comply with their treatment program. In earlier findings (Ingersoll, Orr, Herrold, & Golden, 1986), adequacy of metabolic control is related to conceptual level as reflected in responses to Hunt's Paragraph Completion Method (Hunt, Butler, Noy, & Rosser, 1978). Additionally, willingness of the diabetic adolescents to engage in self-managerial behaviors related to good metabolic control is also related to levels of cognitive social maturity. Those adolescents with IDDM at more advanced levels of cognitive social maturity are more likely to self-regulate their insulin dosage. Researchers using Loevinger's (1976) measure of ego development, which is also a measure of general social maturity, have found a linear relationship between level of ego development and feelings of adequacy in adolescents with diabetes (Hauser et al., 1979; Powers, Hauser, Schwartz, Noam, & Jacobson, 1983).

Beyond assessing cognitive antecedents to good metabolic control, evidence suggests that the affective environment of the adolescents with IDDM has an impact on metabolic control. Early studies relating stress to IDDM were directed at whether major stressful events precipitated diabetes (Daniels, 1939; Dunbar, Wolfe, & Rioch, 1936; Menninger, 1935) or whether there was an "oral diabetic personality" (Rosen & Lidz, 1949; Stein & Charles, 1975a, 1975b). Both approaches proved fruitless (Dunn & Turtle, 1981; Johnson, 1980). Alternatively, early studies (Hinkle, Evans, & Wolf, 1951a, 1951b) found stress to elevate blood glucose levels, although recent investigators (Kemmer et al., 1986) were unable to obtain disturbances in glycemic control with short-term stressors. On the other hand, Surwit and Feinglos (1983, 1984) demonstrated that blood glucose levels could be reduced through relaxation training. Hence, it is reasonable to ask: "Do stressful events disrupt good metabolic control?"

Previous research demonstrates that life changes are stressful and may disrupt positive social and emotional adjustment (Holmes & Rahe, 1967; Johnson, 1986). Among chronically ill children, the stresses of life changes may be even more disruptive (Coddington, 1972). Beyond disrupting normal adjustment, stressful events may deplete the chronically ill adolescents' emotional reserves and interfere with their positive health maintenance. Among children and adolescents with IDDM, number of stressful events is related to adequacy of metabolic control (Chase & Jackson, 1981). Among adults, significant life stressors are associated with increased risk of disease complications (Grant, Kyle, Teichman, & Mendels, 1974) and chronically elevated blood glucose levels (Bradley, 1979).

The focus of the analysis reported here is on the combined effects of level of cognitive maturity and stressful life events on metabolic control and self-managerial behaviors. Quality of metabolic control is operationalized as total glycosylated hemoglobin level (HbA_1), a measure of average blood glucose concentrations over an extended period; higher HbA_1 levels reflect poorer metabolic control. Self-managerial behaviors are operationalized as self-adjusting of insulin dose in response to changes in diet, exercise, or home blood glucose readings.

A complete model of the contributions of cognitive maturity and stressful life events (with sex of the adolescent and age as demographic variables) takes the form of Fig. 8.1. That is, sex contributes directly to cognitive maturity that, in turn, contributes to self-adjustment and metabolic control. Sex also contributes to variance in each of the outcomes as well as to variance in stressful events. As such, the model is not parsimonious. Not all lines of relationship persist. Sex is related to cognitive maturity and to quality of metabolic control. In our previous findings, males score higher on the Hunt measure, and adolescent females have higher mean HbA_1 levels. There is no reason to speculate about gender

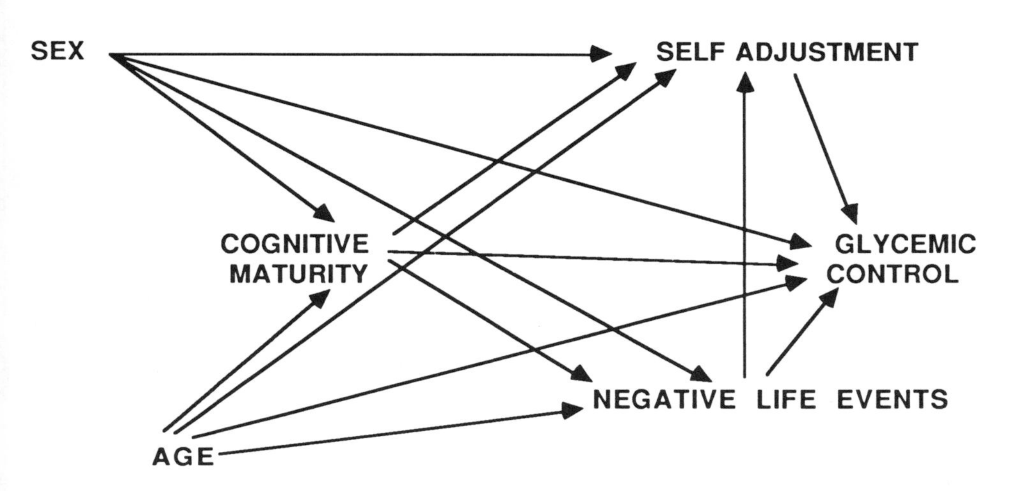

FIG. 8.1. Potential effects of cognitive maturity and negative life events on metabolic control.

differences in self-management. Age is a direct contributor to cognitive maturity because it is a strongly developmentally related variable. Age, however, does not contribute to glycemic control or to self-adjustment beyond variance accounted for by cognitive maturity.

Cognitive maturity is the central contributing variable, providing direct contributions to variance in both self-managerial behaviors and metabolic control, the latter contribution a function of unexplained variation in behavioral management. Cognitive maturity moderates the interpretation of stressful events. Because cognitive maturity is antecedent to more mature coping responses, stressful events are less disruptive to those at advanced levels of cognitive maturity. Finally, stressful life events contribute negatively to normal self-management and result in poor metabolic control.

METHODS

Subjects for this study were 120 adolescents with IDDM recruited from adolescents treated at the James Whitcomb Riley Hospital for Children of the Indiana University Medical School, and through community-based diabetes support groups and newspaper advertisements placed in a college newspaper. All subjects were informed of the nature of the study and what was expected of them. For subjects under 18 years of age, parental permission was also obtained. Informed consent procedures were approved by the Institutional Review Board of Indiana University.

Cognitive Maturity

Each subject was administered the Paragraph Completion Method (PCM) as a measure of global cognitive-social maturity (Hunt et al., 1978). The PCM is a semi-projective instrument requiring written responses to six open-ended topical stems to assess the individual's concepts and beliefs regarding conflict, uncertainty, rules, and authority. Responses were scored by trained raters using a 4-point scale. Low scores reflect immature and egocentric cognitions. Low to moderate scores reflect a high degree of dependency, conformity, and acquiescence to authority and social control. Moderate to high scores reflect greater tolerance for ambiguity and conflict. High scores indicate an understanding and appreciation of the interdependence of social behavior and of the mutuality and reciprocity of outcomes. Following procedures defined in the PCM manual, the final cognitive maturity score is the arithmetic average of the top three item scores. Scores for the sample had a mean of 1.37 and a standard deviation of 0.50. Interrater reliability for scoring of the subjects' responses was 0.83 using an interclass correlation coefficient (Frick & Semmel, 1978).

Life Events

The number and intensity of significant life events experienced by the subjects was assessed using the Adolescent Life Events Inventory (ALEI) (Johnson & McCutcheon, 1980). The instrument asks the respondent to indicate which among several life events he or she has experienced within the past 6 months and the extent to which the event was positive, negative, or neutral. Unlike some other instruments that depend upon clinical judgments of stressfulness, the ALEI permits the adolescent to define the degree of and direction of affect related to specific stressful events.

Self-Managerial Behaviors

Self-management of diabetes was measured by subjects' indication of how frequently they self-adjusted their insulin dose under conditions of increased exercise, altered diet, and elevated (or low) blood sugars. A composite sum was used as an index of insulin self-adjustment.

Metabolic Control

Adequacy of metabolic control was measured through total stable glycosylated hemoglobin (HbA_1). HbA_1 reflects an average daily blood glucose concentration over a period of the previous 60 to 90 days. Higher HbA_1 levels indicate poorer continuous metabolic control. Blood samples were drawn using a droplet of blood extracted from a finger prick. The sample was assayed for total glycosylated hemoglobin (Abraham et al., 1978) at the Immunoassay Core of the Indiana University Diabetes Research and Training Center.

RESULTS

Data analyses reveal that level of cognitive social maturity, as measured by performance on the PCM, and reported negative life events are both significant linear contributors to variance in glycosylated hemoglobin levels (see Table 8.1). As in our previous study, those adolescents at higher levels of cognitive social maturity are more likely to be in better metabolic control, that is, have lower glycosylated hemoglobin levels. The data also indicate that those who reported more frequent negative life events and who rated those events as more negative are more likely to be in poorer metabolic control, that is, have higher HbA_1 levels. Total positive life events is not related to metabolic control. Further examination of the zero-order relationships also reveals that the tendency of those at lower levels of cognitive maturity is to report a higher frequency of and more intense negative life events.

TABLE 8.1
Pearson Correlation Coefficients Relating Independent Variables and Metabolic Control

	Sex	*Age*	*PCM*	*NLE*	*ADJ*
Age	.039				
Cognitive maturity (PCM)[1]	−.184*	.409***			
Negative life events	.049	.122	−.156		
Self-adjusts insulin	−.162*	.235**	.384***	−.015	
Glycosylated hemoglobin (HbA_1)	.312***	−.103	−.461***	.253***	−.422***

[1]Paragraph Completion Method.
*$p < .05$
**$p < .01$
***$p < .001$

The data also reveal zero-order relationships among sex, age, and metabolic control. Analysis of mean HbA_1 levels for males ($\bar{X} = 9.84$, $SD = 1.56$) and females ($\bar{X} = 11.06$, $SD = 1.92$) indicates overall better metabolic control among males ($F = 9.84, p < .005$). These differences are found across low, moderate, and high levels of cognitive maturity.

The zero-order relationships were submitted to structural equation modeling using LISREL (Joreskog & Sorbom, 1984). In addition to the two central variables of concern (cognitive maturity and negative life events), sex, current age, and age of onset were entered as exogenous variables. LISREL permits the simultaneous test of several linear structural equations that define hypothesized contributions of a set of independent variables to variance in an outcome measure, in this instance, glycosylated hemoglobin levels. The resulting linear structural model is presented with respective contribution weights in Figure 8.2. Only statistically significant path coefficients were retained. The composite linear model yielded a squared multiple correlation coefficient of 0.324 ($p < .001$) with glycosylated hemoglobin as the outcome variable indicating that 32% of variance in metabolic control was accounted for through the linear contribution of the input variables.

Further study of the coefficients reveals that the effect of age observed at the bivariate level is indirect. That is, age is related to cognitive maturity that is, in turn, related to metabolic control. The partial relationship of age and metabolic control controlled for cognitive maturity is reduced to 0.00. A small, marginal relationship ($p < .10$) is noted between age of onset and level of cognitive maturity. The relation, not included in the path diagram because it is not statistically significant, nonetheless conforms to a small set of studies (Ryan, Vega, & Drash, 1985) that suggest increased risk of long-term cognitive impairment as a result of very early onset of the disease. Subjects' sex retains its independent contribution to variance in metabolic control among adolescents with IDDM; that is, females are in less good metabolic control.

The contribution of cognitive maturity and stressful life events retains direct

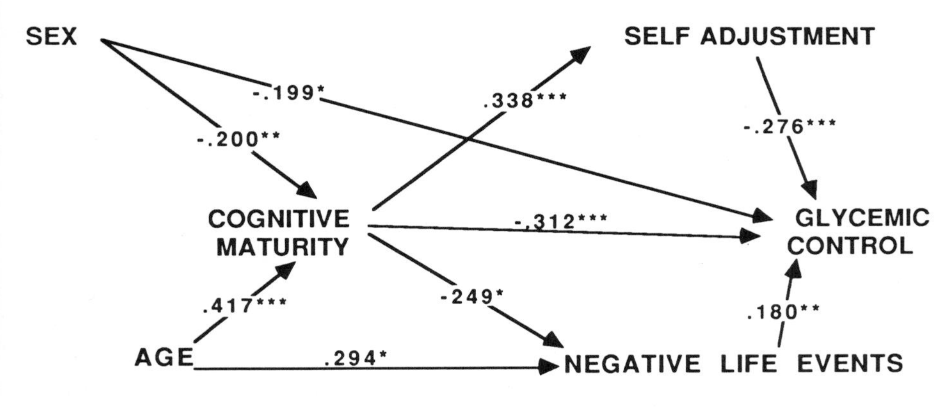

*$p < .05$
**$p < .01$
***$p < .001$

FIG. 8.2. Path diagram of recursive model for effects of cognitive maturity and negative life events on metabolic control.

variance in glycemic control. By far the dominant linear contribution is from cognitive maturity. In addition, cognitive maturity yields an indirect contribution through reported negative life events. Those at earlier levels of cognitive maturity are more likely to report a higher frequency of negative life events. Negative life events, in turn, yields a direct contribution to glycemic control. Those with more frequent negative life events are in poorer metabolic control.

There is reason to speculate that the effects of cognitive maturity and negative life events are nonlinear; those at early levels of cognitive maturity are more adversely affected by negative life events than those at more advanced levels of cognitive maturity. Those at advanced levels of cognitive social maturity are assumed to have more complex coping skills. Hence, the effects of serious negative events are mitigated by more mature coping responses. An analysis of variance of HbA_1 control by three levels of cognitive maturity and two levels of negative life events reveals no statistical interaction to support such a hypothesis.

As in our earlier analysis (Ingersoll et al., 1986), cognitive maturity also is related to the adolescents' willingness to engage in self-managerial behaviors that are presumed antecedent to positive metabolic control. Subjects in this study were questioned about a variety of health care behaviors, some directly related to a diabetic treatment plan. A composite index of self-care behaviors was created that included whether the subject carried sugar, wore a medical identification bracelet, self-adjusted insulin, and whether family and friends were informed of how to react in case of a diabetic emergency. This composite was directly related to cognitive maturity ($r = .192$, $p < .05$). On the other hand, reported levels of participation in a second composite of general health related behaviors (smoking, drinking alcohol, coffee, tea) was not related to cognitive maturity ($r = -.079$).

DISCUSSION

Adolescents with IDDM are a particularly useful target population within which to assess the effects of cognition and stress on health related outcomes. Like adolescents in general, adolescents with IDDM experience a rapid transition in their personal status. They must restructure their personal sense of self to accommodate radical alterations in their physical and intellectual self, and they must adapt to increased demands that they assume adult roles in society (Orr & Ingersoll, 1988; Ingersoll, 1989).

Dealing with the experience of a chronic illness, such as diabetes, during the adolescent transition interacts with the normal developmental tasks of the adolescent transition. Hence, although it is currently well accepted that adolescence is not inherently a period of storm and stress, many adolescents experience a range of emotional and behavioral risks (Ingersoll & Orr, 1988, 1989). Stressful events are expected to disrupt normal coping responses. The evidence found in these data that negative life events adversely contribute to a measure of metabolic control in a population of adolescents, whose metabolic control is already in jeopardy, serves to confirm previous studies and also the hypothesis that stress may disrupt adolescents' ability to cope with complex decisions related to good diabetes control.

Although adolescents with IDDM are frequently told that with proper maintenance of their diet, exercise, and insulin they can live a relatively normal life, the truth is that maintenance of a diabetic regimen is not easy. The regimen requires a complex set of decision-making behaviors that are contingent upon adequate understanding of the dynamics of the disease plus the ability to assess the simultaneous effects of multiple variables. It is, therefore, not surprising that a general measure of cognitive maturity is so strongly related to overall metabolic control.

In the past, investigators have tried to link chronic poor diabetes control or acute variations in blood sugar to disruptions in cognition and information processing (Rovet, Ehrlich, & Hoppe, 1987, 1988; Ryan, 1988; Holmes, 1987). That is, research into the relationship of diabetes control and cognitive function is directed by the question, "Does quality of diabetes control affect cognition?" The orientation of our research is, in contrast, directed by the question, "Does cognition affect quality of diabetes control?"

These data indicate that developmental psychological maturation variables that operate independently of chronic illness significantly affect patients' abilities to achieve positive metabolic control. The functional relationship between cognitive maturity and metabolic control is highly significant and replicable. It should be noted that the relationship between cognitive maturity and metabolic control is not simply a general maturational effect due to physiologic age. First, the relationship of chronologic age is mediated by cognitive maturity; its bivariate relationship is only indirect. Second, there is evidence that cognitive maturity is independent of physical maturity when chronological age is statistically controlled

(Orr, Brack, & Ingersoll, 1988). Hence, it is insufficient to attribute differences in metabolic control to differences in physical maturity. On the other hand, there are gender differences in metabolic control. Girls are in poorer metabolic control than boys. Although it is tempting to attribute the male–female differences to altered insulin resistance as a function of hormonal differences, that attribution is speculative at this time. In any case, gender differences in metabolic control are not readily attributed to psychosocial differences.

The existence of a direct contribution of cognitive maturity to metabolic control should be interpreted with some caution. It is hazardous to assume direct causality. Instead, the relationship likely reflects differing levels of adaptability to variations in the adolescents' diabetes and general environment. Indeed the indirect link between cognition and control through insulin self-adjustment serves to affirm that view. The indirect link of cognition and control through the contribution of negative life events also suggests differential ability to adapt to and cope with unexpected stressors. The remainder of a direct, uninterrupted link in the path diagram is assumed to reflect other, unmeasured adaptive response patterns.

Although the primary orientation of these analyses is on the contribution of cognition to diabetes control, some tentative evidence of the converse has been found. Ryan (1988; Ryan et al., 1985) has hypothesized that repeated hypoglycemic seizures, especially during the early childhood years, contribute to neuropsychological impairment. In a longitudinal analysis based on a small sample of young children with IDDM (Golden et al., 1989), evidence suggests that even repeated episodes of mild, asymptomatic hypoglycemia may have adverse, but relatively specific, effects on intellectual development. Whether the limited relationship between age of onset of the disease and general cognitive maturity as measured by the PCM is a reflection of this relationship is unclear. At a broad level, however, neuropsychological effects of repeated hypoglycemia do not appear pervasive but rather selective.

In some sense, the observation of stable relationships between level of cognitive social functioning, stress, and adolescents' abilities to adapt to the demands of a complex diabetes regimen raises as many issues as it answers. The strong linear contribution of cognitive complexity to a metabolic outcome may be itself indirect. That is, cognitive complexity may be antecedent to complex behaviors that are, in turn, antecedent to good metabolic control. Indeed, our earlier data (Ingersoll et al., 1986) indicate that adolescents' ability to apply a complex insulin-adjustment algorithm is related to cognitive maturity. When the effects of age are statistically controlled, the converse, however, is not true. If cognition operates as the primary mediator of adolescents' abilities to adapt to a complex health environment, what does this say with reference to our mode of response (e.g., methods of clinical intervention and education)? We are unlikely to substantially alter adolescents' level of cognitive social maturity. Are those at lower levels of cognitive complexity thereby doomed to poor metabolic control? Alternatively, are there differing patterns of intervention that are ideally suited to individuals at each level of conceptual maturity? The solution appears to rest in the latter perspective. That is, there is an apparent idealized match between the level of environmental structure and the adolescents' level of conceptual complexity. Those at lower levels of conceptual complexity are more likely to benefit from highly structured, supportive environments with limited response uncertainty. Those at higher levels of conceptual complexity are more likely to benefit from less structured interventions that emphasize autonomous decision making (Hunt & Sullivan, 1974). In the case of clinical intervention, the environment is composed not only of the composite of rules for compliance but also a set of authoritative support systems. In the long run, modifying clinicians' responses may be more productive in facilitating compliance than attempting to manipulate adolescents' psychosocial status.

ACKNOWLEDGMENTS

Funded in part by the Indiana University Diabetes Research and Training Center, PHS Grant P60AM20542-07.

REFERENCES

Abraham, E. C., Huff, T. A., Cope, N. D., Wilson, J. B., Brensome, E. D., & Huisman, T. H. J. (1978). Determination of glycosylated hemoglobin (HbA_1) with a microcolumn procedure. *Diabetes, 27,* 931-937.

Amiel, S. A., Sherwin, R. S., Simonson, D. C., Lauritano, A. A., & Tamborlane, W. V. (1986). Impaired insulin action in puberty. *New England Journal of Medicine, 315,* 215-219.

Bibace, R., & Walsh, M. E. (1979). Developmental stages in children's conceptions of illness. In G. C. Stone, F. Cohen, & N. E. Adler (Eds.), *Health psychology* (pp. 285-301). San Francisco: Jossey-Bass.

Bloch, C. A., Clemons, P., & Sperling, M. A. (1987). Puberty decreases insulin sensitivity. *Journal of Pediatrics, 110,* 481-487.

Bradley, C. (1979). Life events and the control of diabetes mellitus. *Journal of Psychosomatic Research, 23,* 159-162.

Chase, H. P., & Jackson, G. G. (1981). Stress and sugar control in children with insulin-dependent diabetes mellitus. *Journal of Pediatrics, 98,* 1,011-1,013.

Coddington, D. C. (1972). The significance of life events as etiologic factors in the diseases of children. II: A study of a normal population. *Journal of Psychosomatic Research, 16,* 205-213.

Daneman, D., Wolfson, D. H., Becker, D. J., & Drash, A. L. (1981). Factors affecting glycosylated hemoglobin values in children with insulin-dependent diabetes. *Journal of Pediatrics, 99,* 847-853.

Daniels, G. E. (1939). Present trends in the evaluation of psychic factors in diabetes mellitus. *Psychosomatic Medicine, 1,* 527-552.

Dunbar, H. B., Wolfe, T. D., & Rioch, J. M. (1936). Psychiatric aspects of medical problems. *American Journal of Psychiatry, 93,* 649-656.

Dunn, S. M., & Turtle, J. R. (1981). The myth of the diabetic personality. *Diabetes Care, 4,* 640-646.

Eiser, C. (1985). *The psychology of childhood illness.* New York: Springer-Verlag.

Frick, T., & Semmel, M. I. (1978). Observer agreement and reliabilities of classroom observational measures. *Review of Educational Research, 48*, 157–184.

Golden, M. P., Ingersoll, G. M., Brack, C. J., Russell, B. A., Wright, J. C., & Huberty, T. J. (1989). Longitudinal relationship of asymptomatic hypoglycemia to cognitive function in IDDM. *Diabetes Care, 12*, 89–93.

Grant, I., Kyle, G. C., Teichman, A., & Mendels, J. (1974). Recent life events and diabetes in adults. *Psychosomatic Medicine, 36*, 121–125.

Harvey, O. J., Hunt, D. E., & Schroeder, H. M. (1961). *Conceptual systems and personality organization*. New York: Wiley.

Hauser, S. T., Pollets, D., Turner, B. L., Jacobson, A., Powers, S., & Noam, G. (1979). Ego development and self-esteem in diabetic adolescents. *Diabetes Care, 2*, 465–472.

Hinkle, L. E., Evans, F. M., & Wolf, S. (1951a). Studies in diabetes mellitus II: Life history of three persons with labile diabetes and the relation of significant experiences to the onset and course of the disease. *Psychosomatic Medicine, 13*, 160–183.

Hinkle, L. E., Evans, F. M., & Wolf, S. (1951b). Studies in diabetes mellitus III: Life history of three persons with labile diabetes and the relation of significant experiences to the onset and course of the disease. *Psychosomatic Medicine, 13*, 184–202.

Holmes, C. S. (1987). Metabolic control and auditory information processing at altered glucose levels in insulin-dependent diabetes. *Brain and Cognition, 6*, 161–174.

Holmes, T. H., & Rahe, R. H. (1967). The social readjustment scale. *Journal of Psychosomatic Research, 11*, 213–218.

Hunt, D. E., Butler, L. F., Noy, J. E., & Rosser, M. C. (1978). *Assessing conceptual level by the Paragraph Completion Method*. Toronto: Ontario Institute for Studies in Education.

Hunt, D. E., & Sullivan, E. V. (1974). *Between psychology and education*. Hillsdale, IL: Dryden Press.

Ingersoll, G. M. (1989). *Adolescents* (2nd ed.). Englewood Cliffs, NJ: Prentice-Hall.

Ingersoll, G. M., & Orr, D. P. (1988). Adolescents at risk. In J. Carlson & L. Lewis (Eds.), *Counseling the adolescent* (pp. 7–20). Denver, CO: Love.

Ingersoll, G. M., & Orr, D. P. (1989). Behavioral and emotional risk in early adolescents. *Journal of Early Adolescence, 9*, 396–408.

Ingersoll, G. M., Orr, D. P., Herrold, A. J., & Golden, M. P. (1986). Cognitive maturity and self-management among adolescents with insulin-dependent diabetes mellitus. *Journal of Pediatrics, 73*, 620–623.

Johnson, J. H. (1986). *Life events as stressors in childhood and adolescence*. Beverly Hills, CA: Sage.

Johnson, J. H., & McCutcheon, S. (1980). Assessing life stress in older children and adolescents. Preliminary findings with the Life Events Checklist. In I. G. Sarason & C. D. Speilberger (Eds.), *Stress and anxiety* (Vol. 7, pp. 111–125). Washington, DC: Hemisphere.

Johnson, S. B. (1980). Psychosocial factors in juvenile diabetes. *Journal of Behavioral Medicine, 3*, 95–116.

Joreskog, K. G., & Sorbom, D. (1984). *LISREL VI: Analysis of linear structural relationships by maximum likelihood, instrumental variables, and least squares methods*. Mooresville, IN: Scientific Software.

Kemmer, F. W., Bisping, R., Steingruber, H. J., Baar H., Harttmann, F., Schlachecke, R., & Berger, M. (1986). Psychological stress and metabolic control in patients with Type I diabetes mellitus. *New England Journal of Medicine, 314*, 1,078–1,084.

Loevinger, J. (1976). *Ego development*. San Francisco: Jossey-Bass.

Mann, N. P., & Johnston, D. I. (1984). Improvement in metabolic control in diabetic adolescents by the use of increased insulin dose. *Diabetes Care, 7*, 460–464.

Menninger, W. C. (1935). Psychological factors in the etiology of diabetes mellitus. *Journal of Nervous and Mental Disorders, 81*, 1–13.

Orr, D. P., Brack, C. J., & Ingersoll, G. M. (1988). Pubertal maturation and cognitive maturity in adolescents. *Journal of Adolescent Health Care, 9*, 273–279.

Orr, D. P., & Ingersoll, G. M. (1988). Adolescent behavior and development: A biopsychosocial view. *Current Problems in Pediatrics, 18*, 442-499.

Powers, S. I., Hauser, S. T., Schwartz, J. M., Noam, G. G., & Jacobson, A. M. (1983). Adolescent ego development and family interaction: A structural-developmental perspective. In H. D. Grotevant & C. R. Cooper (Eds.), *Adolescent development in the family*. San Francisco: Jossey-Bass.

Rosen, H., & Lidz, T. (1949). Emotional factors in the precipitation of recurrent acidosis. *Psychosomatic Medicine, 11*, 21.

Rovet, J. F., Ehrlich, R. M., & Hoppe, M. (1987). Intellectual deficits associated with early onset of insulin-dependent diabetes mellitus in children. *Diabetes Care, 10*, 510-515.

Rovet, J. F., Ehrlich. R. M., & Hoppe, M. (1988). Specific intellectual deficits in children with early onset diabetes mellitus. *Child Development, 59*, 226-234.

Ryan, C. M. (1988). Neurobehavioral complications of Type I diabetes. *Diabetes Care, 11*, 86-93.

Ryan, C. M., Vega, A., & Drash, A. (1985). Cognitive deficits in adolescents who developed diabetes early in life. *Pediatrics, 75*, 921-927.

Schroeder, H. M., Driver, M. J., & Streufert, S. (1967). *Human information processing*. New York: Holt, Rinehart & Winston.

Stein, S., & Charles, E. (1975a). A study of early life experiences of adolescent diabetics. *American Journal of Psychiatry, 128*, 700-704.

Stein, S., & Charles, E. (1975b). Emotional factors in juvenile diabetes: A study of early life experiences of nine adolescent diabetics. *Psychosomatic Medicine, 1*, 547-552.

Surwit, R. S., & Feinglos, M. N. (1983). The effects of relaxation on glucose tolerance in non-insulin dependent diabetes. *Diabetes Care, 6*, 176-179.

Surwit, R. S., & Feinglos, M. N. (1984). Relaxation induced improvement of glucose tolerance is associated with decreased plasma cortisol. *Diabetes Care, 7*, 203-204.

9

Ego Development Paths and Adjustment to Diabetes: Longitudinal Studies of Preadolescents and Adolescents With Insulin-Dependent Diabetes Mellitus

Stuart T. Hauser
Harvard Medical School, Joslin Diabetes Center

Alan M. Jacobson
Harvard Medical School, Joslin Diabetes Center

Janet Milley
Joslin Diabetes Center

Donald Wertlieb
Tufts University

Joseph Wolfsdorf
Harvard Medical School, Joslin Diabetes Center

Raymonde D. Herskowitz
Harvard Medical School, Joslin Diabetes Center

Phillip Lavori
Brown University

Robin L. Bliss
University of Minnesota

In this chapter we trace how the onset of a significant chronic illness in adolescence touches individual development and emotional adjustment. Adolescents have diverse responses to the advent of this new, largely unexpected illness that pervades many facets of their lives, within their families and among their peers. Insulin-dependent diabetes mellitus is a chronic metabolic illness that involves the diagnosed patient and his or her family life. The complex interplay of medical, developmental, and social forces is especially apparent when the patient is a child or adolescent. Our studies examine how individual and family dimensions intersect with the onset and clinical course of diabetes in preadolescent and adolescent patients (Hauser et al., 1989, 1990; Hauser, Jacobson, Wertlieb, Brink, & Wentworth, 1985; Hauser et al., 1979; Hauser, Powers, Jacobson, Schwartz, & Noam, 1982; Wertlieb, Hauser, & Jacobson, 1985). An important individual dimension is ego development, a line of socioemotional development associated with numerous aspects of adaptation in children and adults (Browning, 1986; Frank & Quinlin, 1976; Hauser et al., 1984; Noam et al., 1984; Rosnafsky, 1981).

We have been especially interested in how ego development is influenced by and influences the patient's diabetes. Our perspective, based on the extensive theoretical and empirical work of Loevinger and her associates (Loevinger, 1979; Loevinger & Wessler, 1971), construes ego development as involving a series of qualitatively differing stages. General trends in ego development can be described in terms of increases in internalization of rules of social intercourse, cognitive complexity, tolerance of ambiguity, and objectivity. In addition, the individual's impulse control becomes progressively guided by self-chosen long-term intentions, accompanied by an enhanced respect for individual autonomy and an interest in genuine mutuality.

Early studies using this measure of ego development involved normal samples and addressed basic psychometric questions of reliability and validity (Hauser, 1976; Loevinger, 1979). Recently, a number of research groups, including our own, have reported findings from clinical samples (Browning, 1986; Frank & Quinlin, 1976; Kirshner, 1988). These extensions from healthy populations to those with psychiatric and medical conditions are not surprising, in light of the fact that ego development refers to clinically relevant dimensions, such as impulse control, anticipation, responsibility-taking, and social judgment. These are the very features highlighted in analyses of impaired individual functioning. For instance, a hallmark of serious psychopathology is erratic or minimal impulse control, attribution of responsibility to others, and poor social judgment, such as unawareness of the impacts of one's words and actions upon another person (cf. Browning, 1986 and Rosnafsky, 1981 for fuller discussion of these connections).

In short, there are strong theoretical grounds for expecting ego development to be intertwined with varying forms of psychopathology. But what is the relevance of this line of development to physical illness? Several medical and life cycle considerations must be addressed in thinking about this broad question. The kind of medical illness and the developmental era of the patient (e.g., child, adolescent, early or late adult) will significantly shape our answer. Whether the illness appeared suddenly or was gradual in onset, whether it is usually "expected" at a particular point in the life cycle, and the specific nature of the illness – metabolic, infectious, traumatic – are all dimensions that may influence and be influenced by the patient's socioemotional development (ideas touched on in a paper by

Schwab and Bradnan, 1979). Through our focus on children and adolescents with diabetes we begin to answer this important question about interfaces between medical illness and individual psychological development. Our intent is to identify developmental processes and specific aspects of adaptation, *not* the presence, absence, or degree of psychopathology.[1]

With advancing ego development, the individual's conscious concerns move from the concrete to the abstract. Time orientation shifts from the immediate to the long range, and impulses are experienced as controllable. Moreover, with progress in his or her ego development, the individual becomes more sensitive to cognitive and affective nuances. There are a number of ways that these developmental shifts can influence the child and adolescent's adjustment to diabetes, as well as meeting the demands of diabetes management. With respect to impulse control, for instance, individuals at the earliest stages of development (impulsive, self-protective) are, at best, beginning to delay gratification. Most often, rules regarding impulse control are seen as externally imposed and irrelevant. Many aspects of diabetes management involve control of impulse: dietary restrictions, special times of glucose monitoring, planning exercise, and postponing parties. Children and adolescents at lower levels of ego development may find these constraints especially disturbing and almost impossible to adhere to.

Another connection between ego development and diabetes has to do with assessing the health risk of various activities. Veering from one's diet or neglecting to self-administer insulin can lead to serious short-term medical problems, such as slowed growth, diabetic ketoacidosis, and hypoglycemia. Moreover, such persistent dietary and medical indiscretions can potentially contribute to visual or renal complications many years in the future. For someone functioning at higher levels of ego development (conformist, self-aware, conscientious, autonomous), anticipation of these short-term problems plus possible long-term future consequences is conceivable. These strengths will enable an adolescent to thoughtfully envision the dangers that may eventually follow dietary or medication indiscretions. On the other hand, brief time perspectives, concrete thinking, and disinterest in abstract ideas (all characteristics of the early stages) can interfere with an adolescent's ability to anticipate potential harm resulting from such actions. Distorted and frightened visions of the future may impair a young patient's rational planning, such as, when an adolescent is convinced that severe complications await him or her (e.g., blindness), irrespective of attentiveness to diet or insulin. These difficulties with anticipation are heightened by the tendency of patients at early stages to not recognize uncertainties and to anchor thoughts and feelings in current experience. Tangible, immediate rewards are important not imagined long-term ones. In other words, judgments about appropriate manage-

[1]Pursuing a psychopathology orientation has led to inconsistent findings, as several reviews and empirical contributions have recently noted (cf. Hauser & Pollets, 1981; Hauser et al., 1984; Jacobson et al., 1986).

ment of illness and satisfaction with the restrictions imposed by the chronic illness, will be more problematic for adolescents at early levels of ego development. There are, then, several reasons to expect that ego development will be linked with favorable adjustment (advanced stages) or difficulties (early stages) in adjusting to the taxing demands imposed by diabetes.

Besides the impact of ego development on the child and adolescent's diabetes adjustment, there is a second direction of influence. There are reasons to expect that diabetes will affect ego development. The onset of this illness, with its multifold impact upon life style and possibly longevity, may delay or disrupt continued progression in ego development. Although there is limited evidence of significant child or adolescent psychopathology associated with diabetes (Hauser & Pollets, 1981; Jacobson, Hauser, Powers, & Noam, 1985; Jacobson et al., 1986), our previous findings indicate that adolescents with diabetes are functioning at lower levels of ego development in comparison to age matched nondiabetic patients (Hauser et al., 1984; Jacobson, Hauser, Powers, & Noam, 1982). Although the diabetic adolescents are at higher ego development levels than those found in adolescents with known psychopathology (Hauser et al., 1984), they nonetheless differ from physically healthy high school students of the same age.

This ego development finding remains unexplained, yet it certainly suggests that the onset and presence of insulin-dependent diabetes influences individual development, leaving impacts simply not visible when we look through lenses sensitive only to psychiatric symptoms and psychopathology. In this chapter, we present our efforts to extend understanding in this area, drawing upon observations of newly diagnosed patients (not present in the previous studies) to determine whether this developmental difference represents an immediate regressive response to the onset of illness or a more cumulative slowing in development. Moreover, because our new studies include an age- and sex-matched acute illness comparison group, we can clarify the extent to which developmental effects are in response to new strains accompanying the advent of unexpected, and likely unwanted, medical care providers and their institutions (clinics and hospitals).

In summary, we focus on two questions in this chapter: (a) How is the patient's adjustment to diabetes shaped by his or her level of ego development? and (b) How is this level of development influenced by the onset and continued presence of diabetes? Because we observe the patients' ego development each year, we can also pursue a line of inquiry that considers *paths* of development. In addition to examining links between yearly "slices" of development, we conceptualize and study the individual patient's form of change over time. Does this path of development differ for adolescents with diabetes? How does a patient's developmental pattern influence his or her adaptation to diabetes? We have recently advanced the argument that another way to think about ego development is with respect to individual patterns of change, patterns that can be identified from underlying theoretical considerations (Hauser, Powers, & Noam, 1991; Hauser, Powers, Noam, & Bowlds, 1987). Through this conceptual step, we can generate an array of developmental paths. This form or profile of development that each individual shows represents his or her developmental curve, or *trajectory*. These trajectories refer to individual patient's profiles of stages over the first years after diagnosis. We operationalize several theoretically meaningful trajectories. The first trajectory is referred to as *early arrest* in ego development. At the time of diagnosis, the patient is functioning at one of the earliest (pre-conformist) ego stages and remains at one of these stages over the first 2 to 3 years after diagnosis. A second trajectory is the *steady conformist*. Here, the patient begins at one of the conformist stages and remains at this level over the next 2 to 3 years after diagnosis. A third trajectory, *progressive ego development*, represents a patient's shifts upward from one of the earliest or intermediate stages over the years of assessment. There is also the *regressive ego development* trajectory, where the patient shifts downward from one set of stages (e.g., from conformist to preconformist) over the years following his or her diagnosis. Finally, there is the trajectory that we term (after Erikson, 1959) *psychosocial moratorium*, where the individual at first decreases and then increases in his or her level of ego development.

Although we are interested in how ego developmental stages at the time of diagnosis may predict subsequent functioning, we expect that these trajectories are most compellingly connected with adjustment to diabetes over time. Because these developmental patterns are based on several observations over time, they more accurately reflect the patient's course of development during the adolescent years.

METHODS

The findings we will report later are drawn from our study of children with diabetes and children who first present as acutely ill. We began studying these children (from 9 to 16 years old) and their families in the years immediately prior to adolescence and in the early to mid-adolescent years, and we will be following them into late adolescence and early adulthood. Our longitudinal data set includes a range of individual and family variables such as self-esteem, pubertal and cognitive development, psychopathology, locus of control, family coping, and family interactions. We have reported on several of these dimensions in previous papers about adolescents with diabetes (Hauser et al., 1985, 1986; Jacobson et al., 1986, 1990; Wertlieb et al., 1985). This is our first presentation of findings regarding links between ego development and the onset and subsequent course of diabetes.

Sixty-two boys and girls, recruited within 12 months of the onset of diabetes, comprise the diabetes sample. They are compared with a group of 68 children, who within the last 12 months had a serious medical problem from which there was complete recovery. This medical problem required a clear alteration in their daily activities: two or more visits to a physician, hospitalization, loss of at least one day in school, or, during vacation periods, one missed day of outside activities.

These children, who do not differ significantly in age or sex from the diabetes sample, were recruited from a local health maintenance organization. Of the 126 children recruited, 54% ($n = 68$) entered the study and were no longer ill when studied. Subjects were identified through either provider referrals or case records that were reviewed by the research team. The diagnostic breakdown of the acute illness sample was: fractures (48%), infections (15%), appendicitis (13%), lacerations and other injuries (24%). Patients who presented for treatment for the same acute medical problem within the preceding 6 months were excluded from the sample.

There is a specific rationale for choosing these patients as a comparison group rather than the more typical normal control group. We knew from our previous studies that, in terms of ego development, children with diabetes differ from adolescents who are healthy high school students (Hauser et al., 1984; Jacobson et al., 1982). One possible reason for this difference, we reasoned, has to do with the experience of illness and the impact of the health care system. Does the encounter with the physician and health provider have an impact on its own that is independent of the specific illness? By using an acute illness group, we could begin to disentangle medical care effects from those of the chronic illness (diabetes) itself.

The two samples do not differ in terms of age, gender, or time following diagnosis. On entering the study, when these first psychosocial assessments were obtained, the diabetic sample had a mean duration of diabetes of 5.0 ± 3.9 (*SD*) months; and the acute illness group had an average of 5.4 ± 2.6 (*SD*) months postdiagnosis. There is a difference in socioeconomic status. The diabetic group has fewer upper middle-class families and more working- and lower-class families. Table 9.1 shows these demographic features. Because of this social class difference, our analyses control for social class in order to avoid confounding social class with illness differences. Moreover, in light of the intermittent reports raising the possibility of a complex association between intelligence and ego development (Hauser, 1976; Loevinger, 1979), we also control for both verbal and performance intelligence level.

A final set of sample analyses monitors selective mortality in our sample. We compared patients who participated in all 3 years with those who dropped out after 2 years. In both patient groups, analyses of subjects missing from Year 3 do not significantly differ from the other subjects with respect to sex, age, ego development, or self-esteem. In addition, the ego development trajectories formed for 2 years do not differ from those formed with all 3 years of ego development observations. We are also currently working on other ways of accounting for missing data (Little & Rubin, 1987), such as the use of specially designed correction factors, which will be applied in future longitudinal analyses of these two groups of patients.

Ego development was assessed with the Washington University Sentence Completion Test (WUSCT), a 36-item instrument administered to all patients and parents on entering the study. Conceptual and psychometric features of this measure

TABLE 9.1
Demographic Characteristics of the Diabetic and Acute Illness Samples

	Daibetes (n = *62)*	*Acute Illness* (n = *68)*
Gender		
Boys	30	43
Girls	32	25
Age	12.8 (2.0)[a]	12.9 (1.8)
Social class[b]		
Upper middle	27 (20.8)	46 (35.4)
MIddle and lower middle	20 (15.4)	16 (12.3)
Working and lower	15 (11.5)	6 (4.6)

[a]Mean (standard deviation).
[b]Using Hollingshead (1957) 2 factor index, frequencies; percentages in parentheses; chi-square = 8.99 ($p < .01$).

have been considered in numerous publications (Hauser, 1976; Loevinger, 1979). Protocols were scored separately by items and then reassembled by reliable raters. Two scores were derived from each protocol. The first, the patient's ego stage, was calculated on the basis of the items' distribution of ego stage scores, using the ogive rules given by Loevinger and Wessler (1971). These stages vary from the *earliest* preconformist (impulsive, self-protective, transitional) to the *intermediate* conformist (conformist, self-aware), and to the most *advanced* post-conformist (conscientious, autonomous, integrated) levels. The obtained *stage score* is used to form trajectories and in selected other analyses of stages (e.g., comparing specific years, looking at extremes in relation to diabetes adjustment). The second score, the *item sum score*, represents the cumulative score of all items in a protocol, and is thus a polar dimension (as opposed to milestone) and an equal interval variable. As such, it is more amenable to correlational and regression analyses that are also reported in this chapter (cf. Hauser, 1976; Hauser et al., 1984).

Diabetes adjustment was measured with a self-report measure constructed by Sullivan (1979a, 1979b). This 68-item instrument (the DAS) taps the child and adolescent's views of his or her attitudes, feelings, and behaviors pertaining to diabetes. Previous psychometric studies (Sullivan, 1979a, 1979b) have shown strong correlations between these scales and the child's self-esteem, as well as various indices of depression. Five subscales have been derived from prior factor analyses: independence, peer adjustment, school adjustment, family relationships, and attitudes toward diabetes and the body. Specific items that comprise one of the adjustment subscales (peer adjustment) include: "I tell my friends at home I have diabetes"; "My friends at home deliberately tempt me to eat foods I shouldn't eat"; "I enjoy eating with my friends"; "My nondiabetic friends understand me"; "My friends at home tease me about my diabetes"; "It's harder to make friends when you have diabetes."

Intelligence was assessed through the vocabulary and block design subtests of the Wechsler Child Intelligence Scale-Revised. A number of studies have shown insignificant correlations between overall ego development and intelligence (Hauser, 1976; Loevinger, 1979). Yet there is reason to believe that high intelligence may be a necessary, but not sufficient, factor for achieving high levels of ego development (Hauser, 1976). Consequently, we account for possible effects of the patients' intelligence on ego development by using verbal and performance IQ scores as covariates in our ego development analyses. By controlling for these dimensions, we are in a better position to conclude that any ego development differences between patients with diabetes and those with an original acute illness do *not* simply represent intelligence differences.

RESULTS

Ego Development in Adolescents With Diabetes and Adolescents With an Acute Illness

In the first year, the preadolescents and adolescents with diabetes express significantly lower ego development item sum scores after social class and verbal performance or overall IQ differences were controlled. This difference is also present in Year 2 but is not found in the following year. The diminishing difference between the two groups is confirmed by a repeated measures analysis of variance revealing a nonsignificant difference over the 3 years. This 3-year profile is illustrated in Fig. 9.1.

One way to grasp these differences is by more closely examining the discrete *stages* of ego development revealed by annual assessments. As seen in Fig. 9.2, in Year 1 almost three quarters of the diabetic patients are functioning at the earliest (preconformist) stages of ego development. On the other hand, the acute illness patients are evenly divided between the earliest and next most advanced (conformist) stages of ego development. The distribution of this significant difference between the two patient groups is shown in Fig. 9.2.

In the following years, this pattern of earlier ego development for the diabetic youth is less dramatic. Nonetheless, it is important to note that by Year 3 a larger proportion of the diabetic adolescents continue to function at the earlier stages, and none of these patients are functioning at the highest (postconformist) stages. In other words, it is as though the diabetic adolescents are experiencing some kind of barrier to progression to the postconformist levels of ego development.

We also find clear differences in ego development *trajectories*, consistent with the stage findings.[2] The most striking contrast involves arrests in ego develop-

---

[2]Fuller discussion of the meaning of these ego development trajectories is found in a recent book on this topic (Hauser et al., 1991).

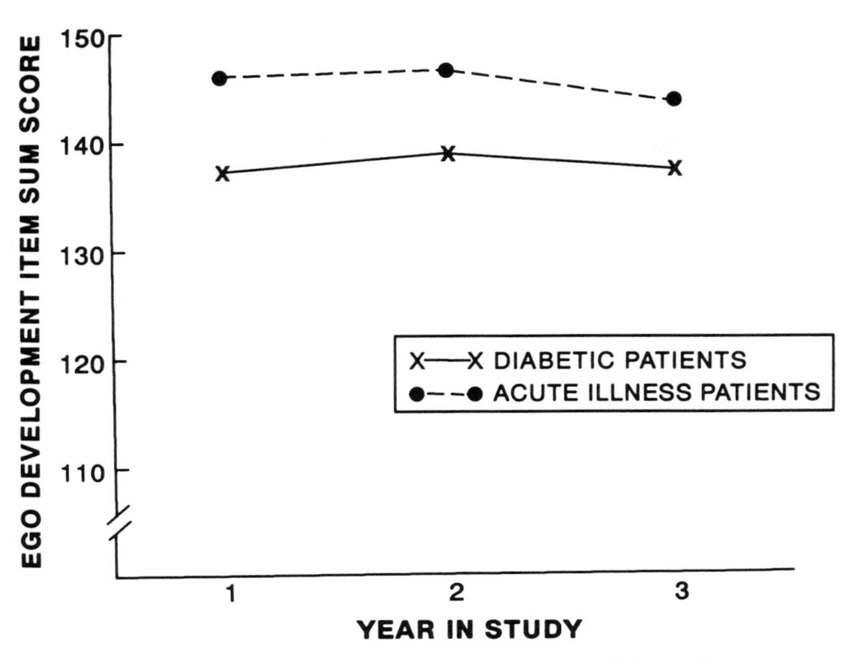

FIG. 9.1. Ego development of adolescents with diabetes and an initial acute illness.

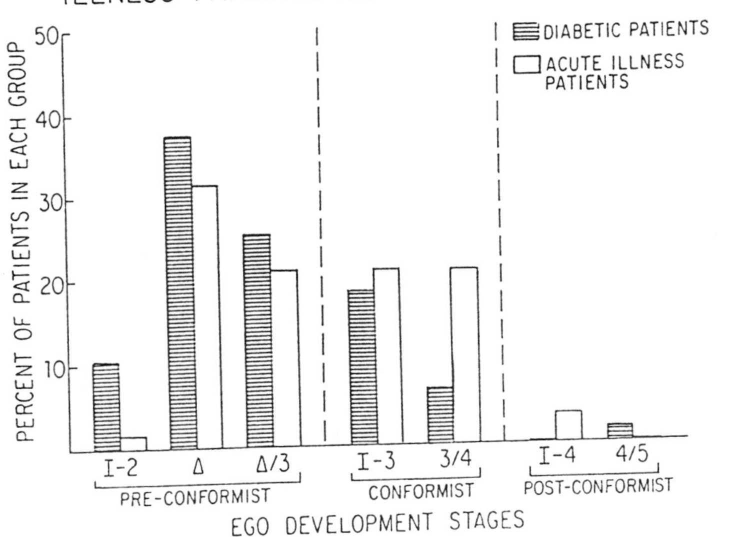

FIG. 9.2. Ego development stages of adolescents with diabetes and initial acute illness near time of diagnosis.

ment. Nearly 50% of the diabetic patients show an early arrest in ego development. The other type of arrest is an attenuated one, steady conformist, and is present in almost equal numbers for the diabetic and non-diabetic groups. A second noteworthy contrast concerns those developmental paths that reflect either regressive change or vicissitudes in ego development (psychosocial moratorium). A higher proportion of adolescents with acute illness express these patterns. Thus, besides contributing to early arrests and possibly limiting development beyond the intermediate stages, one other influence of the diabetes may be to dampen "experimentation"; this might appear as regression or unstable development. These significantly different ($\chi^2 = 4.81$; $p < .03$) patterns of trajectories are illustrated in Figure 9.3.

Although important, it is also apparent that these group differences do not fully capture the complete picture of how these adolescents differ in their development. Through hearing the voices of several adolescents with diabetes and acute illnesses, we can more fully appreciate how these patients describe their feelings, their perceptions of the world, and their perceptions of those closest to them.

Boys and girls with diabetes express the following thoughts and feelings in response to varied sentence stems:

If I can't get what I want I scream.

When people are helpless they get really scared; they feel alone and weak; I say to myself, glad it isn't me.

A pregnant woman gets so fat; shouldn't do aerobic dancing or take drugs; should be careful with diet and exercise.

I feel sorry for the little girl; people who are blind; for people who are really sick and poor; for people who have terminal illnesses and those who use diseases for a crutch; for the dead cat.

At times she worried about her daughter; me; too much; my health.

A woman should always be very careful.

The thing I like about myself is not to die early.

Sometimes she wished that she could do that too; she could be like them; I was never born; she could live in another world.

When I am with a man I get sick.

Rules are not fun and very sickening.

Boys and girls with an acute illness respond to the incomplete sentences with very different themes:

If I can't get what I want I complain sometimes, but always understand; I try harder.

I feel sorry for the helpless and the sick; when I beat someone.

He felt proud that he didn't get caught.

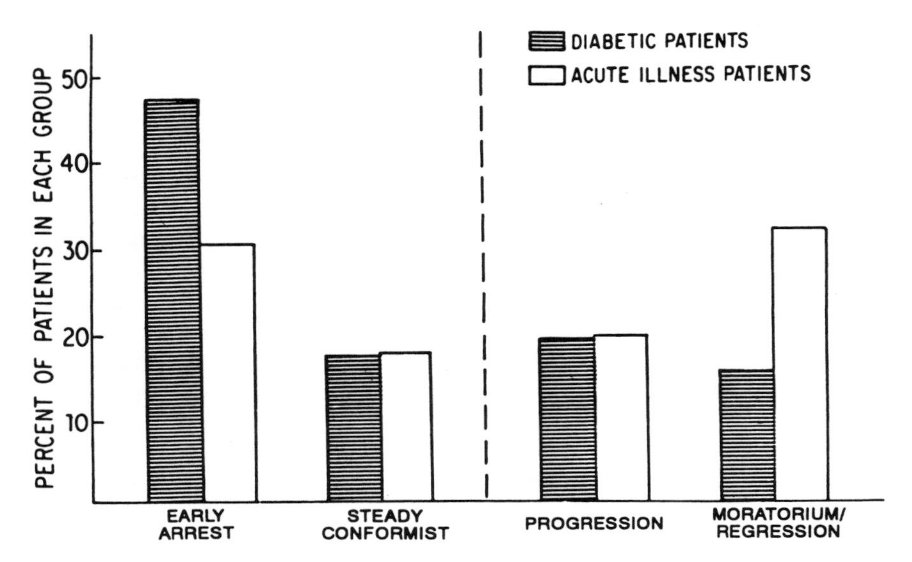

FIG. 9.3. Ego development trajectories of adolescents with diabetes and initial acute illness.

At times he worried about losing the game.

Rules are important to be kept; made to be.

We already know that the diabetic and acute illness patients are at different initial levels of ego development. Now we see how they differ. Through this first inspection of the ways they complete their sentence stems, the patients with diabetes call attention to their conscious awareness of loss, caution, and sequelae of illness (health, terminal illness, early death, death). On the other hand, the adolescents with an acute illness write of many adolescent-specific concerns, varying from complaining to getting away with breaking rules and persistence. This more informal perusal of themes closely parallels a more systematic content analysis of differences between adolescent diabetic and nondiabetic patients (Hauser et al., 1979).

Overall, then, the preadolescents and adolescents with diabetes differ in several important ways from those patients who had a recent acute illness. The two groups are distinguished along the lines of their initial ego development levels, ego development trajectories, and conscious concerns.

Ego Development and Adjustment to Diabetes

What does ego development level have to do with the adolescent's adjustment to diabetes? Here we no longer focus on whether diabetic adolescents differ from the acutely ill. We know that their development at first appears to be lagging behind that of the acutely ill. But we do not know what the *clinical significance* of this finding is, particularly with respect to how they are handling their chronic illness.

We can probe relations between ego development and diabetes adjustment in several ways. First, we can inquire about immediate links. What is the influence of current ego level to diabetes adjustment? We divided the patients into two homogeneous ego level groups, those at the earliest preconformist stages (impulsive, self-protective, and transitional) and those at the conformist stages (conformist and self-aware). In each of the 3 years of the study, we found (after controlling for age differences) that the preconformist patients express significantly lower levels of overall adjustment and specific adjustment towards peer relationships and independence. In addition, 3 years after diagnosis, this group of patients with diabetes also expresses lower adjustment to school and attitudes toward the body. Table 9.2 details these concurrent relations between ego development and diabetes adjustment.

A second set of questions involves *prediction*: To what extent does knowing a child's level of ego development close to the time of diagnosis predict subsequent problematic or favorable adjustment? Using repeated measures analyses of covariance (again controlling for age), we found that patients with diabetes who are functioning at the earliest stages (preconformist) at the time of diagnosis show significantly lower overall independence, and school adjustment, as well as marginally lower peer adjustment, when all 3 years adjustment scores are considered.

TABLE 9.2
Concurrent Ego Stage and Diabetes Adjustment

	Year in Study					
Ego Stages	*1*		2		*3*	
Diabetes Adjustment Scale	*Pre*	*Con*	*Pre*	*Con*	*Pre*	*Con*
Overall adjustment[a]	108.2*	91.4	105.3***	91.7	110.2***	89.7
Independence[a]	21.0*	16.9	20.6***	15.9	20.8***	16.0
Peer[a]	20.2*	15.6	20.3***	16.1	20.2***	15.3
School[a]	19.2	16.1	17.7	15.9	19.1***	15.9
Diabetes and body	20.6	26.2	29.0	28.6	31.9***	27.1
Family	17.5	16.6	17.7	15.3	18.1	15.4

Note: Pre refers to Preconformist; Con to conformist.
Using Duncan's Multiple Range test, controlling for Type I Comparison-wise error rate:
*$p < .05$
**$p < .007$
***$p < .002$

[a]Patients with ego development arrests also have significantly lower adjustment scores on this scale.

A second approach to these longitudinal observations draws on the developmental curves, the trajectories. We now know that initial ego development predicts subsequent diabetes adjustment. But how is the form of this development associated with a patient's adjustment to diabetes over the years? Consistent with the preceding Year 1 predictive findings, patients who remain at the earliest stages (early arrests) are persistently lower in their overall adjustment as well as adjustment to independence, school, and peer relations. This last set of analyses, then, drawing simultaneously on the longitudinal ego and diabetes adjustment measures, reveals that the patients whose development is arrested in the earliest stages represent a distinctive subgroup, expressing lower adjustment to diabetes than any of the other ego trajectory subgroups of patients, as shown for overall and independence adjustment in Figure 9.4.

These findings suggest that patients who begin at lower ego development stages and those who remain at these stages over the following years are at-risk for initial and subsequent difficulties in adjusting to their diabetes. Once more, actual responses to these ego development test sentence stems convey a more complete picture of patients who are in this early arrest trajectory.

Judy, an early adolescent, describes herself in the following ways during the first 2 years of the study:

I am so lonely.

My mother and I never talk.

My father is a pain.

The thing I like about myself is nothing.

My main problem is everything.

What gets me into trouble is food.

When they avoided me I got very upset.

When they avoided me I could care less.

I feel sorry for that little girl.

Rules are so hard to follow.

At times she worried about me.

Being with other people is sometimes uncomfortable.

Themes of loneliness, sadness, low self-esteem, and general discomfort are palpable in these answers. It is hardly surprising that this same girl reports low adjustment across a number of domains associated with her diabetes.

Jim, also an early adolescent whose diabetes was diagnosed at the start of his teenage years, expresses different thoughts and feelings:

The thing I like about myself is everything.

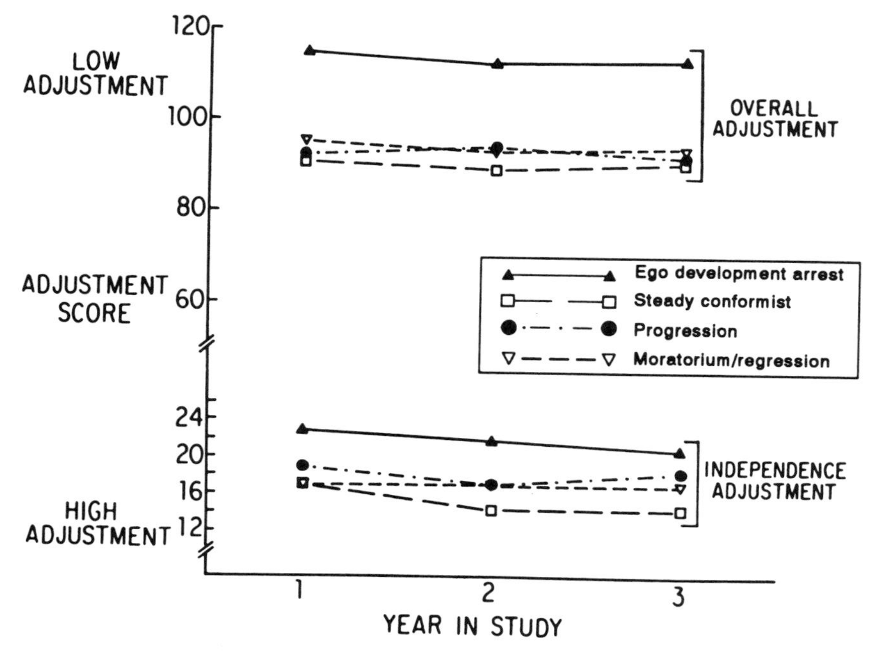

FIG. 9.4. Ego development trajectories and diabetes adjustment.

My main problem is I can't control my temper.
What gets me into trouble is I scream a lot.
If I can't get what I want I scream.
I just can't stand people who cry.
When people are helpless I never get involved.
I feel sorry for the dead cat.
Rules are made to be broken.
Education is boring.

Although Jim does not express low self-esteem and difficulties in personal relationships, his conflicts over controlling his impulses ("I scream"), his visions of difficulty ("dead cats"), and his clear lack of any interest in altruism or feelings toward others (not being able to stand people who cry, not getting involved with people who are helpless) stand out. These observations of two adolescents suggest that it is unlikely that we will discover a single, fine-grained portrait characterizing diabetic adolescents who are arrested in their ego development. On the other hand, several features of these patients are clearly visible: low self-esteem, interpersonal conflicts, and impaired impulse control. Perhaps most important is the fact that their way of understanding themselves and their surroundings places them at a disadvantage with respect to adjusting to their diabetes.

DISCUSSION

Diabetes and Development

These findings do not lead to the conclusion that adolescents with diabetes, or a subgroup of them, are in some way "pathological" or severely disturbed. No age norms have been established for ego development, and we doubt that the initial ego development differences we report represent severe deviations in developmental status. Numerous studies compare diabetic adolescents with non-diabetics (Hauser & Pollets, 1981; Jacobson et al., 1986; Johnson, 1980). Few indications of striking psychopathology are reported across the varied studies. What the current findings emphasize is that near the time of diagnosis and 1 year later, preadolescent and adolescent patients with diabetes express lower levels of ego development than comparable youngsters who have had a recent acute illness. This is not an isolated finding. In fact, a similar observation has been reported in several different analyses (Hauser, Jacobson, Noam, & Powers, 1983; Hauser et al., 1979; Jacobson et al., 1982).

Several approaches can be taken in interpreting these results. First, it is possible that social class, intelligence, parental ego development, or other family demographic factors are determinants of these results. (Could we have inadvertently sampled an unusual group of diabetic adolescents – ones who are younger, lower in intelligence, or from less privileged backgrounds?) Do these differences lead to lower levels of development? Being sensitive to this possibility of confounding, each of these factors is controlled in our analyses. Where possible, these differences are experimentally controlled, using samples with the same age and similar sex distribution. With respect to intelligence level, verbal and performance IQ is statistically controlled in all analyses. In terms of social class, the diabetic adolescents are from slightly lower middle-class backgrounds and are somewhat overrepresented with respect to working and lower class strata. Consequently, we also control for class differences.

Finally, one can raise the possibility that the ego development of the parents of the diabetic adolescents is lower. These patients might then be in an environment where there is lower ego development within their families, and they either resemble their parents generally or are especially vulnerable during times of stress (onset of diabetes), with lower levels of development as a consequence of this vulnerability. We measured the ego development levels of all parents and found no differences between the two groups. Given all of this evidence, we believe it is improbable that the finding of lower ego development levels and a greater proportion of arrests among the diabetic adolescents can be dismissed as a consequence of sampling bias. Further strengthening the case against these results reflecting sociodemographic confounds are our other analyses revealing no differences between the diabetic and acute illness samples in terms of birth order or family size. We are, therefore, left with an important and recurrent finding that requires explanation.

A second interpretation is that the diabetes itself leads to neuropsychological deficits that include cognitive and perceptual impairments. Such findings have been reported by Ryan and associates (Ryan, Vega, & Drash, 1985) for diabetic adolescents who developed diabetes prior to age 5, especially if they had experienced severe hypoglycemia. This explanation might be applicable to our previous findings, where we studied adolescents who had diabetes of varying duration. Even there, however, we did not find that duration significantly influenced ego development level. In this newest study we find the lower ego development level present from the very beginning of diabetes. It is unlikely that a sufficient number of serious hypoglycemic episodes could have occurred within this brief time span.

A third interpretation leads us to the impact of this new chronic illness upon the functioning of the child. It is highly improbable that before onset all of the diabetic children were functioning at lower ego development levels than their acutely ill counterparts. Hence, the more likely possibility is that the diabetic patients are experiencing a regression in their ego development. A new set of strikingly antiadolescent demands have been imposed on these adolescents: complex dietary prohibitions and recommendations, exercise prescriptions, self or parental bodily intrusions (injections), and heightened attentiveness to bodily fluids (urine, blood). These demands run directly counter to new adolescent yearnings for autonomy and closer peer relationships (Powers, Hauser, & Kilner, 1989). Moreover, these adolescents are presented with the dangers of insulin reactions, diabetic acidosis, and possible long-term complications. Most immediately disturbing for these young patients may be the daily insulin injections that they (or their parents) must now administer.

The introduction and accumulation of so many stressors could be expected to lead to new preoccupations and conflicts, rather than to new psychological explorations and expansiveness about inner experiences, perceptions, and relationships. There may be even less energy available for such interests. In a recent paper, Vaillant and McCullough (1987) suggest that the strongest correlates of ego development in adults may have to do with intuitiveness, psychological mindedness, and creativity. Rather than diminished ego development being a clear sign of psychopathology, they argue that those functioning at higher levels of ego development have impressive strengths. Perhaps such strengths become luxuries in the face of the onslaught of a serious and pervasive chronic illness. Although we cannot confirm it at this point, this explanation certainly is appealing, in light of our other evidence that there is no obvious psychopathology or marked behavioral impairment for the children and adolescents with diabetes.

It may be that we are witnessing an initial turning away from the very considerations that mark progressive ego development, because of new preoccupations and distractions or because of an even more deliberate strategy to subtly withdraw and thereby protect a more vulnerable self. The current data cannot clarify the basis of this hypothetical withdrawal, metaphorically a turtle pulling into its shell. However, whatever the cause, it is clear that this phenomenon represents a restriction in the expression of overall potential development in adolescence; a constriction that loosens but does not vanish in later years.

Yet another explanation, not inconsistent with the preceding one, deals with the impact a new chronic illness has upon the functioning of the family. Most likely there are major shifts in intrafamilial processes, possibly in the family's way of dealing with the world and the family's way of interacting with the index patient. For instance, in an analysis of families drawn from the first year of this project (Hauser et al., 1986), we found significantly higher levels of enabling processes, such as explaining, active understanding, and accepting on the part of diabetic families, when compared with families of the acute illness patients. It is possible that what appears to be stronger enabling and accepting on the part of the family might actually reflect overprotectiveness and consequent restrictions of autonomy, as the family is trying so hard to be helpful and cooperative with one another and especially toward the new patient. Such shifts in familial processes might then undermine those more autonomous strivings towards differentiation that are so important in adolescence, and especially characteristic of the higher stages of ego development. Unwittingly, the family may be obstructing the long-term development of their son or daughter through being so responsive to perceived special short-term needs of their chronically ill adolescent.

We are in an excellent position to pursue these interpretations about family processes because our annual observations include measures of global variables, such as family atmosphere (Hauser et al., 1985; Moos, 1974), and more discrete variables, such as ways of family coping (Hauser et al., 1988) and family interaction patterns (Hauser et al., 1986). Indeed, analyses currently underway investigate these issues: How do the families of the diabetic patients differ from the nondiabetic ones at different phases of the illness? How do these differences affect the overall functioning and developmental trajectories of the diabetic children and adolescents?

Ego Development and Adjustment to Diabetes

Returning to the results showing dramatically different levels of adjustment for diabetic children who are at lower levels of ego development at the time of diagnosis, there is less to puzzle over and more to take seriously with respect to applying these findings. The findings indicate that children and adolescents functioning at the earliest stages of ego development may be important targets for early interventions. Also explanations offered to these patients, and treatment plans, must be tailored and carried out much differently than for those patients functioning at higher levels. Intuitively, most clinicians know this. The best health care providers shape their explanations, suggestions, and demands to the functioning and psychology of each individual patient. But, too often, health care providers lapse into more mechanical ways, minimizing or neglecting such individual differences.

The findings suggest that it is at everyone's peril—the health care provider, the patient, and the family—when health providers (or parents) deal with diabetes management in automatic ways, such as warning all teen age patients about later complications of renal disease or blindness. The diabetic adolescent whose development is transiently arrested (early ego stages at diagnosis) or is more tenaciously arrested (early arrest trajectory) feels at the mercy of his or her feelings or is involved in troubling peer relationships. For him or her, such warnings are meaningless at best or annoyingly irrelevant. The dire results being predicted by the health care provider are a long way off, and not at all consistent with his or her immediate concerns. Moreover, these threats or warnings are abstract ones, and do not meet the needs of the day.

We do not know how to change the individual's level of ego development. However, we can use our knowledge of his or her level of ego development to tailor how we respond to, instruct, or even at times do therapy with particular individuals. This is perhaps the strongest message that these results have to deliver: The importance of taking seriously the diabetic patient's current level of ego development in order to determine level of risk for problems in adjusting. Knowing this information about the individual's development may then guide personal interactions and medical interventions at each office visit and over the long run.

REFERENCES

Browning, D. L. (1986). Psychiatric ward behavior and length of stay in adolescent and young adult patients: A developmental approach to prediction. *Journal of Consulting and Clinical Psychology, 54*, 227–230.

Erikson, E. (1959). *Children and society*. New York: Norton.

Frank, S. J., & Quinlin, D. M. (1976). Ego development and female delinquency: A cognitive developmental approach. *Journal of Abnormal Psychology, 85*, 505–510.

Hauser, S. T. (1976). Loevinger's model and measure of ego development: A critical review. *Psychological Bulletin, 83*, 928–955.

Hauser, S. T., Jacobson, A. M., Lavori, P., Wolfsdorf, J. I., Herskowitz, R. D., Milley, J. E., Bliss, R., Wertlieb, D., & Stein, J. (1990). Adherence among children and adolescents with insulin-dependent diabetes over a four year longitudinal follow-up: II. Immediate and long-term linkages with the family milieu. *Journal of Pediatric Psychology, 15*, 527–542.

Hauser, S. T., with Powers, S. I., & Noam, G. G. (1991). *Adolescents and Their Families: Paths of Ego Development*. New York: The Free Press.

Hauser, S. T., Jacobson, A. M., Noam, G. G., & Powers, S. I. (1983). Ego development and self-image processes in early adolescence: Longitudinal studies of diabetic and psychiatric patients. *Archives of General Psychiatry, 40*, 325–332.

Hauser, S. T., Jacobson, A. M., Wertlieb, D., Brink, S., & Wentworth, S. (1985). The contribution of family environment to perceived competence and illness adjustment in diabetic and acutely ill adolescents. *Family Relations, 34*, 99–108.

Hauser, S., Jacobson, A. M., Wertlieb, D., Weiss-Perry, B., Follansbee, D., Wolfsdorf, J., Herskowitz, R., Houlihan, J., & Rajapark, D. (1986). Children with recently diagnosed diabetes: Interactions within their families. *Health Psychology, 5*, 273–296.

Hauser, S. T., Jacobson, A. M., Wertlieb, D., Wolfsdorf, J., Herskowitz, R., Vieyra, M., & Orleans, J. (1989). Family contexts of self-esteem and illness adjustment in diabetic and acutely ill children. In C. Ramsey (Ed.), *Family Systems in Medicine* (pp. 469–484). New York: Guilford.

Hauser, S. T., Paul, E., Jacobson, A. M., Weiss-Perry, B., Vieyra, M., Rufo, P., Spetter, D., DiPlacido, J., Wolfsdorf, J., & Herskowitz, R. (1988). How families cope with diabetes in adolescence: An approach and case analyses. *Pediatrician, 15*, 80–94.

Hauser, S. T., & Pollets, D. (1981). Psychosocial aspects of diabetes: A critical review. *Diabetes Care, 2*, 227–232.

Hauser, S. T., Pollets, D., Turner, B., Jacobson, A. M., Powers, S., & Noam, G. (1979). Ego development and self-esteem in diabetic youth. *Diabetes Care, 2*, 465–471.

Hauser, S. T., Powers, S., Jacobson, A. M., Schwartz, J., & Noam, G. (1982). Family interactions and ego development in diabetic adolescents. In Z. Laron & A. Galatzer (Eds.), *Psychosocial aspects of diabetes in children and adolescents* (pp. 69–76). Basel: S. Karger.

Hauser, S. T., Powers, S. I., Noam, G. G., & Bowlds, M. (1987). Family interiors of adolescent ego development trajectories. *Family Perspective, 21*, 263–284.

Hauser, S. T., Powers, S. I., Noam, G. G., Jacobson, A. M., Weiss, B., & Follansbee, D. (1984). Family contexts of adolescent ego development. *Child Development, 55*, 195–213.

Hollingshead, A. B. (1957). Social class index of Social Position (Mimeograph). New Haven, CT: Yale University.

Jacobson, A. M., Hauser, S. T., Lavori, P., Wolfsdorf, J. I., Herskowitz, R. D., Milley, J. E., Bliss, R., Gelfand, E., Wertlieb, D., & Stein, J. (1990). Adherence among children and adolescents with insulin-dependent diabetes: I. The influence of patient coping and adjustment. *Journal of Pediatric Psychology, 15*, 511–526.

Jacobson, A. M., Hauser, S., Powers, S., & Noam, G. (1982). Ego development in diabetics: A longitudinal study. In Z. Laron & A. Galatzer (Eds.), *Psychosocial aspects of diabetes in children and adolescents* (pp. 1–8). Basel: S. Karger.

Jacobson, A. M., Hauser, S., Powers, S., & Noam, G. (1985). The influences of chronic illness and ego development on self-esteem in diabetic and psychiatric adolescent patients. *Journal of Youth and Adolescence, 13*, 489–507.

Jacobson, A. M., Hauser, S. T., Wertlieb, D., Wolfsdorf, J., Orleans, J., & Vieyra, M. (1986). Psychological adjustment of children with recently diagnosed diabetes mellitus. *Diabetes Care, 9*, 323–329.

Johnson, S. B. (1980). Psychosocial factors in juvenile diabetes: A review. *Journal of Behavioral Medicine, 3*, 95–116.

Kirshner, L. A. (1988). Implications of Loevinger's theory of ego development for time-limited psychotherapy. *Psychotherapy, 25*, 220–227.

Little, R. A., & Rubin, D. B. (1987). *Statistical analysis with missing data*. New York: Wiley.

Loevinger, J. (1979). Construct validity of the ego development test. *Applied Psychological Measurement, 3*, 281–311.

Loevinger, J., & Wessler, R. (1971). *Measuring ego development* (Vol. I). San Francisco, CA: Jossey-Bass.

Moos, R. (1974). *Family environment scale*. Palo Alto, CA: Consulting Psychologists Press.

Noam, G., Hauser, S. T., Santostefano, S., Garrison, W., Jacobson, A. M., Powers, S., & Mead, M. (1984). Ego development and psychopathology: A study of hospitalized adolescents. *Child Development, 55*, 184–194.

Powers, S. I., Hauser, S. T., & Kilner, L. (1989). Adolescent mental health. *American Psychologist, 44*, 200–208.

Rosenberg, M. (1965). *Society and the adolescent self-image*. Princeton: Princeton University Press.

Rosnafsky, J. (1981). The relationship of ego development to q-sort personality ratings. *Journal of Personality and Social Psychology, 41*, 99–120.

Ryan, C., Vega, A., & Drash, A. (1985). Cognitive deficits in adolescents who developed diabetes early in life. *Pediatrics, 75*, 921–927.

Schwab, J. J., & Bradnan, W. A. (1979). Life phases in health and illness. In C. P. Patterson (Ed.), *The psychiatric clinics of North America, 2*, 277–288.

Sullivan, B. J. (1979a). Adjustment in diabetic adolescent girls: Development of the diabetic adjustment scale. *Psychosomatic Medicine, 41*, 119–126.

Sullivan, B. J. (1979b). Adjustment in diabetic adolescent girls: Adjustment, self-esteem, and depression. *Psychosomatic Medicine, 41*, 127–138.

Vaillant, G. E., & McCullough, L. (1987). The Washington University Sentence Completion Test compared with other measures of adult ego development. *American Journal of Psychiatry, 144*, 1,189–1,194.

Wertlieb, D., Hauser, S. T., & Jacobson, A. (1985). Adaptation to diabetes: Behavior symptoms and family context. *Pediatric Psychology, 11*, 463–479.

New Perspectives on Health and Development

10

Wellness, Illness, Health, and Disease Concepts

Arthur H. Parmelee, Jr.
University of California
Los Angeles

The theme of this volume is not limited to the impact of specific types of illness on social, emotional, and cognitive development in children or adolescence nor to social, emotional, and cognitive stresses as causes of illness. The scope is broadened to include multiple life-span developmental processes from infancy to adulthood and how children's and adults' concepts of wellness, illness, health, and disease are incorporated into these (chapter 1 in this volume: Gochman). Encompassed as an integral part of children's social, emotional, and cognitive developmental processes is the interaction of all social relationships and life events, including the physical perturbations, transient or prolonged, that infants, children, and adolescents and their parents encounter during their life span. In this context, even minor illnesses and injuries such as colds and bruises or cuts that occur from infancy through adolescence play a role in expanding or contracting, however briefly, individual and community relationships at emotional, cognitive, and social levels. These constantly recurring common events usually do not involve the traditional medical system or do so only briefly. By the time a child or adolescent has a severe enough illness or physical problem to significantly involve a physician and other segments of the medical system, he or she already has formulated concepts of self and others that include the numerous experiences with physical problems and illnesses that have been cared for within the family or other child care services. Also included are all the family and community cultural concepts of individual and mutual support systems and responsibilities, as well as appropriate illness and sick role behavior and beliefs about causes of illnesses and their treatments (Bruhn, 1988; Gochman, 1985, 1988; Lerner & Busch-Rossnagel, 1981; Parmelee, 1986, 1989; Turk & Kerns, 1985).

An appropriate extension of current developmental and sociological studies of illness and wellness behavior should be further exploration of the extent of integration of illness, wellness, health, and disease into the general processes of the social development of individuals. Because illnesses are part of the daily life and personal-social development from infancy through the life span, they become a part of each individual's general social competence. Physicians have, however, difficulty in determining when and how biological concepts are included in social concepts. Often the biological explanations of the nature of illnesses and their treatments are not congruent with adults' or children's ability to comprehend biological concepts or with the family and community conceptualizations of illnesses and appropriate illness behavior. Biology of the human body is not easily understood at any age even by experts in the field. In fact, it is likely that most adults do not have clear understandings of the more specific functions of the various organ systems, such as the liver, spleen, pancreas, thyroid, blood cells, and immune system, etc., and their malfunctions. Studies of children's understanding of the biology of growth, body organ functions, reproduction, death, and disease indicate that reasonably sophisticated concepts develop late in childhood (Carey, 1985; Gellert, 1962). Development of these concepts may be after children have rather sophisticated concepts of self, other, and social relationships and have incorporated into these, as personal-social events, their numerous experiences with minor illnesses and injuries and some serious illnesses requiring medical care (Emde, 1989; Maccoby, 1980; Parmelee, 1986, 1989; Sroufe, 1989; Sroufe & Fleeson, 1986; Stern, 1985, 1989; Turiel, 1983).

DEVELOPMENT OF CONCEPTS OF HEALTH, ILLNESS, AND DISEASE

A major problem in studying how children develop concepts of health and disease or wellness and illness is the different meanings children and adults give to these words, as well as how investigators define them in their research. For example, the World Health Organization's definition of health states that "health is a state of complete physical, mental, and social well-being and not merely the absence of disease or infirmity" (World Health Organization, 1958). This is undoubtedly a useful definition for establishing world health policies and for related discussions. It is difficult to disagree with this general definition, but it is equally difficult to use it in thinking about the complex behavioral developmental issues we have been discussing.

There are a number of studies of the development of children's concepts of health, illness, and disease. These have generally been done within a traditional Piagetian construct. In this model the development of children's reasoning about all domains of life experience are expected to parallel each other in sophistication at each stage. Thus, the development of children's reasoning concerning health or illness and diseases should parallel their reasoning concerning the physical world. The findings of these studies confirm a shift in reasoning about illnesses from preoperational in preschool children to concrete operational in early childhood and formal operational at later ages that parallels their reasoning about the physical world. Within this model, children take a centered point of view that is more personal-social early in life and demonstrate more abstract biological reasoning later in childhood and adolescence. However, in these studies there is evidence that some personal-social interpretations persist into adolescence and that the biological constructs are not as advanced as those of the physical world (Bibace & Walsh, 1980, 1981; Brewster, 1982; Carandang, Folkins, Hines, & Steward, 1979; Perrin & Gerrity, 1981; Redpath & Rogers, 1984; Simeonsson, Buckley, & Monson, 1979; Susman, Dorn, & Fletcher, 1987).

In addition, some observations do not fit easily into this general construct. For example, siblings of children with chronic illnesses have a construct of illnesses in general that is not as advanced as their concepts of the physical world in contrast to those of children with healthy siblings (Carandang et al., 1979). One can account for these findings by considering the possibility that the chronically ill children and the siblings of chronically ill children are incorporating their illness concepts into personal-social concepts at different rates than the siblings of children without chronic disease. The mixing of personal-social and biological constructs of health, illness, and disease together in these studies may obscure this. It is possible that personal-social constructs of health, illness, and disease develop independently of biological constructs, have a different rate and trajectory of development, and that personal and family experiences with illness influence this trajectory more than the development of biological concepts (Campbell, 1975, 1978; Carey, 1985; Gelman & Spelke, 1981; Hoffman, 1981; Jacobson et al., 1987; Millstein, Adler, & Irwin, 1981; Millstein & Irwin, 1987).

ILLNESS AND WELLNESS

As a clinician dealing with children and adults I find it helpful to separate the concepts that individuals have of themselves in their personal-social relationships, bodily feelings, and their ability to function socially from society's normative concepts of how people in general should feel and function biologically. For this, it is useful to use the terms wellness and illness to define individuals' concepts of themselves and their personal-social interaction when well or ill. The terms health and disease then are considered normative categories that extend across individuals. Health, even with this limitation, remains a difficult term because it is a mixture of social and biological issues. Disease, on the other hand, is acceptable as a concept that concerns categorizations across individuals of biological or psychological abnormalities. For example, the disease categories measles, diabetes, or schizophrenia have similar signs and symptoms across individuals, a fact that has, of course, advanced the biological understanding and treatment of disease entities greatly (Bruhn & Cordova, 1977; Caplan, Engelhardt, & McCartney, 1981; Eisenberg, 1977; Engelhardt, 1981; Fabrega, 1974; Wilkinson, 1988).

Assuming that the domain of personal-social development that includes concepts of social relationships, self, other, empathy, and prosocial behavior develops significantly differently from the domains of biological and physical concepts (Carey, 1985; Damon & Hart, 1982; Emde, 1989; Gelman & Spelke, 1981; Hoffman, 1975, 1981; Kagan, 1981; Radke-Yarrow, Zahn-Waxler, & Chapman, 1983; Sroufe, 1989; Sroufe & Fleeson, 1986; Stern, 1985; Wilkinson, 1988; Zahn-Waxler, Radke-Yarrow, & King, 1979), then it is important to consider children's development of the concept of wellness and illness separately from those of health and disease, as defined (Parmelee, 1986, 1989). As previously stated, illness is a personal-social experience of change in mood, lowering of energy level, and the inability to carry on usual daily activities, and wellness is primarily the absence of these ill feelings. With the term disease applying only to biological diseases and the term health primarily to the absence of biological disease, one can more easily separate personal-social experiences and biological problems. One can also more readily understand how it is possible to have a biological disease, such as diabetes, and fell well or feel ill in the absence of a biological disease as during separations ("home sickness").

Throughout our lives, both as children and adults, we are primarily concerned with illness and wellness. We decide we are not well but ill when we have a change in our mood states, have lowered energy levels and have difficulty carrying out our daily activities, whether it is play, attending school, or working. Illnesses concern us because they interfere with our usual social activities. We may or may not try to determine whether or not our ill feelings are biologically caused. When we seek medical advice and a biological cause of our ill feelings, and a disease is diagnosed and the appropriate treatment is determined, we still remain predominantly concerned with the personal-social effect of our ill feelings. Whatever disease is diagnosed, worries emerge about our jobs, how our family activities will be managed, and who will take care of our children. Children even more than adults are oriented toward the personal-social impact of the feelings of illness and are more concerned about who will take care of them than the biology of any disease they may have (Apple, 1960; Brodie, 1974; Campbell, 1975; Millstein & Irwin, 1987; Natapoff, 1978; Rashkis, 1965).

FOSTERING HEALTH THROUGH PERSONAL-SOCIAL SUPPORT SYSTEMS

In this volume the impact of the development of cognition and the ego, including the development of autonomy and individuality as expressed by risk taking, is prominent in the discussions of the management of nutrition, diabetes, drug abuse, other health problems, and teen-age pregnancy. The development of social cognition and competence clearly plays an important part in how children, adolescents, and adults strive for health and respond to illness and disease (chapters in this volume by Lozoff; Hauser; Ingersoll, Orr, Vance, & Golden; Irwin & Millstein; & Ingersoll, Orr, Harrold, & Golden, 1986; Irwin & Millstein, 1986; Jacobson et al., 1987). A number of studies indicate that children's understanding of and attitudes toward illness are more a function of family practices leading to general social competence than the family's specific health beliefs or habits (Campbell, 1975, 1978; Mechanic, 1964, 1979, 1980; Pratt, 1973).

The importance of the personal-social nature of illness and wellness rather than the normative concept of health is further emphasized by the observation that many societies, including our own, commonly use a social transgression causal model for illness (Gardner, 1969; Kister & Patterson, 1980; Parsons, 1958; Whiting, 1963; Whiting & Whiting, 1975; Wilkinson, 1988). This aspect of understanding of health, illness, and disease has not been discussed, so I comment on it briefly. Views of moral transgressions in relation to illness range from religious rules to community prudential rules (Emde, Johnson, & Easterbrooks, 1987; Nucci, 1981; Turiel, 1983; Tisak & Turiel, 1984). Although children commonly explain their illnesses by a transgression model, this is often a simple and logical explanation not necessarily accompanied by feelings of imminent justice or guilt and shame. Although we recognize this transgression explanation of illnesses in children, we are slower to acknowledge that as adults we also commonly use a transgression causal model. Nevertheless, we are likely to explain ill feelings on the basis of eating or drinking too much or exercising too little and attribute venereal disease to promiscuity first and only secondarily consider the type of infecting organism. How readily we organize community action programs for certain illnesses or health problems such as sexual abuse and incest, drug abuse, AIDS, and abortions is also, in part, a function of the level of moral transgression society sees as the cause of the individual's problems.

Assuming primarily a personal-social and social competence orientation toward illness and wellness, any support system that helps maintain some continuity in daily activities should help us cope with illness and strive for wellness. For children in particular, continuity of their daily life activity, such as contact with family or friends and play or school activities, even at the most minimal level, is important and helpful. Families generally reorganize when children are ill to provide this personal-social continuity of life and, therefore, of personal identity and self. It should be equally important for child care centers to plan for such family style adaptation to the ill children because the center constitutes their surrogate home. For sick children in child care, it is therefore helpful when they can be with the same teacher and classmates while ill and be able to at least observe the usual center activities when they feel too ill to participate in them. They might also be allowed to participate as much as they feel they can, just as they join family activities at home as soon as some energy returns. To send children with minor illnesses away from their child care center to some new and strange place and person interrupts the continuity in the children's daily lives at a time when they are emotionally vulnerable and are in the greatest need of some semblance of continuity of self and known support systems. The same issues arise when children are hospitalized. In hospitals, in order to encourage children's positive incorporation of illness concepts and coping skills into their personal-social development, we need to deal with their personal-social concerns. We can do this by encouraging their families' participation in their children's care, providing some of their usual play activities including toys from home and contact with school friends, even if only through video tape, and some easy school tasks for older children when they are ready (Brill, Fauvre, Klein, Clark, & Garcia, 1987; Oremland & Oremland, 1973; Plank, 1971).

Biological explanations of disease and how to stay free of disease are essential but are not very salient to adolescents and adults unless placed in the context of the personal-social aspects of illness and wellness. For younger children biological explanations, even when placed within the personal-social context, have limited meaning. Incorporating illness care into regular family empathic child-rearing practices is therefore probably the most constructive way to further their future illness and wellness activities. Children learn from their families what an appropriate "sick role" is and when it is important to reduce one's activities, lose some autonomy, and let others care for one in order to get well (Campbell, 1975, 1978). Within the family they also learn to recognize when others are ill and need to assume the "sick role" and be given empathy and care so that they can get well. An understanding of the fact that others, like ourselves, have periods of illness from a variety of causes when they cannot care for themselves or carry on their usual activities and need the caregiving support of those who are well is important for society as a whole. It is part of the general personal-social development of empathy and prosocial behavior (Whiting, 1963; Whiting & Whiting, 1975; Parmelee, 1986, 1989). A greater understanding of these processes could impact the nature and extent of social and health programs. In addition, education for children should be concerned with helping them maintain wellness and may be most effective when it addresses the personal-social aspects of development. Adults may also be more readily encouraged to accept appropriate care when ill, if important personal-social issues such as job security, sick leave, child care, and homemaker services are sufficiently available to ensure that they can count on some continuity in their and their families' lives during illnesses.

SUMMARY

In summary, a conceptualization of illness and wellness behavior is presented that is based more on the development of each individual's general social competence than the sociological models of health beliefs and perceived vulnerability, yet is complementary to these models. It also deviates from the usual Piagetian model of the development of general cognition as it relates to understanding illness and health and the biology of diseases in that development of reasoning in the social domain that includes illness and wellness has a different rate and trajectory than development of reasoning in domains of biology and the physical world. This conceptualization is more compatible with the experiences of pediatricians who observe from birth through adolescence the development of individual children during well baby and child care and during acute and sometimes chronic illnesses. For these children and their families, all of the physical perturbations ranging from infant feeding difficulties, brief vomiting and diarrhea episodes, minor respiratory illnesses, and the like to the commonly occurring major acute illnesses are lumped together with the many other ongoing life events that are the matrix of children's personal-social development and understanding of social relationships. Illness and wellness behavior are, therefore, from the beginning of life integrated into personal-social development and the development of general social competence (Maccoby, 1981; Parmelee, 1989; Sameroff & Emde, 1989; Wynne, 1984). Consequently, it is important to consider any program that promotes the development of general social competence in children as relevant to appropriate illness and wellness behavior, the prevention of disease, and the promotion of health.

REFERENCES

Apple, D. (1960). How laymen define illness. *Journal of Health and Human Behavior, 1*, 219–225.

Bibace, R., & Walsh, M. E. (Eds.). (1980). Development of children's concepts of illness. *Pediatrics, 66*, 912–917.

Bibace, R., & Walsh, M. E. (Eds.). (1981). *Children's conceptions of health, illness, and bodily functions. New directions for child development* (No. 14). San Francisco: Jossey-Bass.

Brewster, A. B. (1982). Chronically ill hospitalized children's concepts of their illness. *Pediatrics, 69*, 355–362.

Brill, N. S., Fauvre, M., Klein, N., Clark, S., & Garcia, L. (1987). Caring for chronically ill children: An innovative approach to children's health care. *Chronic Illness, 16*, 105–113.

Brodie, B. (1974). Views of healthy children toward illness. *American Journal of Public Health, 64*, 1,156–1,159.

Bruhn, J. G. (1988). Lifestyle and health behavior. In D. S. Gochman (Ed.), *Health behavior: Emerging research perspectives* (pp. 71–86). New York: Plenum.

Bruhn, J. G., & Cordova, F. D. (1977). A developmental approach to learning wellness behavior. Part I. Infancy to early adolescence. *Health Values, 1*, 246–254.

Campbell, J. D. (1975). Illness is a point of view: The development of children's concepts of illness. *Child Development, 46*, 92–100.

Campbell, J. D. (1978). The child in the sick role: Contributions of age, sex, parental status, and parental values. *Journal of Health and Social Behavior, 19*, 35–51.

Caplan, A. L., Englehardt, H. T., Jr., & McCartney, J. J. (Eds.). (1981). *Concepts of health and disease: Interdisciplinary perspectives*. London: Addison Wesley.

Carandang, M. L. A., Folkins, C. H., Hines, P. S., & Steward, M. S. (1979). The role of cognitive level and sibling illness in children's conceptualizations of illness. *American Journal of Orthopsychiatry, 49*, 474–481.

Carey, S. (1985). *Conceptual change in childhood*. Cambridge, MA: MIT Press.

Constitution of the World Health Organization (Preamble). (1958). *The first ten years of the World Health Organization*. Geneva: WHO.

Damon, W., & Hart, D. (1982). The development of self-understanding from infancy through adolescence. *Child Development, 53*, 841–864.

Eisenberg, L. (1977). Disease and illness. *Culture, Medicine and Psychiatry, 1*, 9–23.

Emde, R. N., Johnson, W. F., & Easterbrooks, M. A. (1987). The do's and don't's of early moral development: Psychoanalytic tradition and current research. In J. Kagan & S. Lamb (Eds.), *The emergence of morality in young children* (pp. 245–276). Chicago: University of Chicago Press.

Emde, R. N. (1989). The infant's relationship experience: Developmental and affective aspects. In A. J. Sameroff & R. N. Emde (Eds.), *Relationship disturbances in early childhood: A developmental approach* (pp. 33–51). New York: Basic Books.

Engelhardt, H. T., Jr. (1981). The concepts of health and disease. In A. L. Caplan, H. T. Engelhardt, Jr., & J. J. McCartney (Eds.), *Concepts of health and disease: Interdisciplinary perspectives* (pp. 31–45). London: Addison-Wesley.

Fabrega, H., Jr. (1974). *Disease and social behavior: An interdisciplinary perspective*. Cambridge, MA: MIT Press.

Gardner, Richard A. (1969). The guilt reaction of parents of children with severe physical disease. *American Journal of Psychiatry, 126*, 636–644.

Gellert, E. (1962). Children's conceptions of the content and functions of the human body. *Genetic Psychology Monographs, 65*, 293–405.

Gelman, R., & Spelke, E. (1981). The development of thoughts about animate and inanimate objects: Implications for research on social cognition. In J. H. Flavell & L. Ross (Eds.), *Social cognitive development: Frontiers and possible futures* (pp. 43–66). New York: Cambridge University Press.

Gochman, D. S. (1985). Family determinants of children's concepts of health and illness. In D. C. Turk & R. D. Kerns (Eds.), *Health, illness and families: A life-span perspective* (pp. 23–50). New York: Wiley.

Gochman, D. S. (1988). Health behavior: Plural perspectives. In D. S. Gochman (Ed.), *Health behavior: Emerging research perspectives* (pp. 3–17). New York: Plenum.

Hoffman, M. L. (1975). Developmental synthesis of affect and cognition and its implications for altruistic motivation. *Developmental Psychology, 5*, 607–622.

Hoffman, M. L. (1981). Perspectives on the difference between understanding people and understanding things: The role of affect. In J. H. Flavell & L. Ross (Eds.), *Social cognitive development: Frontiers and possible futures* (pp. 67–81). New York: Cambridge University Press.

Ingersoll, G. M., Orr, D. P., Harrold, A. J., & Golden, M. P. (1986). Cognitive maturity and self-management among adolescents with insulin-dependent diabetes mellitus. *Journal of Pediatrics, 108*, 620–623.

Irwin, C. E., Jr., & Millstein, S. G. (1986). Biopsychosocial correlates of risk-taking behaviors during adolescence. *Journal of Adolescent Health Care, 7*, 82–96.

Jacobson, A. M., Hauser, S. T., Wolfsdorf, J. I., Houlihan, J., Milley, J. E., Herskowitz, R. D., Wertlieb, D., & Watt, E. (1987). Psychologic predictors of compliance in children with recent onset of diabetes mellitus. *Journal of Pediatrics, 110*, 805–811.

Kagan, J. (1981). *The second year: The emergence of self-awareness*. Cambridge, MA: Harvard University Press.

Kister, M. C., & Patterson, C. J. (1980). Children's conception of causes of illness: Understanding of contagion and use of immanent justice. *Child Development, 61*, 839–846.

Lerner, R. M., & Busch-Rossnagel, N. A. (1981). Individuals as producers of their development: Conceptual and empirical bases. In R. M. Lerner & N. A. Busch-Rossnagel (Eds.), *Individuals as producers of their development: A life-span perspective* (pp. 1–36). New York: Academic Press.

Maccoby, E. E. (1980). *Social development: Psychological growth and the parent-child relationship*. San Diego: Harcourt Brace Jovanovich.

Mechanic, D. (1964). The influence of mothers on their children's health attitudes and behaviors. *Pediatrics, 33*, 444–453.

Mechanic, D. (1979). The stability of health and illness behavior: Results from a 16-year follow-up. *American Journal of Public Health, 69*, 1,142–1,145.

Mechanic, D. (1980). Education, parental interest, and health perceptions and behavior. *Inquiry, 17*, 331–338.

Millstein, S. G., Adler, N. E., & Irwin, C. E., Jr. (1981). Conceptions of illness in young adolescents. *Pediatrics, 68*, 834–839.

Millstein, S. G., & Irwin, C. E., Jr. (1987). Concepts of health and illness: Different constructs or variations on a theme? *Health Psychology, 6*, 515–524.

Natapoff, J. N. (1978). Children's views of health: A developmental study. *American Journal of Public Health, 68*, 995–1,000.

Nucci, L. (1981). Conceptions of personal issues: A domain distinct from moral or societal concepts. *Child Development, 52*, 114–121.

Oremland, E. K., & Oremland, J. D. (Eds.). (1973). *The effects of hospitalization on children*. Springfield, IL: Thomas.

Parmelee, A. H., Jr. (1986). Children's illnesses: Their beneficial effects on behavioral development. *Child Development, 57*, 1–10.

Parmelee, A. H., Jr. (1989). The child's physical health and the development of relationships. In A. J. Sameroff and R. N. Emde (Eds.), *Relationships disturbances in early childhood: A developmental approach* (pp. 145–162). New York: Basic Books.

Parsons, T. (1958). Definitions of health and illness in the light of American values and social structure. In E. G. Jaco (Ed.), *Patients, physicians and illness: Sourcebook in behavioral science and medicine* (pp. 165–187). New York: The Free Press.

Perrin, E. C., & Gerrity, P. S. (1981). There's a demon in your belly: Children's understanding of illness. *Pediatrics, 67*, 841–849.

Plank, E. (1971). *Working with children in hospitals*. Cleveland: Case Western Reserve University Press.

Pratt, L. (1973). Child rearing methods and children's health behavior. *Journal of Health and Social Behavior, 14*, 61–69.

Radke-Yarrow, M., Zahn-Waxler, C., & Chapman, M. (1983). Children's prosocial dispositions and behavior. In P. H. Mussen (Series Ed.) & E. M. Hetherington (Vol. Ed.), *Handbook of child psychology: Vol. 4. Socialization, personality, and social development* (4th ed., pp. 469–545). New York: Wiley.

Rashkis, S. R. (1965). Child's understanding of health. *Archives of General Psychiatry, 12*, 10–17.

Redpath, C. C., & Rogers, C. S. (1984). Healthy young children's concepts of hospitals, medical personnel, operations, and illness. *Journal of Pediatric Psychology, 9*, 29–40.

Sameroff, A. J., & Emde, R. N. (1989). *Relationship disturbances in early childhood: A developmental approach*. New York: Basic Books.

Simeonsson, R. J., Buckley, L., & Monson, L. (1979). Conceptions of illness causality in hospitalized children. *Journal of Pediatric Psychology, 4*, 77–84.

Sroufe, L. A. (1989). Relationships, self, and individual adaptation. In A. J. Sameroff & R. N. Emde (Eds.), *Relationship disturbances in early childhood: A developmental approach* (pp. 70–94). New York: Basic Books.

Sroufe, L. A., & Fleeson, J. (1986). Attachment and the construction of relationships. In W. Hartup & Z. Rubin (Eds.), *Relationships and development* (pp. 27–47). Hillsdale, NJ: Lawrence Erlbaum Associates.

Stern, D. N. (1985). *The interpersonal world of the infant: View from psychoanalysis and developmental psychology*. New York: Basic Books.

Stern, D. N. (1989). The representation of relational patterns: Developmental considerations. In A. J. Sameroff & R. N. Emde (Eds.), *Relationship disturbances in early childhood: A developmental approach* (pp. 52–69). New York: Basic Books.

Susman, E. J., Dorn, L. D., & Fletcher, J. C. (1987). Reasoning about illness in ill and healthy children and adolescents: Cognitive and emotional developmental aspects. *Developmental and Behavioral Pediatrics, 5*, 266–273.

Tisak, M. S., & Turiel, E. (1984). Children's conceptions of moral and prudential rules. *Child Development, 55*, 1,030–1,039.

Turiel, E. (1983). *The development of social knowledge: Morality & convention*. New York: Cambridge University Press.

Turk, D. C., & Kerns, R. D. (1985). The family in health and illness. In D. C. Turk & R. D. Kerns (Eds.), *Health, illness, and families* (pp. 1–22) New York: Wiley.

Whiting, B. (Ed.). (1963). *Six cultures*. New York: Wiley.

Whiting, B., & Whiting, J. (1975). Altrustic and egoistic behavior in six cultures. In L. Nader & T. W. Maretzki (Eds.), *Anthropological studies* (pp. 56–65). Washington, DC: American Anthropological Association.

Wilkinson, S. R. (1988). *The child's world of illness: The development of health and illness behavior*. New York: Cambridge University Press.

Wynn, L. C. (1984). The epigenesis of relational systems: A model for understanding family development. *Family Process, 23*, 297–318.

Zahn-Waxler, C., Radke-Yarrow, M., & King, R. A. (1979). Child rearing and children's prosocial initiations toward victims of distress. *Child Development, 50*, 319–330.

11

Intervention Strategies to Promote Healthy Children: Ecological Perspectives and Individual Differences in Development

Lynne V. Feagans
The Pennsylvania State University

This volume presents research perspectives that emphasize the importance of two emerging areas in children's health: (a) the importance of understanding the psychological, ecological, and developmental context in which children live; and (b) an understanding of the individual differences among children at different developmental levels. These perspectives are also part of the emerging literature in child development in general (Cole & Cole, 1989; Feagans & Bartsch, in press; Lerner, 1986, 1989), emphasizing the necessarily complex process of understanding development. It is increasingly clear that both the causes and effects in development are multivariate in nature, including psychological, biological, family, and other contextual influences. Much of the research represented in this volume (Lozoff, chapter 7; Ingersoll, Orr, Vance, & Golden, chapter 8; and Iannotti & Bush, chapter 4) serve as emerging models of the complex nature of trying to understand those factors related to healthy development. The difficult nature of this task is seen by the selection of an appropriate theoretical perspective and the many variables needed in order to have some understanding of the health phenomenon under investigation. This chapter focuses on how the two facets emphasized in this volume relate to the design of future intervention initiatives with children and their families to promote healthy development.

AN ECOLOGICAL APPROACH TO INTERVENTION

An ecological approach to intervention recognizes the importance of context in the success of any approach to human development. Bronfenbrenner (1979) clearly articulated this conception with regard to children. He postulated that children live in several microsystems. These are the major systems where the children operate. For most children this encompasses the home and the school setting. For children with chronic illness, the microsystem of the hospital is also a microsystem during some period of development. The successful adaptation from one setting to the next depends heavily on the next level in the Bronfenbrenner conception, the mesosystem. This mesosystem contains the connections between the microsystems. The better and more facilitative the connections, the easier it is for the children to make the transition from one setting to the next. Parents who are involved with their children's school and have good relations with the teachers form a mesosystem that indirectly helps their children function better. This is also true for the health care system that children and families encounter, although the mechanisms to promote strong mesosystem connections may not be established. As was pointed out in the Hauser, Jacobson, and Milley chapter (chapter 9, this volume), a chronic illness like diabetes may alter the way parents create mesosystems so that the parents become overprotective of their children leading to a restriction in the microsystems the children are able to enter and a restriction on the facilitative connections. The implications for intervention are to try to enhance the mesosystem connections, so that the restrictions on the children are minimal without endangering the health of the children or adolescents. This becomes a delicate balancing act for the successful intervention specialists.

The next level in the Bronfenbrenner conception (1979) is the exosystem. These are settings that the children do not participate in but that influence the children's development. The parents' workplace is an example of such an exosystem that clearly has economic impact on the children but also indirectly affects the parents' ability to take off time from work for the children and influences the children's beliefs about the workplace. The last system is the macrosystem that encompasses the larger societal norms and institutions of our culture that influence in a major way the children's view of the world and their place in it. The cultural view that the field of medicine is only illness focused rather than health promotion focused influences the way in which the children and family view their interactions and advice from the medical profession. All of these biological levels interact in producing healthy or nonhealthy outcomes for children.

INDIVIDUAL DIFFERENCES AMONG CHILDREN AND ADOLESCENTS

The individual child exhibits certain characteristics while functioning within a setting. These characteristics (like emotionality, self-esteem, and activity level) clearly influence the reactions that are evoked in the setting. Each setting also contains demands and expectations for each individual that enter the setting. For instance, the demands for certain behaviors in the hospital setting are quite different from those demands in the home setting. Children of all ages vary on how well their characteristics fit with the setting. Clearly children sometimes vary their characteristics and behavior from setting to setting to fit with the expectations and demands of the environment (Lerner, 1986, 1989). The settings themselves are usually less responsive to change than the individual child. For instance, a very active child who fits well in the home setting where there is freedom to move about the house and outside may find the confines of a hospital difficult to adjust to because there is little tolerance of high activity level.

This fit between the individual and the environmental setting is seen as developing over time in the form of feedback loops (Schneirla, 1957). Thus the environment gives feedback to the individual about how well he or she fits with the particular setting. This in turn affects the individual's characteristics that in turn affect the reactions from the setting. This continual feedback loop leads to good or poor outcomes, depending on the characteristics of the individual and the responsiveness of the setting to help the child fit well (Lerner, 1989). The Ingersoll et al. chapter in this volume reports that the cognitive maturity of diabetic adolescents is highly related to metabolic control. Thus, individual differences in one characteristic (cognitive maturity) is clearly important in the responsiveness of the individual to the demands of the medical system for diet and other responsible behavior.

Certain settings accommodate individual differences better than others. Unfortunately many settings (hospitals, schools, etc.) tolerate only a narrow range of behavior, making it difficult for individual children to fit well the demands of these settings. Both the school and many medical settings require a narrow range of behavior that leads to negative emotional and social outcomes on the part of children whose characteristics do not fit well to the setting. In addition, many solutions for disease states are medically regimented and do not take into consideration the settings in which the children live. Iron deficiency (Lozoff, chapter 7, this volume) is medically the same in the United States, Guatemala, and Costa Rica, but, as Lozoff illustrates, the effects of iron deficiency are different because of the culture and environment in which the mother and infant live. This also implies that the way in which intervention solutions would be designed to eliminate iron deficiency would be quite different in the three countries.

The challenge is to develop interventions that promote health, by not only targeting the individual, but targeting the fit between the individual and the settings in which she or he functions. This is done by changing the environment and/or by developing strong mesosystems among settings to ensure that the children make the best fit in each of the major settings in which they participate. For instance, a diabetic adolescent who has delayed cognitive maturity may warrant a change in the structure of the environment that establishes a more supportive and less autonomous dietary and medical regime in order to get the maximum fit between the individual characteristics of the adolescent and his or her environment. Fox (chapter 3, this volume) emphasizes the need for more research on the fit between the individual and family environment, with respect to temperament and parental behavior. He concludes by saying

> In first attempting to describe dimensions of individual differences in infant temperament, Thomas and Chess (1977, 1980) underscored the need to examine the "goodness of fit" between infant temperament and parent behavior. There are only a handful of studies (Bates, Maslin, & Frankel, 1985; Crockenberg, 1981) that have attempted to directly examine the interaction of infant temperament and maternal behavior in determining security of attachment. More of these studies are clearly necessary. The goal of research should no longer be to demonstrate the importance of infant temperament in determining attachment classification. Rather efforts should be made to understand how the interaction of temperament and caregiver behavior produces the unique and interesting behavior observed over so many studies in the Strange Situation.

Fox's argument is even more true of interventions that are generally designed for children of a particular age without accounting for the large individual differences among children in developmental level. Of even less concern in many interventions is a focus on the different environments in which children must function. The interventions need to be adapted so that the children's health can be maintained at home, at school, and in the neighborhood. All these settings provide different demands and opportunities for growth, especially for children with varying degrees of stress (due to medical or psychological/environmental stressors). There needs to be sensitive interventions that fit with the needs of the individual in changing environments. An emphasis on the development of strong mesosystems among the settings would also enhance the effectiveness of any intervention approach.

DEVELOPMENTAL LEVELS OVER TIME

Although it is important to have interventions that fit the individual needs of the children and their environment, it is also important to recognize that the individual and the environments are changing over time. Thus, interventions need to be developmentally and contextually sensitive. For instance, children with middle ear disease in later childhood who are in relatively quiet environments may have no effects from the mild hearing loss associated with this disease. On the other hand, young infants and toddlers who are at a critical period for language development and who participate in noisy environments like a daycare center may truly suffer developmental effects in language because of this rather mild disease (Feagans, Blood, & Tubman, 1988).

Parmelee (chapter 10) asserts that children with and without illness need continuity in their daily life activity so that contact with family and friends is maintained. These contextual features of the children's network also change over time and thus, interventions designed to promote health need to be developmentally sensitive. As children grow older, the need for the contact with friends and family is important, but the kind of contact may change as the children become more independent and see the need for more peer contact. This change needs to be reflected in the changes in the intervention for the children and their families.

The interventions of the future need to reflect the complexity of human development that is represented in this volume. The interventions need to focus on health not only illness, and they need to take into account the contextual and individual differences that are evident in all children. Trying to develop interventions that fit the characteristics of the individual child and her/his environments as well as fit the changing needs of the individual over time is certainly a challenge for the future. The development of these interventions requires not only professionals from different fields but the working together of the researcher/theoretician with the practitioners. The synergistic interaction among theory, research, and practice as represented in this volume should produce interventions that lead to the best health for all children.

REFERENCES

Bates, J. E., Maslin, C. A., & Frankel, K. A. (1985). Attachment security, mother–child interaction, and temperament as predictors of behavior problem ratings at three years. In I. Bretherton & E. Waters (Eds.), *Growing points of attachment theory and research* (pp. 167–193). *Monographs of the Society for Research in Child Development, 50*(1-2, Serial No. 209).

Bronfenbrenner, U. (1979). *The ecology of human development*. Cambridge, MA: Harvard University Press.

Cole, M., & Cole, S. R. (1989). *The development of children*. New York: Freeman.

Crockenberg, S. B. (1981). Infant irritability, mother responsiveness, and social support influences on the security of infant–mother attachment. *Child Development, 52*, 857–865.

Feagans, L. V., Blood, I., & Tubman, J. G. (1988). Otitis media: Models of effects and implications for intervention. In F. Bess (Ed.), *Hearing impairment in children* (pp. 347–374). Parkton, MD: York Press.

Feagans, L. V., & Bartsch, K. (in press). A framework for examining the role of schooling in early adolescence. In R. M. Lerner (Ed.), *Early adolescence: Perspectives on research, policy, and intervention*. Hillsdale, NJ: Lawrence Erlbaum Associates.

Lerner, R. M. (1986). *Concepts and theories of human development* (2nd ed.). New York: Random House.

Lerner, R. M. (1989). Developmental contextualism and the life-span view of person–context interaction. In M. H. Bornstein & J. S. Bruner (Eds.), *Interaction in human development* (pp. 217–230). Hillsdale, NJ: Lawrence Erlbaum Associates.

Schneirla, T. C. (1957). The concept of development in comparative psychology. In D. B. Harris (Ed.), *The concept of development* (pp. 78–108). Minneapolis: The University of Minnesota Press.

Thomas, A., & Chess, S. (1977). *Temmperament and development*. New York: Brunner/Mazel.

Thomas, A., & Chess, S. (1980). *The dynamics of psychological development*. New York: Brunner/Mazel.

Author Index

A

Abraham, E. C., 125, *130*
Adler, N. E., 81, 82, 85, 87, 89, 91, 92, 94, 96, *98, 99, 100,* 157, *163*
Ainsworth, M. D. S., 32, 33, 35, 42, 45, *48*
Alansky, J. A., 34–36, *50*
Alexander, F., 106, *108*
Amiel, S. A., 121, *130*
Andreas, D., 36, *50*
Antonovsky, A., 14, *20*
Apple, D., 158, *161*
Aral, S. O., 78, *96*
Arasteh, J. D., 2, *7*
Aro, H., 107, *108*

B

Baar, H., 122, *131*
Bachman, J. G., 80, 81, 88, 94, *99*
Badger, B. F., 54, *73*
Bakow, H., 35, *51*
Baranowski, T., 13, *20*
Barglow, P., 34, 36, 48, *52*
Bartlett, H. M., 14, *20*
Bartsch, K., 165, *169*
Bates, J. E., 48, *49,* 168, *169*
Baum, A., 18, 19, *20, 21*
Baumrind, D., 76, 86, *96, 97*
Bayley, N., 112, *118*
Beck, A., 89, *101*
Becker, D. J., 121, *130*
Becker, M. H., 13, *21,* 54, *73*
Beckwith, L., 115, *119*
Beirness, D. J., 82, *99*
Bell, R. Q., 32, 39, *49*
Bell, S. M. V., 32, *48*
Bell, T. A., 77, *97*
Belloc, N. B., 16, *21*
Belsky, J., 34, 42, 44–46, *49,* 115, *119*
Bennett, T., 75, 77, *98*
Ben-Sira, Z., 14, 15, *21*
Bentler, P. M., 83, *100*
Berenson, G. S., 71, *73*
Berger, M., 122, *131*
Berndt, T. J., 53, *72*
Bibace, R., 4, *7, 22,* 53, *72,* 122, *130,* 157, *161*
Billy, J. O. G., 86, 88, 92, *97, 102*
Bishop, G. D., 15, *21*
Bisping, R., 122, *131*
Blehar, M., 33, 35, 45, *48*
Bliss, R., 137, *150, 151*

Bloch, C. A., 121, *130*
Blood, I., 168, *169*
Blos, P., 53, *72*
Blue, J., 91, *101*
Blyth, D. A., 75, 88, 90, *97, 98, 101*
Bowlby, J., 27, 28, *30,* 31, 32, *49*
Bowlds, M., 136, *151*
Boxer, A., 89, *100*
Boyer, C., 85, *101*
Brack, C. J., 129, *131*
Bradley, C., 123, *130*
Bradnan, W. A., 135, *152*
Bradshaw, D., 34, *50*
Brensome, E. D., 125, *130*
Breslow, L., 16, *21*
Bretherton, I., 33, *49*
Brewster, A. B., 157, *161*
Bridges, L. J., 34, 46, 48, *49, 52*
Brill, N., 160, *161*
Brindis, C., 75, 77, *98*
Brink, S., 134, 137, 149, *151*
Brittenham, G. M., 111–113, 117, *119*
Broberg, A., 46, *50*
Brodie, B., 158, *161*
Brodt, S., 75, 77, *98*
Bronfenbrenner, U., 165, 166, *169*
Brooks-Gunn, J., 80–90, 92, *97*
Brown, R. E., 117, *119*
Browning, D. L., 134, *150*
Bruhn, J. G., 12, 14, *21,* 54, *72,* 155, 158, *161*
Brunswick, A. F., 107, *108*
Buckley, L., 11, *23,* 157, *163*
Bulcroft, R., 90, *97*
Burbach, D. J., 12, *21*
Burke, G. L., 81, *98*
Burt, J. J., 13, *21*
Busch-Rossnagel, N. A., 155, *162*
Bush, D. M., 54–60, 62, 90, *97*
Bush, J. W., 105, *109*
Bush, P. J., *72, 73*
Buss, A. H., 43, *49*
Butler, L. F., 122, 124, *131*
Butts, J. D., 90, 92, *102*

C

Calkins, S. D., 47, *49*
Campbell, J. D., 11, 12, *21,* 54, 58, *72,* 157–160, *161*
Caplan, A. L., 158, *161*
Carandang, M. L. A., 157, *161*
Carey, S., 156–158, *161*
Carney, C., 58, *72*
Cassidy, J., 45, *51*
Cataldo, M. F., 2, *7*
Cates, W., Jr., 78, 96, *97*
Centers for Disease Control, 77–80, 82, *97*
Chadud, P., 112, *120*
Chapman, M., 158, *163*
Charles, E., 122, *132*
Chase, H. P., 123, *130*
Chase-Lansdale, L., 42, 46, *51*
Chess, S., 48, *52,* 168, *169*
Chrousos, G. P., 89, *101*
Clark, S., 160, *161*
Clarke, M. C., 34, 36, *52*
Clausen, J. A., 89, 90, *97*
Clemons, P., 121, *130*
Coddington, D. C., 123, *130*
Cohn, L., 81, 82, 85, 89, 91, 94, *98, 99, 100*
Cole, M., 165, *169*
Cole, S. R., 165, *169*
Colton, M. B., 38, *49*
Comite, F., 91, *101*
Connell, J. P., 34, 46, 48, *49, 52*
Connolly, G. N., 81, *97*
Conrad, P., 15, *21*
Constitution of the World Health Organization, 158, *162*
Contento, I. R., 11, *22*
Converse, S. A., 15, *21*
Cope, N. D., 125, *130*
Cordova, F. D., 158, *161*
Cornelius, S., 53, 71, *73*
Corry, T., 46, *50*
Costa, F., 87, *99*
Covington, M. V., 83, *97*
Cresanta, J. L., 71, *73*
Crockenberg, S. B., 48, *49,* 168, *169*
Croft, J. B., 81, *98*
Cutler, G. B., Jr., *101*

D

Daitzman, R., 93, *97*
Dallman, P. R., 111, *119*

Damon, W., 158, *162*
Daneman, D., 121, *130*
Daniels, G. E., 122, *130*
Davidson, F. R., 54–60, *72, 73*
Davidson, R. J., 37, 38, *49, 51*
Davies, M., 84, *99*
deAndraca, I., 112, *120*
Derryberry, D., 36, 43, *51*
Dielman, T. E., 13, *21,* 54, *73*
Dienstbier, R., 5, *7*
Dingle, J. H., 54, *73*
DiPlacido, J., 149, *151*
Dolcini, P., 81, 82, 85, 89, 91, 94, *99, 100*
Donelson, A. C., 82, *99*
Donovan, J. E., 86, 87, *97, 99*
Dorn, L. D., 4, *8,* 89, *101,* 157, *163*
Drash, A. L., 126, 129, *130, 132,* 148, *152*
Driver, M. J., 122, *132*
Drotar, D., 2, *7,* 13, *21*
Dunbar, H. B., 122, *130*
Dunn, S. M., 122, *130*
Dvir, R., 33, 46, *51*

E

Easterbrooks, M. A., 159, *162*
Eastman, G., 53, 71, *73*
Egeland, B., 117, *119*
Ehrlich, R. M., 128, *132*
Eichorn, D. H., 89, 90, *97*
Eisenberg, L., 158, *162*
Eiser, C., 106, *108,* 122, *130*
Elkind, D., 91, *97*
Elliott, D. W., 84, *97*
Elster, A. B., 75, *98*
Emde, R. N., 156, 158, 159, 161, *162, 163*
Englehardt, H., Jr., 158, *161, 162*
Ensminger, M. E., 84, *97*
Eppinger, H., 37, *49*
Epstein, L., 85, *97*
Erikson, E. H., 29, *30,* 53, *73,* 137, *150*
Escalona, S. K., 117, *119*
Estes, D., 33, 46, *51*
Evans, F. M., 122, *131*

F

Fabrega, H., Jr., 158, *162*
Faust, M. S., 89, *97*
Fauvre, M., 160, *161*
Feagans, L. V., 165, 168, *169*
Feinglos, M. N., 122, *132*
Feiring, C., 42, 47, *51*
Felt, D., 90, *97*
Finman, R., 38, *49*
Fleeson, J., 156, 158, *163*
Fletcher, J. C., 4, *8,* 157, *164*
Folkins, C. H., 157, *161*
Follansbee, D., 134–139, 149, *151*
Forrest, J. D., 79, *98*
Forsstrom, B., 46, *50*
Fox, N. A., 34, 36–39, 43, 47, *49, 50, 52*
Frank, S. J., 134, *150*
Frankel, K. A., 48, *49*, 168
Freedman, D. W., 71, *73*
Freud, S., 31, *50*
Frick, T., 124, *131*
Friedman, I. M., 82, *98*
Frodi, A. M., 42, 46, *50, 51*
Furstenberg, F. F., Jr., 80, *97*

G

Gans, J. E., 75, *98*
Garcia, L., 160, *161*
Gard, P. D., 71, *73*
Gardner, R. A., 159, *162*
Garduque, L., 42, *49*
Garn, S. M., 118, *119*
Garrison, W., 134, *151*
Gaveras, L. L., 75, *98*
Geiser, D., 5, *7*
Gelfand, E., 137, *151*
Gellert, E., 10, *21,* 156, *162*
Gelles, M., 37, *50*
Gelman, R., 157, 158, *162*
Gerrity, P. S., 54, *74*
Gilstrap, B., 46, *49*
Gochman, D. S., 2, *7,* 9, 11–13, 16–19, *21, 22,* 54, 59, *73,* 155, *162*
Golden, M. P., 122, 127, 129, *131,* 159, *162*
Goldsmith, H. H., 34–36, 48, *50*
Gomez, I., 112, *119*
Goossens, F. A., 42, *50*
Grant, I., 123, *131*
Grantham-McGregor, S., 117, *119*
Graves, E. J., 76, *98*
Greenberger, E., 53, *73*
Greene, J. W., 108, *109*

Greydanus, D. E., 76, *98*
Grossmann, K., 35, 42, *50*
Grossmann, K. E., 35, 42, *50*
Guilkey, D. K., 80, *99*
Gunnar, M. R., 36, *50*

H

Haan, N., 90, *97*
Halperin, F., 117, *119*
Hamburg, B. A., 88, *98*, 107, *108*
Hamburg, D. A., 88, *98*
Hardy, J. B., 83, *102*
Harrold, A. J., 159, *162*
Hart, D., 158, *162*
Hartman, K., 15, *22*
Harttmann, F., 122, *131*
Harvey, O. J., 107, *108*, 122, *131*
Haurin, R. J., 84, *100*
Hauser, S. T., 122, *131*, *132*, 134–140, 143, 147–149, *150*, *151*, *152*, 157, *162*
Hayes, C. D., 79, 89, *98*
Hayes-Bautista, D. E., 12, *22*
Healthy People, 76, *98*
Hecht, S. S., 81, *97*
Helu, B., 114, *119*
Henningfield, J. E., 81, *97*
Herrold, A. J., 122, 127, 129, *131*
Herskowitz, R. D., 134, 137, 149, *150*, *151*, 157, *162*
Hess, L., 37, *49*
Hines, P. S., 157, *161*
Hinkle, L. E., 106, *108*, 122, *131*
Hirsch, M. B., 83, *102*
Hirschman, R. S., 15, *22*
Hofferth, S. L., 89, *98*
Hoffman, A., 107, *109*
Hoffman, D., 81, *97*
Hoffman, M. L., 157, 158, *162*
Hollingshead, A. B., 139, *151*
Holmes, C. S., 128, *131*
Holmes, K. K., 77, *97*
Holmes, T. H., 123, *131*
Honig, A. S., 114, *119*
Honzik, M. P., 90, *97*
Hoppe, M., 128, *132*
Horowitz, C. J., 55, *73*
Horvath, W. J., 13, *21*, 54, *73*
Houlihan, J., 137, 149, *151*, 157, *162*
Howanitz, P., 114, *119*
Hrncir, E., 42, *49*
Huber, F., 42, *50*
Huberty, T. J., 129, *131*
Huff, T. A., 125, *130*
Huisman, T. H. J., 125, *130*
Humphries, C. L., 107, *109*
Hunt, D. E., 107, *108*, 122, 124, 130, *131*
Hunter, S. M., 81, *98*
Hwang, C., 42, 46, *50*, *51*

I

Iannotti, R., 2, *7*, 13, *21*, 54, 60, 62, *72*
Ingersoll, G. M., 122, 127–129, *131*, *132*, 159, *161*
Inoff-Germain, G., 89, *101*
Irwin, C. E., Jr., 3, *7*, 28, *30*, 75–78, 81, 82, 85–87, 89–96, *98*, *99*, *100*, *101*, 157–159, *162*, *163*

J

Jackson, G. G., 123, *130*
Jacobson, A. M., 122, *131*, *132*, 134, 135, 137, 138, 139, 143, 147, 149, *150*, *151*, *152*, 157, *162*
Jenkins, R. R., 90, 92, *102*
Jessor, R., 28, 29, *30*, 82, 83, 86, 87, 92, *97*, *99*
Jessor, S. L., 29, *30*, 82, 83, 86, 87, 92, *99*
Jimenez, E., 112, 116, 117, *119*
Jimenez, R., 112, *119*
Johnson, J. H., 122, 123, 125, *131*
Johnson, S. B., 2, *7*, 13, *21*, 147, *151*
Johnson, W. F., 159, *162*
Johnston, D. I., 121, *131*
Johnston, L. D., 80, 81, 88, 94, *99*
Jonah, B., 79, *99*
Jordan, W. S., 54, *73*
Joreskog, K. G., 126, *131*

K

Kagan, J., 37, 38, *49*, *50*, 158, *162*
Kahn, J. R., 80, *99*
Kalnins, I., 12, *22*
Kandel, D. B., 81, 83, 84, 87, *99*, *101*, *102*
Kandel, R. F., 53, 54, *73*

Kaplan, G. D., 62, *74*
Kaplan, N., 45, *51*
Kaplan, R., 105, *109*
Katlic, A. W., 54, *73*
Keating, M. T., 118, *119*
Kegeles, S. M., 81, 82, 85, 89, 91, 94, *98, 99, 100*
Kemmer, F. W., 122, *131*
Kerns, R. D., 155, *164*
Kestenbaum, R., 36, *50*
Kilner, L., 148, *152*
Kimmerly, N. L, 34, 43, *50*
King, R. A., 158, *164*
Kinsbourne, M., 38, *50*
Kirschenbaum, D. S., 14, *23*
Kirshner, L. A., 134, *151*
Kister, M. C., 159, *162*
Klein, N. K., 115, *119,* 160, *161*
Klepper, S., 54, *73*
Kogan, N., 28, *30*
Kolbe, L. J., 18, *22*
Kovalskys, J., 114, *120*
Krafchuk, E. E., 35, *51*
Krasnegor, N. A., 2, *7,* 13, *21*
Krauskoph, D., 112, *119*
Ku, L. C., 79, *101*
Kuhnert, P. M., 112, *119*
Kyle, G. C., 123, *131*

L

Lacey, B. C., 37, *50*
Lacey, J. I., 37, *50*
Lamb, M. E., 33, 42, 46, *50, 51,* 118, *119, 120*
Lang, S., 36, *50*
Larson, M., 36, *50*
Lau, R. R., 15, *22,* 54, *73*
Lauritano, A. A., 121, *130*
Lavori, P., 137, *150, 151*
Leech, S. L., 13, *21,* 54, *73*
Lefever, G. B., 34, 36, 48, *52*
LeMare, L., 36, *51*
Lerner, R. M., 5, *7, 8,* 88, *99,* 155, *162,* 165, 167, *169*
Lesser, G. S., 53, *73*
Leventhal, H., 15, *22*
Levitt, M. J., 34, 36, *52*
Lewis, C. E., 79, 90, *99*
Lewis, M., 43, 47, *51*
Lewis, M. A., 79, 90, *99*
Lewkowicz, K. S., 33, 46, *51*
Lidz, T., 122, *132*
Lipowski, Z. J., 106, *109*
Lira, M. I., 117, *119*
Little, R. A., 138, *151*
Livson, N., 90, *100*
Loevinger, J., 122, *131,* 134, 138–140, *151*
Logan, J. A., 83, *99*
Lollis, S., 36, *51*
Loriaux, D. L., 89, *101*
Love, R., 12, *22*
Lozoff, B., 111–113, 116, 117, *119, 120*
Lynch, J. H., 96, *101*

M

Maccoby, E. E., 156, 161, *162*
Maddux, J. E., 3, *8*
Maides, S. A., 62, *74*
Maiman, L. A., 54, *73*
Main, M., 42, 45, *51*
Mangelsdorf, S., 36, *50*
Mann, N. P., 121, *131*
Marshall, W. A., 88, *99*
Maslin, C. A., 48, *49,* 168, *169*
Matarazzo, J. D., 2, *8,* 16, *22*
Matheny, J. P., Jr., 113, *119*
Matthews, K. A., 2, *7,* 13, 18, *21, 22*
Mayhew, D. R., 82, *99*
McCartney, J. J., 158, *161*
McClish, D. K., 112, *119*
McCullough, L., 148, *152*
McCutcheon, S., 125, *131*
McNeil, D., 90, *100*
Mead, M., 134, *151*
Mechanic, D., 54, *73,* 107, *109,* 159, *163*
Melamed, B. G., 2, *7,* 13, 18, *21, 22*
Mendels, J., 123, *131*
Meng, A. L., 14, *23*
Menninger, W. C., 122, *131*
Merzel, C. R., 107, *108*
Meyer, M., 58, *73*
Michela, J. L., 11, *22*
Miller, H. G., 83, *100*
Miller, P. Y., 84, *100*
Milley, J. E., 137, *150, 151,* 157, *162*
Millstein, S. G., 2, 3, *7,* 13, *21,* 29, *30,* 81, 82, 85–87, 89–96, *98, 99, 100, 101,* 157–159, *162, 163*

Monson, L., 11, *23,* 157, *163*
Moos, R., 149, *151*
Mora, L. A., 112, *119*
Morris, N. M., 86, 88, 92, *101, 102*
Morse, B. J., 84, *97*
Moses, L. E., 83, *100*
Mosher, W. D., 78, *96*
Mott, F. L., 84, *100*
Mussen, P. H., 90, *97*

N

Nader, P. R., 13, *20, 22*
Nagy, M. H., 10, *22*
Natapoff, J. N., 9, *22,* 53, 54, *73,* 158, *163*
National Center for Health Statistics, 75–77, 79, *100*
National Institute on Drug Abuse, 81, *100*
Newacheck, P. W., 75, *100*
Newcomb, M. D., 83, *100*
Newman, W. P., 71, *73*
Noam, G. G., 122, *131, 132,* 134–136, 138–140, 143, 147, *150, 151*
Nottelmann, E. D., 89, *101*
Noy, J. E., 122, 124, *131*
Nucci, L., 159, *163*

O

Ohm-Smith, M. J., 89, *101*
O'Malley, P. M., 80, 81, 88, 94, *99*
Oremland, E. K., 160, *163*
Oremland, J. D., 160, *163*
Orleans, J., 134–137, 147, *151*
Orr, D. P., 122, 127–129, *131, 132,* 159, *162*
Osgood, D. W., 88, *100*
Oski, F. A., 114, *119*
Owen, M. T., 42, 46, *51*

P

Padeh, B., 14, *21*
Parcel, G. S., 12, *21,* 54, 58, *72, 73*
Parke, R. D., 46, *51*
Parmelee, A. H., Jr., 53, *73,* 155, 156, 158, 160, 161, *163*
Parsons, T., 159, *163*
Patterson, C. J., 159, *162*
Paul, E., 149, *151*
Pearlin, L. I., 14, *22*
Perales, C. G., 112, *120*
Perrin, E. C., 54, *73,* 157, *163*
Petersen, A. C., 88–90, *97, 100*
Peterson, L., 12, *21*
Peterson, R. A., 2, *7,* 13, *21*
Piaget, J., 29, *30*
Plank, E., 160, *163*
Pleck, J. H., 79, *101*
Plomin, R., 43, *49*
Pollets, D., 122, *131,* 134–136, 143, 147, *151*
Popiel, D., 2, *7,* 13, *21*
Porges, S. W., 37, *50, 51, 52*
Powell, C. A., 117, *119*
Powers, S. I., 122, *131, 132,* 134–136, 138–140, 143, 147, 148, *150, 152*
Prabucki, K. M., 115, *119*
Pratt, L., 13, *22,* 53, 54, 71, *73, 163*
Pratt, W., 79, *101*
Prohaska, R. R., 15, *22*

Q

Quinlin, D. M., 134, *150*

R

Radke-Yarrow, M., 158, *163, 164*
Rahe, R. H., 123, *131*
Rajapark, D., 137, 149, *151*
Rashkis, S. R., 10, *22,* 158, *163*
Rauste-von Wright, M., 107, 108, *109*
Redpath, C. C., 157, *163*
Reinglos, M. N., *132*
Reznick, J. S., 37, *50*
Rieser-Danner, L., 34, *50*
Rindfuss, R. R., 80, *99*
Rioch, J. M., 122, *130*
Roberts, M. C., 3, *8*
Robins, L. N., 87, *101*
Rodriguez, R., 75, 77, *98*
Rodriguez, S., 117, *119*
Rogers, C. S., 157, *163*
Rosen, H., 122, *132*
Rosenbaum, E., 84, 87, *101*
Rosenberg, M., 62, *73, 152*

Rosenfeld, A. A., 107, 108, *109*
Rosenstock, I. M., 13, *21,* 54, *73*
Rosnafsky, J., 134, *152*
Rosser, M. C., 122, 124, *131*
Roter, D. L., 15, *22*
Rothbart, M. K., 35, 36, 43, *51*
Routh, D. K., 2, *7,* 13, 18, *21, 22*, 106, *109*
Rovet, J. F., 128, *132*
Rovine, M., 34, 39, 44–46, *49*
Rubin, D. B., 138, *151*
Rubin, K. H., 36, *51*
Rufo, P., 149, *151*
Russell, B. A., 129, *131*
Ryan, C. M., 126, 128, 129, *132,* 148, *152*
Ryan, R. M., 96, *101*
Ryan, S. A., 81, 88, 93, *99*

S

Sagi, A., 33, 42, 46, *51*
Sallis, J. F., *22*
Sameroff, A. J., 35, *51,* 161, *163*
Santostefano, S., 134, *151*
Saron, C., 37, *51*
Saucier, J. -F., 11, 22, 54, 59, *73*
Sawin, D. B., 46, *51*
Schachter, J., 89, *101*
Schaefer, E. S., 118, *118*
Schaffer, C. E., 37, *51*
Schaffer, J. E., 78, *96*
Schaffer, W. D., 34, 43, *50*
Schlachecke, R., 122, *131*
Schlossberger, N., 90, *101*
Schneirla, T. C., 167, *169*
Schooler, C., 14, *22*
Schroeder, H. M., 107, *108,* 122, *131*
Schwab, J. J., 135, *152*
Schwartz, G. E., 2, *8,* 17, *22*
Schwartz, J. M., 122, *132,* 134, *151*
Seifer, R., 34, 36, 48, *52*
Semmel, M. I., 124, *131*
Shafer, M. A., 78, 85, 89, *99, 101*
Shalwitz, J., 89, *101*
Shapiro, E. G., 107, 108, *109*
Sherwin, R. S., 121, *130*
Shoham, R., 33, 46, *51*
Shore, L., 89, *101*
Siimes, M. A., 111, *119*
Silverberg, S. B., 53, 71, *74,* 96, *101*
Simeonsson, R. J., 11, *23,* 157, *163*
Simmons, R. G., 62, *73,* 90, *97, 101*
Simon, W., 84, *100*
Simonson, D. C., 121, *130*
Singh, S., 79, *98*
Sledden, E. A., 3, *8*
Slovic, P., 93, *101*
Small, S. A., 53, 71, *73*
Smith, E. A., 83, 88, *101, 102*
Snidman, N., 37, *50*
Sonenstein, F. L., 79, *101*
Sonis, W. A., 91, *101*
Sorbom, D., 126, *131*
Spangler, G., 35, *50*
Spelke, E., 157, 158, *162*
Sperling, M. A., 121, *130*
Spetter, D., 149, *151*
Srinivasan, S. R., 71, *73*
Sroufe, L. A., 42, 45, *51, 52,* 117, *119,*
156, 158, *163*
Stabler, B., 18, *22*
Stayton, D. J., 32, *48*
Stein, J., *150, 151*
Stein, S., 122, *132*
Steinberg, L., 53, 61, 71, *73, 74,* 92, *101*
Steingruber, H. J., 122, *131*
Stekel, A., 114, *120*
Stern, D. N., 156, 158, *163*
Stevenson, M. B., 118, *120*
Steward, M. S., 157, *161*
Stifter, C. A., 36, 37, 39, 47, *50, 52*
Stimson, G., 15, *23*
Stone, E. J., 71, *74*
Stone, G., 2, *8*
Straus, A. M., 38, *49*
Streufert, S., 122, *132*
Suess, G., 35, *50*
Sullivan, B. J., 139, *152*
Sullivan, E. V., 122, 130, *131*
Surwit, R. S., 122, *132*
Susman, E. J., 4, *8,* 89, *101,* 157, *164*
Sutton, D. B., *50*
Swain, S. O., 79, *101*
Sweet, R. L., 78, 89, *101*

T

Talbert, L. M., 86, 92, *102*
Tamborlane, W. V., 121, *130*
Tamir, A., 85, *97*

Tanner, J. M., 88, *99*
Taylor, D. G., 46, *49*
Taylor, S. E., 18, *23*
Teichman, A., 123, *131*
Thomas, A., 48, *52,* 168, *169*
Thompson, R. A., 34, 48, *52*
Tisak, M. S., 159, *164*
Tobin-Richards, M., 89, *100*
Tonkins, R. S., 29, *30*
Tubman, J. G., 168, *169*
Tuma, J. M., 106, *109*
Turiel, E., 156, 159, *164*
Turk, D. C., 155, *164*
Turner, B., 122, *131,* 134, 143, 147, *151*
Turner, C. F., 83, *100*
Turner, R., 87, 90, 92, 96, *98, 101*
Turtle, J. R., 122, *130*

U

U.S. Preventive Services Task Force, 76, *102*
Udry, J. R., 86, 88, 92, *97, 101, 102*
Unzer, L., 35, *50*
Urrutia, J. J., 111–113, 117, *119*

V

Vaillant, G. C., 148, *152*
Van Cleave, E. F., 90, *97*
van Ijzendoorn, M. H., 42, *50*
Vaughan, E., 28, *30,* 76, 77, 87, *99*
Vaughn, B. E., 34, 36, 48, *52*
Vega, A., 126, 129, *132, 152*
Vieyra, M., 134–137, 147, 149, *151*
Viteri, F. E., 111–113, 117, *119*
Volling, B. L., 46, *49*
von Wright, J., 107, 108, *109*
Voors, A. W., 71, *73*

W

Waldrop, M. F., 39, *49*
Walker, B., Jr., 81, *97*
Walker, L. S., 108, *109*
Wall, S., 33, 35, 45, *48*
Wallach, M. A., 28, *30*
Wallston, B. S., 62, *74*
Wallston, K. A., 62, *74*
Walsh, M. E., 4, *7,* 53, *72,* 122, *130,* 157, *161*
Walter, T., 112, 114, *120*
Wartner, U., 42, *50*
Waters, E., 33, 35, 42, 45, *48, 51, 52*
Watt, E., 157, *162*
Webb, B., 15, *23*
Webber, L. S., 71, *73*
Weber, R. A., 34, 36, *52*
Weiss, B., 134–136, 138, 139, *151*
Weiss, S. M., 2, *8,* 17, *22*
Weiss-Perry, B., 137, 149, *151*
Weller, G. M., 39, *49*
Wenger, M. A., 37, *52*
Wentworth, S., 134, 137, 149, *151*
Wertlieb, D., 134–137, 147, 149, *150, 151, 152,* 157, *162*
Wessler, R., 134, 139, *151*
Westney, Q. E., 90, 92, *102*
Weston, D. R., 42, *51*
Whiting, B., 159, 160, *164*
Whiting, J., 159, 160, *164*
Wilkinson, S. R., 158, 159, *164*
Williams, I., 90, 92, *102*
Williamson, G. D., 71, *73*
Wilson, J. B., 125, *130*
Winn, D. M., 81, *97*
Winnicott, D. W., 31, *52*
Wish, E., 87, *101*
Wittig, B. A., 32, *48*
Wolf, A. W., 111–113, 116, 117, *119, 120*
Wolf, S., 122, *131*
Wolfe, T. D., 122, *130*
Wolfsdorf, J. I., 134–137, 147, 149, *150, 151,* 157, *162*
Wolfson, D. H., 121, *130*
Wright, J. C., 129, *131*
Wright, L., 3, *8*
Wynne, L. C., 161, *164*

Y

Yamaguchi, K., 81, 83, 87, *102*

Z

Zabin, L. S., 83, *102*
Zahn-Waxler, C., 158, *163, 164*
Zastowny, T. R., 14, *23*
Zuckerman, A. E., 55, *73*
Zuckerman, M., 93, *97, 102*

Subject Index

A

Abusable substances, 71
Accidents, 77
Acquired immune deficiency syndrome (AIDS), 83
Acute illness, 136, 140–150
Adrenocorticotropin hormone, 4
Adult Risk-Taking Scale, 62
Alcohol, 59–66, 80–81
  autonomy, 59, 64–66
  availability, 65–66
  use, 80–81
Anemic, 114–115
Attachment, 5–6, 27, 31–48
  concordance in, 47
  discordance of, 42
  insecure, 6, 32, 40–48
    ambivalent/angry, 33, 44
    avoidant, 33, 41–43
    resistant, 41–43, 47
  secure, 6, 28, 32, 40–48
Autonomous, 135
Autonomy, 6, 10, 27–30, 53–74, 148
  definition of, 53
Autonomy of medicine use scale, 69

B

Bayley Scales of Infant Development, 112–113
  Infant Behavior Record, 113–114, 117
  Mental Development Index, 112, 114
  Psychomotor Development Index, 112
Beck Depression Inventory, 37
Behavioral health, 1–7
  definition of, 17
Behavioral medicine, 2, 17–18, 106
  definition of, 2, 17
Behavioral pediatrics, 2
Behavioral reactivity, 37, 40–41
Biopsychosocial development, 75, 88
Biopsychosocial models, 92
Blood glucose, 123

C

Children's Health Locus of Control Scale, 58
Chronic illness, 65, 133, 138, 144, 149
  in adolescence, 133
Cigarette Autonomy, 59, 64–66
Cigarettes, 81

Cocaine, 81
Cognition, 4, 9, 27, 106, 123
  cognitive abilities, 4
  cognitive complexity, 106
  cognitive maturity, 107, 121–129
  concrete operational thinking, 29
  definition of, 9
  formal operational thought, 4, 27, 29
Cognitive development, 105
Conformist, 135
Contraceptives, 80
  use of, 80
Coping, 20
  cognitive aspects of, 14
Corticotropin releasing hormone, 4
Cortisol, 4

D

Developmental levels, 168–169
Developmental perspective, 3
  cognitive processes, 3
  emotional processes, 3
Developmental tests, 111
Developmental trajectory in risk behaviors, 87
Deviant behavior, 87
Diabetes, 7, 133, 138, 140–150
  adjustment, 139
Diabetic, 121
Disease, 157
  processes, 105

E

Ego development, 133–150
  diabetes adjustment, 136
  stages of, 137
    conformist, 139, 144
    postconformist, 139
    preconformist, 137, 139, 144
    progressive ego development, 137
    psychosocial moratorium, 137
    regressive ego development, 137
    steady conformist, 137, 142
Electroencephalogram, 37
Emotions, *see also* Perceived vulnerability, 20, 37
  emotional expressivity, 37
  stress-related, 4
    arousal, 4
Enabling processes, 149
Experience of illness, 138

F

Family, 20
  atmosphere, 149
  interaction patterns, 149
Frustration, 41, 47

G

Gender differences, 107, 123, 129
Glycemic control, 123, 127
Glycosylated hemoglobin level (HbA_1), 123–127
Goodness of fit, 48

H

Health, 10, 13–14, 155–161, 165–169
  as a motive, 14
  definition of, 10
  developmental level, 156
  mental well-being, 156
  motivation, 13
  physical well-being, 156
  Piagetian approach, 156, 160
  reasoning about, 156, 161
  social well-being, 156
Health behavior, 2, 15–18, 27–28, 53–54
  definition of, 2
  research, definition of, 16–17
Health-belief model, 11
Health beliefs, 54
Health cognitions, 9–16, 20
  family, 12
  origins of, 12
Health control, 27
Health-germane motives, 13
  definition of, 13
  motivation, 20
Health Locus of Control, 58, 62–65
Health problems, 75
  adolescent related, 75
Health providers, 150
Health psychology, 2, 18
Health risks, 27

Health status indicators, 75
  definition of, 75
Heart period, 40
Hemoglobin, 114, 125
Homicide, 77
Hypoglycemia, 135, 148

I

Illness, 54, 157–161, 166–167
  attitudes toward illness, 157
  causes of, 10
    infection, 10
  chronic, 157, 166
    diabetes, 166–167
  definition of, 10
  families, 157, 161
  hospitalization, 160, 166–167
  minor, 157
  personal-social, 157, 161
  respiratory, 54
  sick role, 160
  transgression explanation, 159
Illness and Injury Risk Taking, 58
  Risking Illness, 58, 65–66
  Risking Injury, 58, 61, 64
Illness behaviors, 53
Individual differences, 165–169
  feedback loops, 167
  fit, 167–168
Infant personality, 43
Infant reactivity, 37, 41, 47
Infectious diseases, 77–78
  sexually transmitted diseases, 77
    Chlamydia trachomatis, 78
    Neisseria gonorrhoea, 77–78
Injuries, 77, 79
  types of, 77, 79
    intentional, 77, 79
    unintentional, 79
Insulin, 125, 128
  resistance, 121
Insulin dependent diabetes mellitus (IDDM), 121, 126–129, 133
Intelligence, 140, 147
Intervention, 165–169
  developmentally sensitive, 169
  ecological approach, 165–167
    demands of settings, 167
    exosystem, 166
    macrosystem, 166
    mesosystem, 166–167
    microsystem, 166
Invulnerability, 75
I.Q., 116
Iron, 113
Iron deficiency, 7, 113–114, 167
Iron deficiency anemia, 107, 111–118
  anemic infants, 111

L

Life events, 125
Life-span developmental perspective, 5
  contextual, 5
  goodness of fit, 5
  organismic, 5
Life stress, 108
  perceived, 108

M

Marijuana, 81
Maturation, 94
  meaning of, 95
  measures of, 94
  timing of, 94–95
Medicine, 54, 56, 60
  abusable substances, 56, 60
  use, 54, 56
    autonomy of use, 54–69
    intention to use, 56
Medicine Knowledge, 58, 64
Metabolic control, 121–129
Morbidity, 75–78
  in adolescence, 75–78, 91
    risk taking, 76
  prevalence, 77
    hospital discharge rates, 77
Mortality, 75–78
  gender differences, 77
  in adolescence, 75–78
    increases in, 75
Mother-infant interaction, 115
Mother's Perceived Vulnerability, 63
Mother's Risk Taking, 62
Motor and recreational vehicle use, 79
Motor development, 111

N

Negative life events, 123, 126–128
Neonatal Behavioral Assessment Scale, 35
Nutrition, 54–55, 70–72
  nutritional deficiency, 111
  nutritional intake, 54, 71

P

Paragraph Completion Method, 124
Parasympathetic, 37
Peer group, 93
Peer relationships, 148, 150
Perceived vulnerability, 11, 59, 64
  health problems, 11
Perceptions of risk, 93
Perceptual impairments, 148
Personality, 106
Personal relationships, 146
Physical maturation, 89–90
Poisoning, 77
Preadolescents, 143
Problem behaviors, 82
  syndrome of, 82
Problem behavior theory, 86
  definition of, 29
Psychodynamic, 105
Psychological mindedness, 148
Psychophysiological recording, 37
  heart rate, 37
  heart rate variability, 37
Psychophysiological symptoms, 107
Psychosocial development, 90
  developmental tasks, 90
Psychosomatic medicine, 105
  psychosomatic approach, 105–106
Puberty, 91–92, 107
  timing of, 91–92

R

Renal disease, 150
Risk, 27
Risk behaviors (*see* Risk taking)
Risk taking, 6, 28–29, 75
  behaviors, 28–30, 75–76, 82, 92
    covariation of, 82–86
    model, 75
    morbidity and mortality, 29
    types of, 76
  definition of, 76
  intentional nature, 28
    decision making, 28
Rosenberg Self-Esteem Scale, 62

S

Self-esteem, 62, 65–66, 145–146
  Mother's Self-Esteem, 62
Self-medication, 28
Self-reliance, 69
Sensation seeking, 93
Sexual activity (*see* Sexual behavior)
Sexual behavior, 79–80, 83
  incidence, 79–80
    gender differences, 79
    increases in, 79
    racial differences, 79
Sexual intercourse, 84
Smokeless tobacco, 81
Smoking, 85
Social class, 147
Sociodemographic variables, 57, 62
  family composition, 57–58
Socioeconomic status (SES), 55–69, 138
Strange Situation paradigm, *see also* Attachment, 28, 36, 41–48
  insecurity, 36, 45–46
  reactive and nonreactive, 36
  security, 45–46
Stress, 107, 122–123
  life changes, 122–123
  short-term stressors, 122
Stressful life events, 121–128
Substance use, 82–84
  co-occurrence with, 82
    motor vehicle injuries, 82–83
    vehicle use, 82
Substance use and abuse, 80–81
  age of onset, 81
  patterns, 83
  rates of use, 80
Suicide, 77

T

Temperament, 6, 28, 34–48, 168
Testosterone, 86

Timing of maturation, 93
Tolerance of ambiguity, 106
Trauma, 77

V

Vagal tone, 37, 40
Vehicle use (*see* Motor and recreational vehicle use)

W

Wechsler Child Intelligence Scale-Revised (WCIS-R), 140
Wellness, 157–161

Y

Youth risk, 27